THE COMPLETE
CITIES OF ANCIENT EGYPT

STEVEN SNAPE

THE COMPLETE
CITIES OF ANCIENT EGYPT

242 illustrations, 193 in color

For Joyce

Half-title Middle Kingdom model of workers baking and butchering.

Title page Mudbrick settlement and artifacts uncovered at Ayn Asil in the Dakhla Oasis.

Right Reconstruction of a house in the pyramid town at Giza.

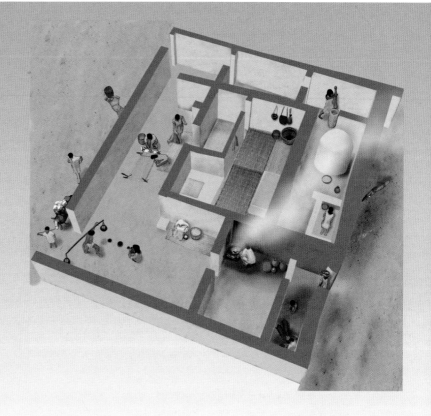

The Complete Cities of Ancient Egypt © 2014
Thames & Hudson Ltd, London

Published in the United Kingdom in 2014 by
Thames & Hudson Ltd, 181A High Holborn,
London WC1V 7QX

First published in 2014 in hardcover in the United
States of America by Thames & Hudson Inc.,
500 Fifth Avenue, New York, New York 10110

thamesandhudsonusa.com

Library of Congress Catalog Card Number 2014931272

ISBN 978-0-500-05179-5

Printed and bound in China by Toppan Leefung
Printing Limited

CONTENTS

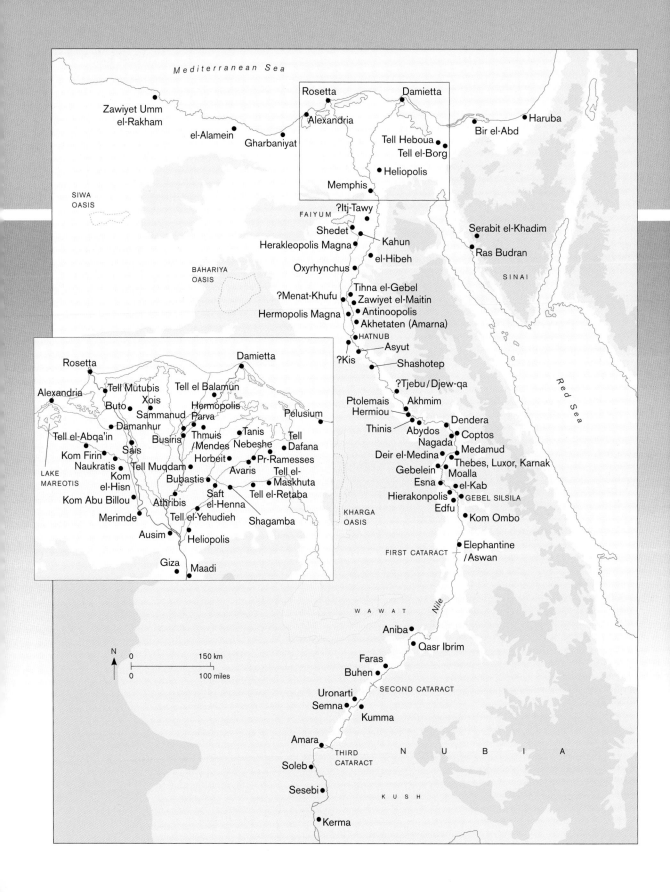

Mediterranean Sea

Rosetta
Damietta
Zawiyet Umm el-Rakham
Alexandria
Haruba
el-Alamein
Bir el-Abd
Gharbaniyat
Tell Heboua
Tell el-Borg
Heliopolis

SIWA OASIS

Memphis

?Itj-Tawy
FAIYUM
Serabit el-Khadim
Shedet
Kahun
Herakleopolis Magna
Ras Budran
el-Hibeh
SINAI
BAHARIYA OASIS
Oxyrhynchus
Tihna el-Gebel
?Menat-Khufu
Zawiyet el-Maitin
Hermopolis Magna
Antinoopolis
Akhetaten (Amarna)
HATNUB
Asyut
?Kis
Shashotep

?Tjebu/Djew-qa

Akhmim
Ptolemais Hermiou
Dendera
Thinis
Abydos
Coptos
Nagada
Medamud
Deir el-Medina
Thebes, Luxor, Karnak
Gebelein
Moalla
Esna
el-Kab
Hierakonpolis
GEBEL SILSILA
Edfu
Kom Ombo

KHARGA OASIS

Elephantine /Aswan
FIRST CATARACT

Red Sea

Nile

W A W A T

Aniba
Qasr Ibrim
Faras
Buhen
SECOND CATARACT
Uronarti
Semna
Kumma

Amara
THIRD CATARACT
N U B I A
Soleb
Sesebi
K U S H
Kerma

N
0   150 km
0   100 miles

Inset map:

Rosetta
Damietta
Alexandria
Tell Mutubis
Tell el Balamun
Buto
Xois
Sammanud
Hermopolis Parva
Pelusium
Damanhur
Tell el-Abqa'in
Busiris
Thmuis /Mendes
Tanis
Tell Dafana
Kom Firin
Sais
Nebeshe
Naukratis
Tell Muqdam
Horbeit
Pr-Ramesses
Kom el-Hisn
Avaris
Kom Abu Billou
Bubastis
Tell el-Maskhuta
LAKE MAREOTIS
Athribis
Saft el-Henna
Tell el-Retaba
Merimde
Tell el-Yehudieh
Shagamba
Ausim
Heliopolis
Giza
Maadi

6

Urban Life in Ancient Egypt

I t is easy to think of ancient Egypt as a land filled with tombs and temples built by a people obsessed with death and their gods. This impression is due to a combination of factors, the most important being the choices the ancient Egyptians made in the allocation of resources to different parts of the built environment, which led to the most durable materials being used for their most important structures, temples and tombs, rather than ordinary dwellings; the locations chosen for different types of structure, resulting in the most visible monuments today being those in spaces often set apart from urban life; and the choices, often in favour of spectacular monuments over more 'mundane' settlement sites, made by the archaeologists who have explored the physical heritage of ancient Egypt through excavation and survey.

However, although its great monuments are the defining feature of ancient Egypt to modern observers, to the ancient Egyptians themselves the royal pyramids of the Old Kingdom and the enormous stone temples of the New Kingdom were exceptional, unusual and generally inaccessible parts of their everyday built environment. This book attempts to explore ancient Egyptian cities to try to find what was usual as well as what was unusual. We shall learn that it cannot be truly 'complete' since the destruction of ancient settlement remains has robbed us of much of the archaeological record, but we shall find partial compensation in looking beyond settlements that we might think of as cities to explore towns, villages, indeed a whole variety of locations where the ancient Egyptians lived their lives.

This book will explore the cities and towns of ancient Egypt first by looking at the evidence we have for who built them, why they were built and for whom they were intended. The role of the king as an initiator of major projects (including urban development) is very important, as is the space that was created within cities for temples, the residences of the gods. But we shall also try to understand the ways in which the built environment of cities, towns and villages throughout Egypt was created and adapted by 'ordinary' Egyptians to serve their everyday lives from 3500 BC to AD 641. Finally, we shall take a journey down the Nile, and visit adjacent areas inhabited by the Egyptians to see what remains, and what we know to have once existed, of the cities and towns of ancient Egypt.

Map of Egypt showing the major sites and settlements discussed in this book.

The Call of the Pyramid

Egypt's monuments demand attention. They were designed to impress both men and gods and they continue to awe both the casual tourist and supposedly serious scholar. Indeed, pyramid investigation in its variety of forms has been a permanent feature of Egyptology (in its broadest sense) since its traditional birth as a serious discipline when Napoleon's *savants* invaded in 1798.

Ancient towns were not so immediately attractive to early archaeologists; for one thing it was difficult to find them and when one did it was often in the form of great mounds of potsherds and broken bricks, which did not make an inviting prospect for excavation. An obvious comparison can be seen today at Giza, where the very visible Old Kingdom pyramids have an immediate appeal, although their obvious magnificence is not necessarily equalled by their contribution to a wider understanding of the ancient Egyptians, apart from teaching us of their ability to move vast quantities of stone. By contrast, the pyramid towns at the same site have long been invisible, but are packed with vital information, which has only been recently revealed after careful archaeological excavation and analysis.

Almost as attractive to early explorers were the heavily decorated elite tombs and royal temples that similarly tempted scholars into the study of monumental architecture, its functions and motifs. They also encouraged an interest in two other wide-ranging topics that have had a substantial impact on the development of the intellectual focus of Egyptology.

Pictures and Words

One of these topics was royal and private art in two and three dimensions. To give just two examples, colossal royal sculpture invited studies of the superhuman aspects of Egyptian kingship, while the decorative schemes of elite private tombs with their 'daily life' scenes of ancient Egyptians doing ordinary ancient Egyptian things, seemed to offer a way of understanding many aspects of the political, social and religious lives of non-royal people.

Excavations at the town attached to the tomb of the Old Kingdom Queen Khentkawes at Giza, in the shadow of the pyramids of Khafre and Khufu.

To a large extent, the decoration and contents of tombs became a substitute for
settlement sites in the study of a range of domestic and industrial activities – until fairly
recently it was commonplace to read accounts of, say, baking and brewing in ancient
Egypt that were based not on archaeological finds from real bakeries and breweries,
but on the illustrations of such activities on the walls of private tombs, and on wooden
models within those tombs. This source of evidence, to some degree, it was thought,
negated the necessity of digging for the badly preserved remains of such structures given
that they were illustrated in such glorious colours, often in a strip-cartoon-like way.

The second topic was even more pervasive. Monuments – from royal temples to
private tombs – were covered by, and filled with objects containing, hieroglyphic text.
The 'daily life' scenes would be less informative if they did not also carry explanatory
'captions' and the colossal statues would be significantly more enigmatic if they were
not labelled with the name and titles of their royal or divine owner. The ability to
read hieroglyphic (and other) texts, which was gained early in the modern study of
ancient Egypt, provided the single most important tool in understanding this ancient
civilization. After all, what could be more authentic and more informative than hearing
the Egyptians speaking to us in their own voices?

The funerary papyrus
of the royal scribe
Nakht shows him in
the afterlife with the
ideal accommodation
for a high-ranking
New Kingdom official:
a comfortable house
(right) and a garden
around a pool (left).
Scenes such as this
provide evidence for
what Egyptian homes
would have looked like.

This statue of the governor of the fortress at Zawiyet Umm el-Rakham, Neb-Re (shown here bearing a staff demonstrating his allegiance to the goddess Sekhmet), is an outstanding example of Ramesside sculpture, but also comes from a site that has much to tell us about military settlements in the New Kingdom (see pp. 220–22).

Art history and philology have a cachet even for the settlement archaeologist. It is undeniable that the single most exciting, and informative, object that the present author has excavated from the fortress-town of Zawiyet Umm el-Rakham is the inscribed statue of its governor, Neb-Re. It is also (and this too is relevant to an understanding of the history of Egyptian archaeology) undeniably the most beautiful object from the site and the only one on display in a major museum. That museum is at Luxor, but 100 years ago it might easily have been the British Museum, the Louvre or (since Liverpool University is the institutional sponsor of this particular expedition) the Garstang Museum of

Archaeology. Even more to the point, if this fieldwork had been conducted 100 years ago by the eponymous John Garstang himself, or by Flinders Petrie, the thousands of small objects found at the site would not now be housed in a purpose-built storage facility in the nearby city of Mersa Matruh, as the property of the Egyptian state, but scattered through private and public collections in Britain and beyond.

The Fruitful Cemetery

The work of excavators such as Garstang and Petrie was largely enabled by private patronage from individuals and museums. The objects recovered were divided first with the Cairo Museum, and then with patrons. Although many of these individual patrons were motivated by philanthropic concerns – often they were rich industrialists or merchants who used some of their wealth to endow civic institutions such as art galleries, museums and universities – they were also businessmen who would know the value of a good return on an investment, and their 'dividend' came in the form of ancient objects. For museums, the idea of a return on investment was even more pressing since it could be argued that the overwhelming reason for them subscribing was not philanthropy or the desire to promote research, but to service their core business – putting good-quality objects on display in their museum.

For the excavator in Egypt in the late 19th and early 20th centuries, a balance had to be struck between working at a site they thought was particularly interesting and worthwhile, and in satisfying their paymasters. Different archaeologists managed this with different degrees of success – Petrie was probably best at maintaining the balance between a flow of objects and the investigation of sites that added to knowledge in significant leaps rather than an incremental shuffle.

For the excavator who wanted to keep his backers happy and ensure a regular supply of goodies there was one obvious solution: Egyptian cemeteries were goldmines (sometimes quite literally) owing to a combination of factors, the most important of which were, first, that a particular set of beliefs concerning the afterlife led the Egyptians to place as large a quantity of high-quality objects in their tombs as they could afford and, second, that the objects had a high level of preservation given the desert-edge location of most of these cemeteries, certainly in the Nile Valley. There were, therefore, very practical reasons why excavators were – and still are – drawn to dig up Egypt's ancient cemeteries – they are certain to find objects, often of high quality – in comparison with the much more uncertain and aesthetically less satisfying exploration of Egypt's settlement sites.

The construction of private tombs designed to welcome visitors, in a manner similar to domestic houses, was a consistent feature of mortuary architecture in ancient Egypt. This example, from the Mustafa Kamal cemetery at Alexandria, combines Egyptian traditions with Hellenistic approaches to tomb design and decoration.

Site Survival

Much of the geography and topography of ancient Egypt can be seen as a pair of duals or opposites – Upper and Lower Egypt, the Nile Delta and the Nile Valley, the cultivated land and the desert. The last pairing is one of radical opposites, with the dry sand of the desert, the 'red land', notably different from the Nile-watered rich agricultural soil of the 'black land'. Often the border between the two is strikingly stark and it has often been remarked that it is possible for a person to stand with one foot on the desert and the other on cultivated land. Burial in each of these environments has a dramatic effect on the chances of survival of small objects; as noted above, objects deliberately and carefully placed in tombs that were themselves located on the dry desert, well above the greatest height of the Nile at the time of inundation, had the greatest chance of survival. In contrast, the often broken and discarded objects of everyday life, lost under succeeding levels of Nile silt and regularly soaked by the inundation had the least chance of survival.

Just as with objects, so with sites. One might draw a distinction between tombs and temples on the one hand, built from stone and located above the inundation, and settlement sites on the other, built from mudbrick and organic materials and regularly flooded by the inundation. This is of course a gross oversimplification, but there is still much truth here. Clearly cemeteries could be built far distant from the Nile because

This Ramesside temple at Kom el-Rabi'a at Memphis is a good example of the problems of survival of buildings – even large stone buildings – in the lush vegetation of the Nile Valley and Delta.

their inhabitants had no need for a regular water supply or for ready access to transport links and agricultural land. Neither could their residents move at short notice when an over-high inundation threatened. Towns, cities, villages, in fact any kind of settlement needed the resources that would support a living population, which was, in most cases, a Nileside location. The vagaries of Nile flooding meant a certain flexibility was required on the part of the population – and the rebuilding of wholly or partly flooded houses was probably a regular occurrence. The use of easily workable and cheap building materials – especially mudbrick – was an obvious solution. The key would be the ease of rebuilding, not the attempt to avoid problems in the first place.

Of course some settlements were located away from the Nile, and their inhabitants managed to avoid the problems that beset the majority of ancient Egyptians. However, these tended to be rather special – and specialist – settlements built in otherwise unlikely or inhospitable locations for particular reasons. Deir el-Medina is the most obvious example of this, although the reader will notice a high proportion of the sites described in the Gazetteer – particularly those that are at all well-preserved – fall into this category.

The location of the village of Deir el-Medina – in an inhospitable part of the Theban mountain – has resulted in its astonishing degree of preservation.

15

Other sites, perhaps built on naturally high ground within the Nile Valley or Delta (including the form of sand-island known as a 'turtleback' or *gezira*), perhaps on one of the high levees along the riverbank, or perhaps grown high as a *tell* on the debris of earlier phases of occupation, may have been relatively safe from Nile flooding. Sites such as this, which have survived to the present day, have a very good chance of being buried under modern towns and villages located in those places for exactly the same reasons as their ancient predecessors. Sites in this class (Horbeit in the Delta, or Shutb near Asyut are good examples) have so much modern settlement on them that large-scale archaeological exploration is very difficult.

The rise and fall of the Nile during the inundation was the very heart of the ancient Egyptian agricultural year. The activities of dam-builders at Aswan in the 20th century mean that the Nile no longer fluctuates so dramatically. The Nile is never as high as it used to be, but nor is it ever so low. If ancient sites are no longer flooded as deeply as they were, neither are they as annually high above those same waters. Instead, archaeologists in the floodplain have to cope with a fairly constant but often inconveniently high subsoil water level, which makes the excavation of the deepest (i.e. earliest) levels of ancient sites somewhat problematic.

A Note on Chronology

Throughout this book, dates will be given in a variety of standard forms, most usually by reference to dynasties of kings or longer periods of time ('kingdoms', 'periods' and 'intermediate periods'). While there is still debate as to the fine-tuning of these dating systems to 'absolute' dates (i.e. years BC or AD), there is general agreement on the broad structure of how Egyptian history can be referred to. The most common terms used in this book are as follows:

Late Predynastic Period	*c.* 3500–3000 BC	
Early Dynastic Period	*c.* 3000–2650 BC	Dynasties 1–2
Old Kingdom	*c.* 2650–2175 BC	Dynasties 3–6
First Intermediate Period	*c.* 2175–1975 BC	Dynasties 8–11
Middle Kingdom	*c.* 1975–1640 BC	Dynasties 11–13
Second Intermediate Period	*c.* 1640–1550 BC	Dynasties 14–17
New Kingdom	*c.* 1550–1070 BC	Dynasties 18–20
Third Intermediate Period	*c.* 1070–664 BC	Dynasties 21–25
Late Period	664–332 BC	Dynasties 26–31
Graeco-Roman Period	332 BC–AD 395	

The time when Egypt was ruled by dynasties, i.e. from *c.* 3000 to 332 BC, is also often referred to more generally as the 'dynastic period'.

Settlement Archaeology Today

Though a list of excavators and the cemeteries they have worked in would be a very long roll indeed, significant past excavations at major settlement sites are comparatively few: Petrie's at Kahun and Bruyère's at Deir el-Medina (both of whose work will be discussed later) come to mind. Indeed it is probably true to say that there are currently more settlement sites in Egypt that are the subject of very recent or current fieldwork than the sum total of all such sites in the past – a far from comprehensive list would include major cities and settlements attached to sites best known for their monumental remains at Avaris/Pr-Ramesses, Giza, Memphis, Amarna, Abydos and Elephantine, while significant numbers of smaller or less well-preserved settlement sites are being investigated both on the margins (e.g. Tell Heboua, Zawiyet Umm el-Rakham, Ayn Asil, Amara) and within (too many to list here) dynastic Egypt. With discoveries of the late and early centuries, and a major emphasis on settlement archaeology as an area for research within Egyptian archaeology, now is a good time to appraise what we know about the towns and cities of ancient Egypt.

Modern investigation of archaeological sites involves a range of survey techniques. In order to explore the past landscapes of ancient Thebes, a team led by Angus Graham and Judith Bunbury carries out a programme of augering at Karnak.

PART I

The Rise of the City

What is a City?

In a famous article in 1960, John Wilson, Professor of Egyptology in the Oriental Institute at Chicago University, described ancient Egypt as a 'civilisation without cities'. Even at the time he wrote these words they were not literally true: the monuments of Thebes were clearly part of a significant urban centre, Amarna had been the subject of many decades of archaeological excavation that had uncovered everything a city could need and Memphis showed the fragmentary remains of perhaps the most long-lasting metropolis in the world. In known ancient texts, too, the greatness of ancient Egyptian cities was celebrated, including a city that (in 1960) was not yet known: Pr-Ramesses, founded by Ramesses II as a new royal city in the Eastern Delta.

So what did Wilson mean? He was, essentially, overstating what he thought to be a fundamental aspect of human settlement in ancient Egypt, which was that, unlike Mesopotamia with its individual city states, where the typical pattern was a single major urban centre and a relatively limited agricultural hinterland, Bronze Age Egypt (the largest country of its time) basically consisted of vast tracts of agricultural land, inhabited by a low-density population that had no need for major urban centres. This view was predicated on Egypt having an economy that was fundamentally agricultural.

In fact, at a basic level, this seems to be true. Although it is difficult to be precise about population in the ancient world, whether using percentages or absolute numbers, it is accurate to say that the vast majority of the population of dynastic Egypt worked on the land. Compared with other wealth-producing activities, agriculture was overwhelmingly dominant – much more so than in Mesopotamia where the production and trade in finished goods was of greater significance as an economic activity and as an occupation of the population at large.

Egypt as a Non-urban State

With such an economic basis, it is tempting to think that in Egypt major centres of population were not necessary, since the requirements of an agrarian population could be catered for locally, with relatively few concentrations of non-agricultural activity (i.e. towns and cities) that housed a relatively tiny elite who would, essentially, be both landowners and members of the royal court and government. This picture does, to some degree, seem to characterize Old Kingdom Egypt. At that time, the only real 'city' seems to have been Memphis, which was the centre of government, the residence city of king and elite, and the location of elite burials,

Previous pages
The range of crafts and industries illustrated on the walls of the tomb of the 18th Dynasty vizier Rekhmire at Thebes includes the large-scale production of mudbrick for public buildings.

The stark contrast between desert, agricultural land and river affected both the location of settlement in ancient Egypt, and how the landscape was conceptualized.

including that of the king himself. The elite tombs seem to represent the most obvious way in which national resources (both men and goods) were brought together for the benefit of king, court and capital. However, although this urban picture may hold good in broad terms, in detail there may be additional complexities. First, the natural advantages presented by the Nile meant that Egypt, in most periods of its history, was an agriculturally superabundant state, with relatively little effort on the part of its inhabitants. Per capita yields for agricultural workers are likely to have been enormous compared with those in Mesopotamia, where the less reliable natural irrigation necessitated much more labour-intensive farming methods. Egypt's agricultural superabundance meant that it could 'grow' a large population owing to the high carrying capacity of the super-fertile Nile floodplain. It is possible to imagine a situation where the rural population of Egypt was significantly larger than the numbers of active farmworkers required to produce its food. It may well be the case that the Egyptian countryside was far from underpopulated. Indeed one could argue that what the centre (i.e. the king and court, based in Memphis) required from the rural areas was, in addition to the remittance of rents, taxes and other revenues, the provision of human labour on a very significant scale for the building projects of Old Kingdom Egypt.

So perhaps the question should be, not 'Did Egypt have cities?', but 'What is the nature of those cities?' What is the difference between a village, a town and a city, and to what extent are these divisions relevant to us and to the ancient Egyptians? Perhaps most interesting of all, and it is a question we shall attempt to answer in this book, is whether, away from the major and obvious urban centres such as Thebes, Amarna and Memphis, there existed major population centres that contained within them areas for specialized functions that might mark them out as urban communities rather than simply huge dormitories for an agricultural population.

The Nature of an Egyptian City

How do we define a city? Size of population is important, but this might be relative; in sparsely populated Norway a centre with a population of 20,000 (e.g. Tromso) can be regarded as a city, while in Britain a centre with a population in excess of 100,000 (e.g. Bolton) can be regarded as a large town. Functions are important too: a city is generally regarded as a population centre with a cluster of assets that relate to a region larger than its own immediate hinterland – government is perhaps the most important example of this, but so too (to use examples from medieval

With much settlement remains destroyed, the most obvious visible identifier of an ancient Egyptian city is either its cemeteries or its surviving temple buildings, illustrated here by Luxor Temple.

21

England) are economic institutions (e.g. trade guilds or holding a royal charter recognizing the city as the location of an important market) and cultural institutions (e.g. universities and seats of religious authority such as cathedrals). A capital city is something else again, being defined, generally, as the place where the main centre of government resides. Because of the somewhat peripatetic nature of government in Egypt (not unlike the Tudor rulers on their royal progresses round England, see p. 45) this is not as simple a definition as it might appear. In the Old Kingdom, Memphis was obviously the capital of Egypt. It was the largest – perhaps the only – city, the centre of royal government and elite residence, the hub of specialized functions.

The New Kingdom capital city is more difficult to define: both Memphis and Thebes were centres of royal administration, but for the north and south (including Nubia) of Egypt respectively – and each had an elite population of administrators who served both secular institutions and major religious foundations. Neither could be said to be the ruling centre of the country as a whole, apart from during the few periods when one or other became the place of fixed royal residence. In general, though, the immediate royal court was very mobile and royal progression (in the Tudor sense) through Egypt was the norm. The big exception here is Amarna, as we shall see (pp. 155–63).

The Middle Kingdom presents the rather odd phenomenon of Itj-Tawy, a ruling centre for 12th-Dynasty kings – some of the most powerful and active rulers in Egyptian history – but whose location is still unknown. It is probable that Itj-Tawy represents a 'disembedded capital' comprising a small population of administrators attached to the central royal administration while major economic and religious activity took place elsewhere, especially at Memphis and Thebes. This separation of the 'ruling function' of capital cities from major centres of population/ economic activity/cultural activity may seem odd if the models of, say, London or Paris are used as comparators, but not if Washington DC, Ottawa or Canberra are.

The features that designate a city have been discussed by a number of scholars, some of whom (e.g. Bruce Trigger and David Wengrow)

have produced what might be considered convenient 'checklists' for designating 'citiness'. These attributes include:

1 The presence of an elite who are not directly involved in agricultural production.
2 A relatively high density of permanent population.
3 A significant level of participation in trade/ exchange, including river/sea ports/harbours.
4 A concentration of crafts (and other) specialization.
5 A concentration of administrative functions over a territory greater than the city itself.
6 Control over an agricultural hinterland whose surplus maintains the city.
7 Institutions that promote a sense of specific civic identity.

Rather than 'capital city' the term 'royal city' is often used for ancient Egypt. This is a centre that is established not through natural population growth but by royal edict, for specific reasons. Amarna and Pr-Ramesses are the clearest examples of royal cities because they essentially sprang up during the lifetime of a king at his bidding (not unlike the foundation by royal decree of the Russian city of St Petersburg in the 18th century). While there may be good practical reasons behind the creation of a royal city (Pr-Ramesses was near Egypt's eastern border at a time when relations with Western Asia dominated Egyptian international politics) they can also be seen as somewhat egotistical projections of royal identity – the Akhenaten/ Aten relationship for Amarna (see p. 156), and the elevation of a smallish home town to national prominence in the case of Ramesses II (see p. 203). Thebes is also a 'royal city' inasmuch as it owes its status, particularly its monumental appearance, to the specific relationship between the rulers of the Middle and New Kingdoms and the god Amun(-Re) at his major cult centre. On the other hand, while benefiting from royal patronage, it is hard not to think of cities such as Bubastis in the Eastern Nile Delta or Hermopolis Magna in Middle Egypt as being anything other than organically evolved centres of population, administration and specialized functions within a regional context, making it clear that cities come about both as royal foundations and through organic development.

The Origins of Urbanism in Egypt

Like the term 'city', 'urbanism' and 'urbanization' are not words that are easy to define in very strict terms. The classic definition of urbanization was proposed in 1942 by American demographer Hope Tisdale as

'… a process of population concentration. It proceeds in two ways: the multiplication of points of concentration and the increase in size of individual concentrations.'

In 1965 the American sociologist Philip Hauser added to this definition the concept that as a result of this process the 'proportion of the population living in urban places increases', to avoid the definition covering a situation where the non-urban population grows even faster than the urban population – not what most people think of as the process of urbanization. For ancient Egypt the question of what proportion of the population were city- or town-dwellers at any given period of history is not easy to answer. However, the rise of the city as an important institution can perhaps more confidently be identified as an aspect of ancient Egyptian civilization.

Urbanization and State Formation in Upper Egypt

The first cities in Egypt came out of a background of increasing state formation in the Late Predynastic Period (3500–3000 BC). The best examples of this are in Upper (southern) Egypt and these are also the best-known cities from the period (although Lower (northern) Egypt also had important centres of population before unification (see below)). Archaeologically, the settlements at Nagada and Hierakonpolis are the best preserved from this period and other aspects of the archaeology of these sites – the increasingly rank-differentiated cemeteries containing specialist products of an elite, economically vibrant, politically centralized culture – provide rich evidence for the development of urbanism, state formation and ancient Egyptian 'civilization' in this relatively limited part of the Nile Valley. It must also be noted that it was this region that was

the successful competitor for the control of the whole of Egypt around 3000 BC and, presumably, its vision of urbanism and what constituted a suitable basis for a centralized, agrarian state was what informed the creation of the new capital at Memphis at this time.

Nagada (often spelled Naqada), located 30 km (18½ miles) north of Thebes, was clearly one of the most important regional centres of the predynastic period. Its rich cemeteries provided the data that allowed Flinders Petrie in the final years of the 19th century to undertake the first systematic study of the material culture of the predynastic, allowing him to identify a series of distinct phases, which he named after the site: Nagada I–III. Settlement at Nagada in the Nagada II phase was identified by Petrie in two distinct areas, named by him the 'North Town' and the 'South Town'. The exact nature of these areas – whether they were used for domestic occupation, industrial/agricultural production or the dumping of rubbish – is still not agreed, although the South Town did produce a series of rectangular mudbrick structures that have been identified as houses.

The most important early 'urban' site in Egypt is undoubtedly the ancient Nekhen, modern Kom el-Ahmar ('Red Mound'), best known by its Classical name **Hierakonpolis**, located 80 km (50 miles) south of Thebes on the west bank of the Nile. The Predynastic and Early Dynastic city was spread out over an area running 2.5 km (1½ miles) from north to south along the Nile and, more remarkably, over 3 km (almost 2 miles) from east to west. Within this extensive zone, different clusters of structures developed with their own individual character.

The site was first excavated in a systematic way by the British archaeologists James Quibell and Frederick Green in 1897–99. They were lucky enough to discover a major early temple, which is most famous for the 'Main Deposit', an extraordinary cache of votive material that contained the most important objects for the unification period found anywhere in Egypt. The most famous of these objects are the Narmer Palette and the Narmer and 'Scorpion'

major communal projects) that in later periods were used as motifs designating royal activity. Therefore these objects support the view that Hierakonpolis was not only a major settlement site of Upper Egypt at the time of the unification, but that it was also a political centre – perhaps the capital of a southern kingdom – which produced the leaders who would become kings of a unified Egypt around 3050 BC.

Excavations at Hierakonpolis from 1967 onwards by the American archaeologists Walter Fairservis, Michael Hoffman and Renée Friedman have done much to clarify the extent of early urbanism at Hierakonpolis. The main centre of the city is now referred to as HK 29. It has monumental elements, including a large temple and palace, that would be familiar in general terms, if not in architectural detail, to an Egyptian of the dynastic period. Other parts of the city, located away from HK 29, were specialist centres for industrial production, including kilns for the production of distinctive black-topped pottery and a large brewery. The most visibly impressive monument at Hierakonpolis today is the 'Fort', a huge rectangular enclosure built by King Khasekhemwy of the 2nd Dynasty,

Left In an early example of royal sponsorship of agricultural projects, King 'Scorpion' wields a hoe on this important ceremonial object from Hierakonpolis, the 'Scorpion' Macehead.

maceheads. These over-sized ceremonial objects are covered with relief decoration of two individuals – to whom we refer as Narmer and 'Scorpion' – depicted wearing regalia and behaving in ways (smiting enemies, initiating

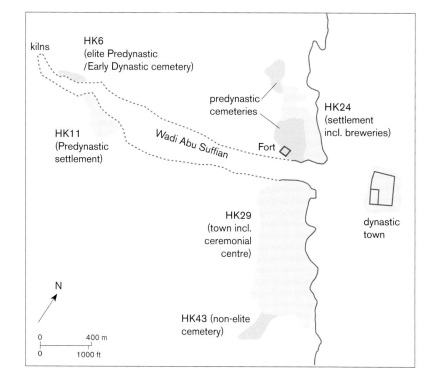

Plan of Hierakonpolis (ancient Nekhen). The extent of the Predynastic and Early Dynastic town (HK 11, 24 and 29) is markedly larger than the later dynastic settlement in the Nile floodplain (middle right).

sometimes described as the oldest standing mudbrick building in the world, which despite its name is of unknown function.

The establishment of Memphis as a national capital at the time of the unification of Egypt brought an end to Hierakonpolis' role as a major royal power-base and, despite some evidence of royal interest in the cult of Horus at the site, the Old Kingdom and later was a time of decline for this important early city.

Grim Northern Towns?

Given the concentration of well-preserved archaeological sites, and especially settlement sites, in Upper Egypt, it is something of a surprise to note that the earliest site in the whole of Egypt that can be properly recognized as a town is the Western Delta site of **Merimde Beni Salama**, excavated by German archaeologist Hermann Junker from 1929 to 1938. This Neolithic town, which was abandoned by 4000 BC, was well placed to take advantage of the contemporary climatic conditions, with the savannah plains that predated the Sahara Desert we know today to the west and the Nilotic Delta to the east. The houses of the latter phase of occupation are substantial, partly subterranean, mud huts, some with door thresholds made from hippopotamus tibia – a resource presumably available from the Delta marshes. Human burials between the houses indicate one way in which Merimde was distinctly different from the usual urban pattern, where settlement and cemetery in Upper (southern) Egypt were separated.

Indeed the heavy dependence Egyptian archaeology has traditionally had on cemeteries as a source of evidence is especially true for the millennia before the unification of Egypt. With a few exceptions – Hierakonpolis the most notable – the predynastic period in Upper Egypt is mainly known from the relatively rich and culturally distinctive burials of the Nagada I–III phases, especially their distinctive ceramic tradition. By contrast, Predynastic burials of Lower (northern) Egypt, which are in any case

The 2nd Dynasty 'Fort' at Hierakonpolis was partly built over a Predynastic cemetery, excavated by John Garstang in 1905–6.

much less well-preserved than the desert-edge cemeteries of Upper Egypt, have provided a much more dour set of grave goods, which are culturally distinct from those of the southern sites. Much of this northern material comes from a series of cemetery sites around Cairo: Wadi Digla, Heliopolis and, especially, **Maadi**. The last site, together with the northwestern Delta site of **Buto**, gave its name to a cultural phase (the Maadi-Buto culture), which was contemporary with Nagada I–II in Upper Egypt. Importantly, as well as burial evidence, there was also a settlement site at Maadi, which was explored between 1930 and 1948. It sits on a natural terrace overlooking the valley below and consists mainly of a narrow strip of simple huts and storage pits.

More recent attention in the search for Predynastic settlement in Lower Egypt has concentrated on a number of sites located on *geziras* (naturally occurring sand-islands) in the Eastern Nile Delta, where work at **Tell Ibrahim Awad**, **Tell el-Issuwid** and **Tell el-Farkha** has

produced sites that are essentially similar to existing Maadi-Buto sites with an emphasis on simple huts (as attested by post-holes) and a significant number of storage pits for agricultural products. A renewed interest recently in the archaeology of Buto has produced evidence for long-distance contacts with the Uruk culture of Mesopotamia; as is also the case at Hierakonpolis, evidence of long-distance contacts has stimulated discussion, although little agreement, on how contact with traders from the early cities of Mesopotamia might have influenced urban development in Egypt itself. Certainly, rapid expansion of many of these settlements at and after the unification, and the extensive use of more substantial mudbrick structures, is striking and may be a development inspired by news of Mesopotamian urban sites from traders.

This view of the German Archaeological Institute at Buto gives a clear sense of the longevity of the city: in the foreground is a mudbrick structure of the 26th Dynasty, while behind it is a building of the Early Dynastic Period.

The Location of Cities

The location of towns and cities in ancient Egypt was dictated by two principal factors; the behaviour of the Nile and the wishes of the king. Royal influence on the location of settlements was graduated. At one end of the spectrum was the ordering of a completely new 'royal city'. Amarna is the best example of this, because of the extent to which it has survived in the archaeological record and the detail we have been given as to the reasons behind its creation. The agenda for this particular piece of urban planning survives on the boundary stelae that the pharaoh Akhenaten commissioned as part of the foundation of the city. In this instance, the desire to 'invent' a new city in which Akhenaten could pursue his particular religious agenda is an extreme example of royal whim causing the considerable resources of the Egyptian state to be marshalled (and the movement of a significant proportion of the Egyptian population, especially among the elite) to create a new and vast metropolis in a few short years.

Royal Cities

Other examples of the creation of cities by royal diktat can be cited; the building of Pr-Ramesses by Ramesses II is one example. Another is the development of Memphis as the major urban hub of Early Dynastic and Old Kingdom Egypt as part of the unification process, although its initial foundation was not directly responsible for its success and longevity – rather, a combination of royal patronage and, perhaps more fundamentally, the fact that it was located at the meeting point of Upper and Lower Egypt set it on the right road to organic growth. Royal encouragement of the development of existing towns and cities can be seen at places such as Thebes where relatively small regional centres were developed on the basis of their connection with the king. In the case of Thebes, its choice as an administrative centre for Upper Egypt and Nubia in the New Kingdom was a side-effect of its being the 'home' of the major cult-centre of the predominant imperial god of the New

The text of the rock-cut boundary stelae of Akhenaten at Amarna (see pp. 157–58) provides one of the clearest statements of royal intentions for the foundation of a city.

Kingdom, Amun-Re, and the patronage of that cult centre at Karnak by virtually every New Kingdom king (not to mention the establishment of royal burial in the Valley of the Kings), and not the other way round. Secular importance followed religious choice and personal connection to the king.

Other examples of royal influence on the initiation and development of settlements include the phenomenon of the creation of settlements to service royal projects. These might be the creation of workers' towns to house labour required for major projects (such as that at Giza in the Old Kingdom, see pp. 179–80), settlements to house staff who would service the constructed royal monuments (e.g. Kahun in the Middle Kingdom, see pp. 64–68) or communities of expert craftsmen who were required for the construction of specialized monuments every generation (e.g. Deir el-Medina in the New Kingdom, see pp. 74–86). Settlements were also needed for other activities that might be categorized as royal or state-driven, including mining and quarrying sites (e.g. the travertine quarries at Hatnub, near Amarna), and military settlements, some of which could be both substantial and self-supporting (e.g. Zawiyet

Umm el-Rakham in the New Kingdom, see pp. 220–22). Royal sites could also 'go organic', as seems to have been the case with the fortress of Buhen, which began life as a royal foundation – a military hub in Egypt's Nubian defences during the Middle Kingdom – but became a thriving organic community in the Second Intermediate Period.

Organic Development

The organic development of towns and cities is the process whereby settlements thrive, or not, owing to their natural advantages. Some towns in Egypt may have flourished because of their connection to trade routes (e.g. Asyut for the Western Desert Oases, Coptos for the Wadi Hammamat routes to gold-bearing regions and the Red Sea), but almost all settlements in Egypt needed to be located by reference to the Nile. Along the Nile Valley and in the Nile Delta some important settlements were successful in becoming regional centres on a level beyond the confines of their district, and sometimes over a very long period. These sites include Coptos and Asyut in Upper Egypt; Hermopolis Magna in Middle Egypt; Memphis; and Bubastis, Mendes

Left A scene of a royal foundation ceremony. The pharaoh Hatshepsut, accompanied by the goddess Seshat, marks out the ground for the building on which this relief appears, the 'Red Chapel' at Karnak.

The source of the Nile was a mystery to the Egyptians. On this relief from Philae it is imagined as the pouring of water by the Nile god Hapy from under the rocks of nearby Biggeh Island.

The dynamic action of the Nile in changing the shape of its floodplain can be seen in this aerial view of 'Banana Island' near Luxor, where silting-up of the channel has resulted in the island becoming attached to the floodplain.

and Sais in the Eastern, Central and Western Delta respectively.

Even for planned settlements, organic growth, often based on their relationship with the movements of the Nile, was a significant factor in their success, or lack of success in the long term. Pr-Ramesses and Memphis are both good examples of the interplay between royal wishes and Nilotic behaviour in the long-term survival of cities. By the end of the New Kingdom, less than 200 years after its foundation, Pr-Ramesses had been abandoned as a major settlement. The movement of Nile branches in the Eastern Delta in the 11th century BC left Pr-Ramesses without the river-harbour that was vital for its functioning as a major trade and military hub, and so its position as the major settlement on the Pelusiac branch of the Nile at the beginning of the Third Intermediate Period passed to the city of Tanis – only a little downstream, but crucially on the Nile. In contrast, the urban centre of Memphis seems to have shifted gradually eastwards during the dynastic period as it followed the Nile, which wandered across its floodplain for at least 2,000 years.

In all cases, the most significant factor for long-term success of cities was, obviously enough,

food supply. When Deir el-Medina ceased to be supported by the supply of provisions (including the most basic, water) by the central administration at Thebes, it became essentially unviable as an organic community. Even in major cities the accessibility of a wide range of high-quality agricultural products is a key attribute; in Papyrus Anastasi III, the city of Pr-Ramesses is praised not for its magnificent monuments, but for its pastoral positioning, allowing easy access to a wide variety of agricultural produce, and with the watery wealth of the river/sea singled out for particular attention (see box overleaf).

The identity of these starving people, shown on the causeway of the Saqqara pyramid of King Unas, has been much debated. Perhaps they represent the vulnerability of marginal lands at a time of climate change towards the end of the Old Kingdom.

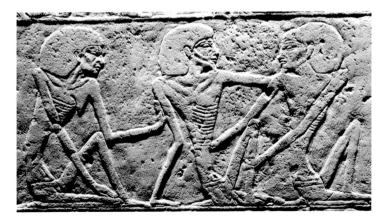

City and Countryside

One of our most vivid descriptions of an ancient Egyptian city is found in this New Kingdom hymn of praise recorded on Papyrus Anastasi III. Our knowledge of what cities looked like, other than by means of archaeological reconstruction, is mainly derived from textual accounts and images found on tomb and temple walls that incidentally portray the urban environment. It is interesting to note, however, that even 'descriptions' such as the one that follows here are more concerned with the benefits of the city's natural environment rather than its physical appearance, so we receive only a limited notion of what cities looked like from original sources.

I have arrived at Pr-Ramesses-miamen (l.p.h.) and found it in [extremely] good condition.

It is a fine district without equal, having the layout of Thebes. It was [Re who founded] it himself.

It is a pleasant place in which to live: its countryside is full of everything good, and it has food and victuals every day.

Its ponds have fishes, its pools have birds.

Its meadows are verdant with herbage: the lades-plant is a cubit and a half in height, and the carob is like the taste of honey in the damp soil.

Its granaries are full of barley and emmer: they approach the sky.

There are onions and leeks of the tr, lettuce of the grove; pomegranates, apples and olives; figs of the orchard, and mellow wine of Kankeme, which is sweeter than honey.

It has red wg-fish of the lake of the Residence that live on lotus-flowers; bdin-fish of the Her-waters; ber-fish together with beg-fish [and] …n-fish of the Peheret-waters; buri-fish [mullet] of the H…-waters of Baal; and huten-fish of the river mouth….

The Lake of Horus [Lake Manzalah?] has salt, and the Pa-Her-waters have natron. Its ships sail forth and moor, [so that] food and victuals are in it every day.

Joy dwells within it, and no one says 'I wish I had….' there. The small in it are like the great.

Come, let us celebrate for its festivals of heaven and its calendar festivals. The papyrus-marshes come to it with papyrus reeds and the Waters-of-Horus with rushes; twigs of the orchards, wreaths of the vine-yards, … birds from the Cataract region. It leans upon … the sea with beg-fish and buri-fish, and [even] their hinterland offers up to it.

The youths of 'Great-of-Victories' [i.e. the city] are in party clothes every day; sweet moringa-oil is upon their heads, and their hair is newly braided. They stand beside their doors, their hands bowed down with foliage and greenery of Per-Hathor and flax of the Pa-Her-waters on the day of the entry of Usimaatre-Setepenre (l.p.h.), Montu-the-Two-Lands, on the morning of the feast of Khoiakh, every man being like his fellow in uttering his petitions.

There is sweet sermet-brew of 'Great-of-Victories'; its debyt-drink is like shaa, its syrup is like the taste of inw, sweeter than honey, beer of Kedy of the port and wine of the vineyards.

It has sweet ointment of the Segbyn-waters and wreaths of the grove.

It has sweet chantresses of 'Great-of Victories' from the school of Memphis.

May one dwell, be happy and move freely about without leaving there!

The Nile marshes were an abundant source of good things for the ancient Egyptians; not just many varieties of fish, but also the papyrus to make fishermen's boats, as in this scene from the Old Kingdom tomb of Kagemni at Saqqara.

Building the City

Egypt, more particularly the Nile Valley between Aswan and Cairo, is blessed with a cornucopia of constructional resources. An ancient Egyptian who made the (sometimes very short) stroll from the edge of the Nile to the edge of the desert would brush past rushes and reeds, which could be used to make matting, roofs, simple shelters and additions to houses; he would walk over the mud of the riverbank, which, combined with the sand of the desert and the chaff of the harvest, could easily produce the small quantities of mudbrick required to build a house or the huge quantities needed to fill the interior of a pyramid; he would see the limestone or, further south, sandstone cliffs that were a convenient local source of easily quarried building stone.

Cities of Mud

The surviving remains of the New Kingdom city of Thebes give a magnificent but misleading impression of ancient Egyptian cities. Along with the royal pyramids of the Old Kingdom, they suggest to the modern visitor that stone was the most commonly used building material in dynastic Egypt. However, this was not the case. Although stone was the ideal material of choice

when building houses for the gods (temples) and houses for the dead (tombs), the vast majority of structures erected in ancient Egypt would have had little, if any, of this comparatively expensive material used within them. Houses for the living were primarily made from a sturdy yet essentially disposable material: mudbrick. This was used in the vast majority of structures inhabited by Egyptians of all classes, from townsfolk in their mudbrick houses to kings in their mudbrick palaces, to soldiers in their mudbrick forts. Some additional elements might be required – wooden roofing beams or stone doorframes or stone column-bases – but, in essence, mudbrick supplied most of a living Egyptian's housing requirements, and also, through granaries and storerooms built on what could be a vast scale, met his storage needs.

Left alone, these structures survive well in the dry Egyptian climate, as ancient mudbrick structures from the predynastic period prove. However, any significant amount of moisture is disastrous, turning the brick back into the damp, formless mud from which it came. For the ancient Egyptians, however, this was not a significant problem. Most mudbrick structures consisted of houses built in ordinary towns and

The three main types of building material used in ancient Egypt – mudbrick, stone and wood – are represented in this wall at Medinet Maadi in the Faiyum. The limited use of wood is indicative of its comparative scarcity.

villages close to the Nile, and were therefore
susceptible to flooding during the inundation,
but such structures could be regarded as
essentially disposable owing to the comparative
ease with which they could be rebuilt.

Mudbrick was the ideal building material for
ancient Egypt. It could be used by a peasant to
build a wall that could turn his house from a
five-room to a six-room dwelling. It could also
be used by a king to fill the vast interior of a
pyramid. It was just a matter of organization.
The peasant making his house alterations
would, perhaps, organize a group of friends or
neighbours to collect the required amount of
soil, which would be taken to a flat, dry piece of
ground, as close as possible to where the brick
was to be used. The most sophisticated tool
required was a simple brick mould: a rectangular
frame of wood, open on both sides, which was
placed on the ground, filled with the mud-mix,
smoothed off and then lifted to leave the wet
brick firm and glistening on the ground.

Because the soil would have been mixed with
water and sand or chaff (or both), the damp
mud would now be firm enough to retain its
shape while it dried. Moreover, the straw chaff
would make the brick porous enough to dry out
thoroughly without cracking, and the addition of
sand or straw would reduce shrinkage. Although
the well-graded silt of the banks of the Nile or
local canals was in many ways ideal, pure Nile
mud shrinks by 30 per cent during the drying
process. The composition of mudbrick varied
considerably, and most bricks were adapted to
make best use of locally available 'ingredients'.
Modern experiments in brickmaking suggest
that the best mix for mudbrick is 1 cubic metre
(35 cubic ft) of soil plus ⅓ cubic metre
(12 cubic ft) of sand and 20 kg (44 lb) of straw.
Once 'struck' the brick would be left to dry for
about three days, turned and allowed to dry for
a further three days, after which it would be ready
for use.

Our understanding of how bricks were
manufactured comes from three major sources.
One is ancient bricks and brick structures
themselves. Another is the study of modern
brickmaking, which operates today in much the
same way it probably did in ancient Egypt –
either a personal or community-based project,

or a more 'official' process, particularly in the
revival encouraged by the work of the Egyptian
architect Hassan Fathy. Another major source of
information is the illustration of the process in
wooden models or on the walls of a few Egyptian
tombs; the scene from the New Kingdom tomb
of Rekhmire (see p. 18) is especially interesting
in that it shows brickmaking for an official, state
project, but the processes involved comprise the
same low-level technology that would have been
used at a village level.

In addition, administrative texts can tell us
what was possible for the official manufacture
of vast quantities of brick for official projects.
Papyrus Reisner I refers to an order for mudbrick
for a royal project during the reign of Senwosret I
(in the Middle Kingdom). It is interesting to note
that the order does not refer to the number of
bricks required, but the volume – 65 cubic cubits
per day, a figure which equates to 34 cubic metres
(45½ cubic yards). The size of bricks is not
known (the same papyrus refers to both 'brick

The simple process of
producing mudbricks
has changed little
over the millennia: the
pile of finished bricks
at Gebelein (above)
could easily have
been produced by the
workers shown in this
wooden model from
the Middle Kingdom
(below) with their
mattocks for digging
out the mud and simple
brick-mould.

and 'large brick'), but the largest size of bricks used in official projects in the Middle Kingdom was *c.* 42 by 21 by 15 cm (16½ by 8¼ by 6 in.), which means the order was for at least 2,600 bricks. Since Fathy reported that a team of four men can produce 3,000 bricks per day, the numbers of people involved in this order need not have been large. However, for other projects the quantities of mudbrick could be enormous; two well-known Middle Kingdom structures, the pyramid of Senwosret III at Dahshur and the fortress of Buhen, were built from 24.5 and 4.6 million bricks respectively.

Cities of Stone

Relatively small amounts of stone were used in most domestic buildings, limited particularly to parts of the structure that were load-bearing (e.g. column-bases) or wear-heavy (e.g. doorframes). The situation was rather different for structures

that were intended to have a longer lifetime than the buildings in most settlements. Projects especially favoured with large-scale use of stone tended to be royal commissions – essentially major temples and royal or elite tombs.

For limited domestic use and the bulk of major constructions, local stone from a conveniently nearby quarry was preferred. This meant one of the two types of 'soft' stone available in the Nile Valley – limestone (from the apex of the Delta as far south as Esna) and sandstone (from Esna south into Nubia). However, the Egyptians were always aware of the balance to be struck between the quality and convenience of building stone; local stone was not necessarily of the best quality, but might be usable for buildings that did not require a high-quality finish. Limestone is the best example of this because it has the widest range of quality of any stone used by the Egyptians, from the extremely fine-grained limestone used in the 'White Chapel' of

The 'White Chapel' of Senwosret I at Karnak is an outstanding example of the use of high-quality limestone. It also contains one of the most important nome lists (see pp. 53–54).

33

The quarrying-marks, showing where layers of sandstone blocks have been removed, are still visible at the extensive Gebel Silsila sandstone quarries, the most important source of building stone for New Kingdom Thebes.

Below Individual quarrying expeditions were often recorded at quarry sites. This elaborate example celebrates the re-opening of the limestone quarries at Masara to supply building stone for the temples of Ptah at Memphis and Amun at Karnak.

Senwosret I at Thebes, to the crude nummulitic limestone (so-called because of its rough coin-like fossil inclusions) found in some of the smaller provincial temples in Middle Egypt.

In terms of the selection of building stone, Thebes is the most interesting case study, given the extent and variety of its New Kingdom monuments. Although Thebes is in a limestone region, the quality of the local limestone is not very high, as it contains many fractures and flint inclusions. For the major building projects of the New Kingdom, therefore, the main quarry was not in the limestone area around Thebes, but was the sandstone workings at Gebel Silsila, 130 kilometres (81 miles) upstream from Thebes, where quarries on both banks of the Nile, located very close to the river, minimized the problems of overland transportation of the stone blocks to river barges (often a difficulty at other quarries).

Granite, chiefly from the Aswan area, was the principal 'hard stone' used in architecture. The other hard stones used in building to a significant degree are quartzite and basalt. These were most often used in specialized contexts, particularly in important elements of the temple, such as entranceways, altars, shrines, obelisks and statues.

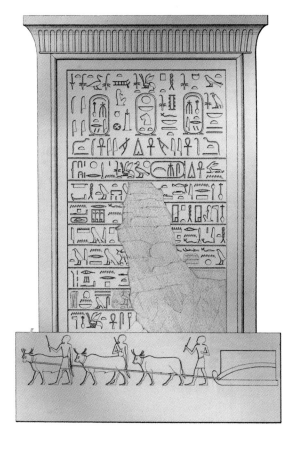

Egyptian Words for Towns and Cities

The Egyptians used a variety of terms to refer to their settlements. Like our own terms ('city', 'town', 'village') they are useful in suggesting what sort of settlement is being referred to, and therefore what the Egyptians considered to be useful categories in the taxonomy of settlement, but, like our own terms, these Egyptian words can be ambiguous in their meaning.

While it would be convenient to equate common Egyptians terms with roughly understandable English equivalents (e.g. *niwt* = 'city', *dmi* = 'town', *whyt* = 'village', probably pronounced niwet, demi, wehyt), any analysis of the ways in which these terms were used by the Egyptians, over what is a very long period, indicates that such an equivalence is an over-simplistic interpretation.

One of the difficulties we face when considering these terms is the fact that we do not know the extent to which they are used in a specific, taxonomic way and that in which they are used rather more loosely. This is not something unique to Egypt: a Briton who was questioned about the difference might comment that cities are generally larger than towns, but if asked why Bolton in Lancashire with a population of 140,000 is a town and Truro in Cornwall with a population of less than 18,000 is a city, they might then flounder around

popular misconceptions about the possession of cathedrals as the distinctive marker of being a city (the cathedral-test is anachronistic; in the UK the sole determining feature of a city is its possession of royal letters patent). More generally, anyone referring to 'London town' or a 'downtown' area of New York is using a colloquial means of referring to two of the largest metropolises in the western world. In a similar way, the term 'Inner City', which appears to be a neutral means of referring to an aspect of a city, has specific connotations in the English-speaking world relating to lower-income residential districts in or close to the city centre; this is a definition that would not apply to, for example, the affluent *Innere Stadt* districts of Vienna.

An example of this type of looseness in an Egyptian context can be seen in the papyrus *Onomasticon of Amenemope*, which provides a list of significant locations during the 21st Dynasty. Under the heading *dmi*, a variety of places are listed, including examples that are described as a *niwt*, a *whyt* and a *hwt* (hwt). To explain this, we need to accept that the word *dmi*, at least in this specific context, is a term that is not part of any ranking order of settlements, but is probably a very loose definition, perhaps denoting 'significant places'. Austrian Egyptologist Manfred Bietak suggests that, in this context, the thing

There are several surviving manuscripts of the *Onomasticon of Amenemope* including this one in the British Museum also known as Papyrus Hood (BM 10202).

the places listed under the heading *dmi* have in common is a topographic or cultic importance, but not necessarily any settlements; he notes that *ẖny* (kheny) – Gebel Silsila, a site important for its quarries and chapels but hardly its population centre – is listed here. One might also note other place names that seem primarily to refer to geographical features rather than population centres, such as individual Nile branches or the marshlands of the Delta. Although, of course, the term *dmi* might mean something else entirely, a topographical significance in the term is also suggested in the following analysis.

Canadian Egyptologist Donald Redford argues that terms for human settlement in ancient Egypt reflect their function and, fundamentally rural, origins. It is certainly the case that Egyptian words for different types of settlement can give an insight into their appearance, functions and origin:

dmi probably derived from the verb 'to touch', indicating a place where ships 'touched' the land, so that a *dmi* is essentially a riverbank settlement. This is confirmed by a common writing of the word, which has as its determinative a sign that often means 'riverbank'. This definition would also work for the *Onomasticon* text we considered above.

i3t (iat, 'mound') a natural description of a settlement located on the flood-plain of the Nile whose vertical growth over a substantial period of time (*tell* formation) would give it an island-like appearance, especially during the inundation when it may well have become an island. This term is reflected in the modern Arabic terms 'Tell' and 'Kom', which refer to mounds formed by long-term settlement.

niwt this is perhaps the most interesting term of all. It is the term most usually associated with very large settlements – cities – and, in the New Kingdom, Thebes became known simply as *niwt*, 'The City'. The hieroglyph for *niwt* ⊗ has often been interpreted as a circular walled town with cross roads but, as Redford has noted, the earliest clear examples of this hieroglyph show that it is formed from four conical huts

Table of sites in the *Onomasticon of Amenemope*.

Modern name	Hieroglyphic text	Transliteration	
Biggeh Island		*snmt*	(Senmet)
Elephantine		*3bw*	(Abu)
Gebel Silsila		*ẖny*	(Kheny)
Kom Ombo		*nbyt*	(Nebyt)
Edfu		*ḏb3*	(Djeba)
Hierakonpolis		*nḫn*	(Nekhen)
El-Kab		*nḫb*	(Nekheb)
Komir		*pr mrw*	(Per meru)
Esna		*iwnyt*	(Iunyt)
Moalla		*ḥf3t*	(Hefat)
Gebelein		*pr ḥwt-ḥr*	(Per Hwt-Hor)
Armant		*iwny*	(Iuny)
Qus		*gsy*	(Gesy)
Coptos		*gbtyw*	(Gebtyu)
Dendera		*int*	(Inet)
Hu		*ḥwt sḫm*	(Hwt Sekhem)
(Wah-Sut)		*w3ḥ-swt (ḫ3-k3-rˁ) m3ˁ-ḫrw*	(Wah-Swt (Khakare) maa-kheru)
Abydos (el-Arabah)		*3bḏw*	(Abdju)
Thinis		*ṯni*	(Tjeni)
Akhmim		*ḫnt-mn*	(Khenet-men)

surrounded by a circular enclosure. The word used to describe the magnificence of imperial Thebes was ultimately derived from the image of a collection of a few simple huts!

ḥnw (khenu) usually translated as 'the (royal) Residence' this word originates in the term for 'interior/inside'. It is a perfect description of the royal 'centre' of palace administration and residence, and was especially associated with the Memphite royal centre of the Old Kingdom and the Middle Kingdom 'residence' at Itj-Tawy.

The detail of the *niwt* town-sign is carefully carved in this writing of the name of Elephantine, Abu.

The *Onomasticon of Amenemope*, after it has finished listing the towns of Egypt, goes on to list different types of dwelling. In order these are:

bḫn (bekhen) 'villa', most usually (as in the Wilbour Papyrus, see pp. 94–96) the building(s) at the core of a country estate.

wḥyt (wehyt) a small settlement equivalent to a village or hamlet, probably originating in the word for 'clan/tribe', and therefore indicating a settlement that was (in theory at least) principally occupied by one extended family.

pr (per) 'house', both as a physical building and, increasingly, in the wider sense of the estate or property of an individual or (often) god.

't (at) originally 'room', it came to mean 'house' in the specific sense of a built structure.

Estimating Population

Working out how many people lived in ancient Egypt is far from an easy task. Despite its documentation-rich bureaucracy, dynastic Egypt has not left us anything like a national census that would tell us how many people lived in the Nile Valley and Delta, nor one for any of its major population centres. With a lack of such direct evidence, various estimates of population have been made on the basis of different types of evidence. However, because of the variability of the available evidence, estimates of the total population of Egypt at different periods vary quite dramatically.

Classical Sources

The clearest statements of the population of Egypt come from Classical historians writing about the country:

'It is said that the reign of Amasis was a time of unexampled material prosperity for Egypt; the river gave its riches to the earth and the earth to the people. The total number of inhabited towns, they say, was 20,000.'

Herodotus, *The Histories* 2: 177, 5th century BC

'In density of population [Egypt] far surpassed of old all known regions of the inhabited world, and even in our own day is thought to be second to none other; for in ancient times it had over 18,000 important villages and cities, as can be seen entered in their sacred records, while under Ptolemy [I] these were reckoned at over 30,000, this great number continuing down to our time. The total population, they say, was of old about 7 million and the number has remained no less down to our day.'

Diodorus Siculus, *Historical Library* I: 31.8, 1st century BC

'This country is extended as far as the Ethiopians … it has 7.5 million men, besides the inhabitants of Alexandria, as may be learned from the revenue of the poll tax.'

Josephus, *Jewish War* 2: 385, 1st century AD

These accounts are broadly in agreement: 20,000–30,000 settlements in the period from the 26th Dynasty to the Ptolemaic Period, with a total population of 7–7.5 million (+/- the population of Alexandria). Our confidence in the accuracy of these figures is supported by Josephus' statement that his population estimate is ultimately derived from poll-tax records. However, the extent to which this figure of between 7 and 8 million can be projected back into the Egypt of Ramesses II, Khufu or Narmer is more than a little problematic.

Carrying Capacity

A method of estimating population based on archaeological evidence, not least in the reconstruction of ancient landscapes, has been attempted by the American geographer Karl Butzer and his figures are the ones most often used as a 'rule of thumb'. His calculations for a particular period are based on:

1 An estimate of the likely total area of cultivable land available at the time in each of the three productive zones of Egypt (Valley, Delta and Faiyum).
2 The 'carrying capacity' of the cultivable land, which is its population density, worked out from knowing what size population could be supported by food production on that area of land.
3 The total population of each region calculated by multiplying its land area by its carrying capacity.

Using this methodology, which admittedly relies on some significant guesstimates for both the amount of available land and its carrying capacity at any given period, the major trends identified by Butzer are:

4000 BC
The Nile Valley and Delta had roughly equal amounts of cultivable land (in the region of 8,000 sq. km, or 3,089 sq. miles, each), but there was a greater population density in the Valley. The Faiyum had a relatively low level of cultivable land (perhaps 100 sq. km, or 39 sq. miles). Total population of Egypt = *c.* **350,000**

3000 BC (Unification)
No significant change to the amount of cultivable land, but a higher population density in all areas. Total population of Egypt = *c.* **870,000.**

2500 BC (Late Old Kingdom)
Increase in cultivable land in the Delta (to about 9,000 sq. km, or 3,475 sq. miles) and continued increase in population density in all areas. Total population of Egypt = *c.* **1.6 million**

1800 BC (height of the Middle Kingdom)
Agricultural efforts by Middle Kingdom kings significantly increased the amount of cultivable land and density of occupation in the Faiyum and in the Delta, together with a slight rise in population density in all areas. Total population of Egypt = *c.* **2 million.**

1250 BC (reign of Ramesses II, New Kingdom)
Significant increase in cultivable land in the Delta (to about 10,000 sq. km, or 3,861 sq. miles) and rise in population density in all areas. Total population of Egypt = *c.* **2.9 million.**

150 BC (Ptolemaic Egypt)
Significant increase in cultivable land in the Delta (to about 16,000 sq. km, or 6,178 sq. miles) and in the Faiyum (perhaps to 1,300 sq. km from the 400 sq. km of the New Kingdom) and rise in population density in all areas. Total population of Egypt = *c.* **4.9 million.**

Urban Population Density

An alternative approach to the 'carrying capacity' method of estimating population is the quantification of the occupied areas of known major settlements. Again, population figures are ascertained by multiplying the size of the occupied area by its population density, but the population density is instead calculated using observations of the urban environment (housing capacity etc.) rather than the food-producing capability of agricultural land. The total urban population can then be extrapolated for any given period. This method, which was also attempted by Butzer, has the advantage of being based on the evidence from identified, known ancient cities, although the assessment of population density within those cities is more problematic.

The 1882 census of Egypt provides a starting point by giving detailed data on the number of settlements, size of settlements and population of those settlements in a country whose population distribution (overwhelmingly rural, with regional centres and one major capital city) might be imagined as being not altogether dissimilar to ancient Egypt from the Old Kingdom onwards. The problem here is in the actual density of the urban settlements – in 1882 six Egyptian cities had a population density as high as 3,000 individuals per hectare, which is probably too high for ancient Egypt – certainly for pre-New Kingdom cities – and Butzer suggests no more than 200 individuals per hectare for Old Kingdom Memphis.

An assessment of known (and assumed) cities and towns, and their likely populations, produces figures for urban populations of 35,000–40,000 for the Old Kingdom, rising to over 500,000 for the Ramesside Period, and about 1 million for the Ptolemaic Period. Butzer compares the figure of 1 million urban Ptolemaic Egyptians with the 7 million total population suggested by Diodorus Siculus and comes up with a proportion of 1:7 for the ratio of urban Egyptians compared with the total population of Egypt. If this figure can be applied to New Kingdom Egypt, Ramesses II would have governed a country of 3–3.5 million Egyptians.

Alternative Estimates

Given the enormous assumptions underlying these figures, and the sometimes patchy archaeological evidence (especially in the Nile Delta), it is hardly surprising that there is no general consensus about these figures. Bruce Trigger put the population of Egypt at the time of unification (3000 BC) as closer to 2 million in contrast with the figure of less than 1 million that was suggested by Butzer; for the New Kingdom Barry Kemp suggests 4–5 million instead of Butzer's 3–3.5 million.

Until the widespread use of red-brick and cement in the later part of the 20th century, most villages in the Nile Valley – like this Nubian settlement at Derr in 1890 – would have seemed little different from their ancient counterparts.

Population Estimates for Individual Towns

Estimates for the whole population of Egypt are difficult to produce with any precision. However, estimates of the population of individual settlements should be more accurate, given the more specific evidence that can be employed. However, even these are far from agreed, and depend on whether the whole of a settlement is occupied at a single time, or whether the archaeological remains represent a shifting pattern of occupation, with partial abandonment and partial occupation, as may have been the case at, for instance, Merimde (see p. 25).

The Middle Kingdom town at Kahun is a good example of a reasonably well-preserved settlement with a range of types of evidence that can be used to estimate its population, as attempted by Barry Kemp. The most obvious first source is the number of houses at Kahun – about 500 smaller houses (including those in missing space). If we assume, as a working hypothesis, that each house was occupied by an average of six people at any one time, we can calculate a figure of c. 3,000 for the entire population. However, a far larger figure is reached in another estimate of population, this one derived from the granaries attached to the 'urban villas' at Kahun: if these were filled to capacity at harvest time, they would be able to supply grain rations to feed a population of between 5,000–9,000 people for a calendar year. Clearly these methods of calculating population are not going to give us any sort of exact figures, but they are useful in providing a range of potential figures, which can be compared against other types of evidence.

The Town of Maiunehes

One of the most important documents for understanding the distribution of settlement at Thebes during the New Kingdom is Papyrus BM 10068. Much of this document deals with robberies from royal tombs that were taking place towards the end of the 20th Dynasty, but it also contains a section dated to 'Year 12, 3rd month of summer, day 13', which bears the title 'Town-register of the West of Niwt [Thebes] from the temple of Menmaatre to the Settlement

of Maiunehes' and contains a list of houses, the names of their owners and the occupations of those owners.

The list begins with 'the house of the temple of King Menmaatre' followed by ten further houses, most of which are occupied by priests. It is tempting to see this as a priestly residential cluster of officials associated with the memorial temple of Seti I at Qurna. The next house listed is 'the house of the temple of Usermaatre-Setepenre', followed by 14 further houses, which again are mostly occupied by priests – perhaps a similar collection for residences of the professional staff attached to the memorial temple of Ramesses II, the Ramesseum.

It is the third group that is most interesting, again beginning with 'the house of the temple of Usermaatre Meryamen' (i.e. the Medinet Habu memorial temple of Ramesses III), but this time followed by 155 houses. The first five are occupied by local high officials, including the Mayor of Western Thebes, Paweraa, and the Scribe of the Army, Kashuti. The remaining 150 houses are occupied by 32 priests of different ranks, but also by a variety of workers, including 12 fishermen, 6 'cultivators', 10 metalworkers, 10 scribes, 6 sandalmakers, 6 gardeners, 3 beekeepers, 4 brewers, 2 woodcutters, 16 herdsmen, 2 goatherds, 6 washermen, 3 potters (or builders?) and 1 physician. This does not look like a skeleton staff attached to a major temple that had seen better days (as seems to be the case with the Seti I and Ramesses II temples listed first), but a real community, with an occupational mix (and evidence of occupational clustering) that one would expect for such a community.

Although once described as 'nothing more than a list of houses with their owners', Papyrus BM 10068 is a vital document for understanding the nature and distribution of settlement in late New Kingdom Thebes.

Although 'Maiunehes' is not defined in this text, it is likely that it is the settlement formed by the houses of this real community. As for the location of that 'settlement', it has long been noted that a 'second stage town' developed within the walls of Medinet Habu, forming a protected community that was the population nucleus of the West Bank of Thebes in the late New Kingdom. We know that Medinet Habu became the home of the 'demobilized' Deir el-Medina community after the abandonment of the royal tombs in the Valley of the Kings. It had long been a place of refuge for the vulnerable and isolated Deir el-Medina community from increasing desert raids by Libyan nomads in the later part of the New Kingdom, and had been an administrative centre for the West Bank

and therefore the place where striking Deir el-Medina workmen would take their complaints. The 'villageization' of the area between the temple and the massive enclosure walls of the Medinet Habu complex should therefore be seen as a natural development for a community living in increasingly uncertain times, seeking both physical and psychological security. It is also unsurprising that this community should continue well into the Coptic Period, at which time it was known as the town of Djeme.

The landscape of western Thebes has not changed greatly since the New Kingdom. The well-defined desert and cultivated land, cut through by the ribbon of river, provide the backdrop for both major temples (the Ramesseum on the desert edge) and the clustered houses of small villages.

PART II

Cities for Kings and Gods

Palaces

For early European explorers in Egypt, it was inconceivable that the massive monumental structures they saw were not obvious evidence of 'oriental despotism' at work creating ego-affirming monuments designed to liken the king with the gods. In particular – and perhaps with the elaborate residences of Ottoman Istanbul in mind – it was easy to think of Egyptian kings creating huge and impressive royal palaces, and in the seminal publication produced after Napoleon's expedition to the country, *Description de L'Egypte,* each of the New Kingdom Theban complexes at Karnak, Luxor and Medinet Habu was described as a 'palais'.

Since the decipherment of the hieroglyphs that adorn their walls, and the archaeological investigations within their precincts, we now know that the major monumental architectural features that so impressed these early visitors were in fact massive temple and mortuary complexes. The urban dwellings of king and subjects were and are harder to identify because

of continued building work on top of ancient sites (sometimes through to the present day) and because, contrary to expectation, the highly stratified hierarchy of ancient Egyptian society was often not evident in its urban landscape: the grandeur Europeans had come to expect in royal building programmes seems to have been reserved for sacred space and funerary complexes.

However, these early visitors were to a very limited extent right in identifying major temples as palaces: Karnak and Medinet Habu did indeed contain royal residences, but only as a comparatively tiny adjunct to what was, overwhelmingly, a residence for gods. The great royal palace, built on the same scale of temples and tombs, was simply not to be seen. There was no direct ancient equivalent of Versailles, Schönbrunn or Buckingham Palace – i.e. a great architectural confection built in or near the capital city of a centralized state, where external appearance reflects the power and dignity of the person or office it houses. The pattern of royal

Previous pages
Aerial view of the Ramesseum, which (like Medinet Habu) acted not only as a royal mortuary temple, but also as a major focus for administrative and economic activity on the West Bank at Thebes.

44

residence in dynastic Egypt was quite different to that of the 18th- or 19th-century European monarch.

Perhaps the best way of thinking about palaces is to consider their different potential functions: as a private dwelling for the ruler and the ruler's family, a place for royal administration and the bureaucracy that supports it, as a venue for ceremonial activity (both public and private). In the Egyptian context (as with others) a fourth major function can be added: the location for production of rare or important goods of intrinsic value or requiring specialist skills.

The Peripatetic Pharaoh

Part of the reason that palaces were so much more than just a residence was that the king was an active, mobile ruler, not just on foreign campaigns (although for a significant number of rulers they seem to have been a regular event),

but throughout Egypt. Egyptian sources refer to the 'Mooring Places of Pharaoh', giving the impression of riverside stopping-places for a king who travelled – unsurprisingly – by river.

In this model of royal residence the major requirement is a relatively large number of relatively small residences that could be equipped at short notice. An example of the preparations required for the imminent arrival of a Ramesside king is found in Papyrus Anastasi IV, which demands, among many other things, nearly 30,000 loaves of bread, 60 sacks of pomegranates, 50 bowls of honey and 100 stands for floral bouquets. It should be noted, however, that these provisions were not just for the king but also for the 'army and chariotry' who were with him. A variation on the movable royal residence is to be found in the fact that towns attached to individual royal pyramids of the Old Kingdom served as multiple important centres of royal administration.

Above and opposite
The 'North Palace' at Amarna has been the subject of many years of excavation. The model (opposite) shows how it may have appeared when complete.

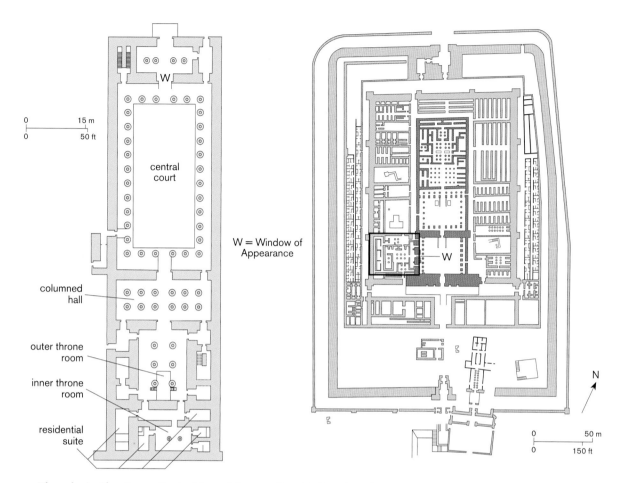

0   15 m
0   50 ft

central
court

W = Window of
Appearance

columned
hall

outer throne
room

inner throne
room

residential
suite

0   50 m
0   150 ft

N

Above left The palace of King Merenptah at Memphis, which appears to have essentially been a building designed for royal audience, with relatively modest living quarters attached.

Above right This small palace (marked by the box) built as part of the mortuary temple complex of Ramesses III at Medinet Habu may or may not have acted as a real royal residence during the king's lifetime, but it was certainly used as such in the Third Intermediate Period.

The only significant exception to this model of constant progress by the king (at least while he was young and vigorous enough to travel) is found at Amarna, where the stated intention of Akhenaten never to leave his new capital finds its archaeological reflection in the extensive palace complexes at the city.

Because the Egyptians did not adopt the model of having a small number of very large multi-functional palaces in a few major centres, individual 'palaces' could have their own distinct character based on its specific, limited functions. The palace of Merenptah at Memphis is a good example of this, essentially consisting of a large audience/reception hall, with a very modest set of personal apartments for the king at the rear.

The palace of Ramesses III at Medinet Habu was also primarily an 'audience palace', but with the additional twist that its connection to an open court of the adjacent mortuary temple provided a very suitable location for more public royal display and reward in the architectural setting of a 'Window of Appearance' where the king presented himself in a manner reminiscent of the balconies favoured by 20th-century totalitarian leaders to appear before a gathered public. Indeed the main way palaces appear in visual art from dynastic Egypt is in tomb scenes showing the rewarding of the tombowner by the king at a 'Window of Appearance'. However, even here the identification of a modest royal residence is by no means straightforward, as some scholars have identified these 'palaces'

attached to New Kingdom mortuary temples as structures for the use of the dead, rather than the living, king.

Building the Palace

Given the requirement that palaces could be built very quickly (in the event of a particular royal progress, or because one king wished suddenly to have a palace in a location not used by his predecessors), but might be used once only, or on a very temporary basis, it is hardly surprising that these buildings were regarded as essentially disposable. Exceptions might be the palaces attached to temples that had a particular long-term connection with the king, meaning that their royal palaces were reused more frequently. This applies particularly to the mortuary temples at Thebes, where both the Ramesseum and Medinet Habu had small palaces as part of their grand scheme – but here, as we have seen, the house of the living king was significantly smaller than the space provided for the god Amun. Owing to the modest nature of royal

palaces, it is sometimes difficult to differentiate archaeologically between residences constructed for kings in important provincial centres and 'palaces' for regional administrators (see Bubastis in the Eastern Delta and Ayn Asil in the Dakhla Oasis).

In most known cases the material of choice for the royal palace, as for the houses of the most humble of the king's subjects, was mudbrick. Just as for ordinary dwellings, the survival of royal palaces in the archaeological record is a matter of accident and, one suspects, atypical examples. However, the ability to construct a palace in a very short time is best attested in Amenhotep III's 'festival palace' complex at Malkata, on the West Bank at Thebes, which was built, used and then abandoned within a relatively short period.

The Palace City

Many New Kingdom urban centres – including Thebes, Memphis, Pr-Ramesses and Amarna – can be referred to as 'Royal Cities' because of the way in which the desires of a king, or a

Above left A 'Window of Appearance' was designed to provide an appropriate setting for the royal reward of officials. This scene, on the walls of Meryra II's tomb at Amarna, shows Meryra being thrown gifts by Akhenaten and Nefertiti.

Above right Window grilles were often made of stone or wood, and can survive in the archaeological record even when the walls in which they were fitted have disappeared. This limestone example comes from the palace of Merenptah (shown in the figure opposite, above left).

The Palace Harem and the Harem Palace

Western conceptions of the harem as an institution tend to be fixated on the erotic possibilities of the creation of an assemblage of sexually available women for the sole access of one male individual. The eastern harem was a regular subject in 19th-century genre painting, and although the harem concerned was usually that of Ottoman Turkey, the range was occasionally extended to include the imagined harem of Pharaoh, portrayed with no less an atmosphere of languorous eroticism.

It is likely that the reality was somewhat different and that the Harem Palace was developed in Egypt as a means of coping with the sheer number of women who were part of the royal household. To take the best-known example, when Princess Gilukhepa came from Mitanni to marry Amenhotep III as a diplomatic bride, the commemorative scarab issued by the king to mark this event also notes that she brought with her 317 'chief women of the harem'. The ancient Egyptian royal harem was not so much a sexual supermarket for the king, but a community that chiefly comprised female and infant members of the king's extended family. A related element of the palace complex was the *Kap*, a royal nursery or school that educated both royal children and those of favoured members of the court. To have been a 'Child of the *Kap*' was an important claim for members of the court in the 18th Dynasty, as it indicated closeness to the king from an early age.

The ancient Egyptian harem differed from the Ottoman variant in an important way. Although it was designed to accommodate significant numbers of royal women, it was not designed to segregate them from the outside world, although the most common word for harem, *ḫnr* (khener),

seems to be derived from the verb 'to restrain'. Instead the harem was a viable institution in its own right, with its own economic assets, income-generating activities and administrative officials. The most important of these activities indicates how these women passed their time: the first mention of what seems to be the earliest Egyptian word for harem, *Ipet*, on a sealing of the First Dynasty (reign of King Semerkhet) refers to a 'weaving workshop of the *Ipet*'.

The production of high-quality linen seems to have been the most important activity at the Harem Palace at Medinet el-Gurob. This site, in the Faiyum, is unusual as a harem because it was located well away from main centres of power. Other buildings known, or suspected, to have housed royal women have been found at Thebes, Memphis and Amarna, but always in association with larger palace complexes. The reasons why Medinet el-Gurob was established a significant distance from the main centres of political power may be to do with a desire to remove potentially competing royal wives and mothers away from those arenas. If this is the case, then the involvement later in the New Kingdom of harem-women in the attempted, and possibly successful, assassination attempt on Ramesses III shows the wisdom of such a policy, particularly when multiple royal wives and numerous royal children had the potential to make the succession to the throne extremely contentious.

Fieldwork carried out at Medinet el-Gurob since 2005 by British Egyptologist Ian Shaw for the University of Liverpool supports the idea of the Harem Palace there as a substantial town with its own production facilities and substantial residential blocks, which prospered from its foundation in the reign of Thutmose III to its eventual abandonment, probably during the reign of Ramesses V.

Surviving architectural remains make it difficult to envisage the internal appearance of royal palaces in ancient Egypt. The 'princesses fresco' from the King's House at Amarna perhaps comes closest – it depicts an informal scene of royal family life, including two daughters of Akhenaten and Nefertiti perched on a cushion.

series of kings, shaped their appearance. An important subset of the royal city is a settlement composed of an extended royal palace with its ancillary buildings. Malkata, which dates to the New Kingdom, is the best surviving example of such a palace-town. The full extent of Malkata is not yet known, but it covered an area of at least 35 hectares (86½ acres) on the West Bank at Thebes. Its centrepiece was the palace itself, 125 by 50 metres (410 by 164 ft), with a series of internal rooms that have been interpreted as a central columned audience hall. At one end of the hall was a small throne room and behind this were the royal apartments (including a bedroom and bathroom). Flanking the central hall were a series of smaller suites, which may have been used to accommodate other important members of the royal household. This palace opened up onto a series of open courtyards. Other structures within this vast complex included further, smaller palaces, an area for the celebration of the king's jubilee-festival, a series of storerooms, workshops, kitchens and bakeries, and houses, the last presumably to be occupied by members

of the court of Amenhotep III. Perhaps most striking was the construction of a huge T-shaped artificial lake (at *c.* 2 by 1 km, 1¼ by ⅔ miles, almost six times the area of the city), now known as the Birket Habu.

Another type of palace-town was built at Deir el-Ballas, located 45 km (28 miles) north of Luxor on the west bank of the Nile and chiefly excavated between 1980 and 1986 by American Egyptologist Peter Lacovara. The site consists of a series of related groups of buildings spread across some small hills and wadis (dried valley beds) over an area about 2 km (1¼ miles) long. The core structure is the 'North Palace' within an enclosure of about 300 by 150 metres (984 by 492 ft). Other parts of the town include large residences, observation towers and what appears to be a workmen's village on the model later followed by Deir el-Medina (see pp. 74–86). Like Malkata, Deir el-Ballas had a short period of occupation, but its purpose seems to have been very different: it was a primarily military staging-post in the Theban wars against the Hyksos in the late 17th and early 18th Dynasties.

Although it now survives as a rather desolate collection of spoil-mounds amid the traces of mud-brick buildings, the palace complex of Malkata built by Amenhotep III is the most extensive royal residence known from ancient Egypt.

Fortified Cities

We have already seen that the evidence for the origin of urbanism in Egypt includes the emergence of heavily defended walled settlements as major political and economic centres. The policy of providing enclosing walls for settlements continued in the Old Kingdom, although the extent to which these were necessary for defence against a genuine external threat has been doubted, apart from at border-towns like Elephantine. Walls do seem to be a defining feature of many Egyptian settlements throughout the dynastic period, particularly small-scale settlements, for reasons that may have had little to do with defence. However, there were clearly situations when a settlement required some form of specialized physical protection from hostile external forces. For most periods of Egyptian history providing that defence was the responsibility of the king.

Nubia in the Middle Kingdom

Perhaps the most sophisticated approach taken by the Egyptians to military architecture was the defence of the Second Cataract region, which was the border between Egypt and its hostile southern neighbour, Nubia, during the Middle Kingdom. Here a series of mutually supportive fortresses was created to form a network of defence. This was in turn backed up by a well-organized logistical system that was embedded within the design of each individual fortress. Some fortresses, such as Semna and Kumma, acted as

a heavily defended frontline and their form was specifically adapted to their location overlooking the Nile, while others had specialist functions, such as Askut, which was effectively a fortified granary. Largest of them all was Buhen, which combined sophisticated external defences with an interior that indicates it was the administrative centre for Lower Nubia in the Middle Kingdom. If anything, Buhen most closely resembles other centrally planned Middle Kingdom settlements, such as Kahun (see pp. 64–68), in its neat rectangular blocks of buildings.

Fortified Settlements in the New Kingdom

In the New Kingdom the evidence is less well preserved and less conveniently gathered than that for the Middle Kingdom Nubian forts. The re-occupied (e.g. Buhen) or newly established (e.g. Sesebi) Egyptian colonial towns of the New Kingdom were provided with thick enclosure walls, but with little of the ingenious defensive sophistication of the Middle Kingdom, suggesting that the threat they faced was, if it existed, low level.

A more serious approach was taken to the creation of fortresses and fortress-towns in frontier areas of genuine threat, including the 'Ways of Horus' chain of fortresses across northern Sinai and a comparable, although solely Ramesside, 'Libyan chain' stretching at least as far west as Zawiyet Umm el-Rakham. This site provides evidence for both military architecture in the face of a serious enemy and the operation of a real town with a mixed population and diverse local economy (see p. 220–22).

However, the end of the New Kingdom saw the emergence of a series of enemies who posed a threat to the interior of Egypt itself. Part of the response to this was the provision of defences for vulnerable towns by surrounding them with a mudbrick wall of an intimidatingly massive height and thickness. This approach was the one adopted in the reign of Ramesses II for the defence of the vulnerable West Delta towns of Tell el-Abqa'in, Kom Firin and Kom el-Hisn

Opposite above and below The Nubian fortress town of Buhen represents a high-point in the architectural complexity of Middle Kingdom military architecture.

Left Although none has survived in the archaeological record, the presence of small watch-tower fortlets in the Early Dynastic Period is indicated by illustrations like this ivory label.

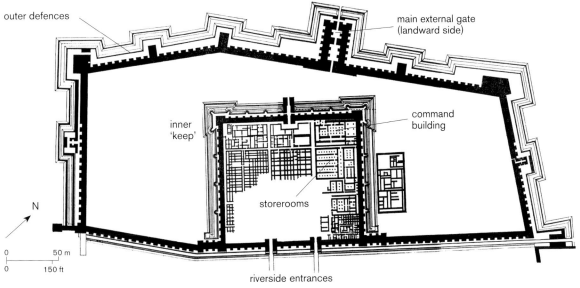

outer defences

main external gate
(landward side)

inner
'keep'

command
building

storerooms

N

0   50 m

0   150 ft

riverside entrances

(see pp. 182–85). Another approach was the strengthening of existing defensive possibilities such as the temple enclosures/'urban citadels' of long-established cities. As a warning to the descendants of the Libyan enemies who had threatened the western Delta in the reign of Ramesses II, Ramesses III ordered the building of mudbrick walls 30 cubits (over 15 metres, 49 feet) in height around the temple enclosures of some of the most important towns in southern Egypt – the temples of Thoth at Hermopolis Magna, Wepwawet at Asyut, Onuris-Shu at This and Osiris at Abydos (this last was fortified so that it was like 'a mountain of iron'). As the guarantor of *maat* (order, and peace) the king could do no less.

At Thebes the enclosure of Ramesses III's mortuary temple at Medinet Habu provides the best model for what the fortresses on the Asiatic

or Libyan borders may have looked like, with their enormous mudbrick walls and intimidating stone gateways. By the end of the New Kingdom this particular temple enclosure, whose external appearance was modelled on that of a fortress, had become the best-known example of a fortress-town in Egypt: a place where the residents of the Theban West Bank could live, protected from external enemies who were now very much an immediate threat.

The great 'migdol' gate of the mortuary temple complex of Ramesses III at Medinet Habu gives a sense of the intimidating but now-denuded gateways of New Kingdom fortresses-towns.

Temple and City

Gods of the Nome

A close relationship with particular deities was an important aspect of regional identity in pharaonic Egypt. This worked in two major ways. The first was the idea that the region, specifically the nome, could be thought of as a personified deity. These gods and goddesses would have no name other than that of the region itself, usually displayed as a standard on their heads when they were depicted in two or three dimensions. These regional personifications had in fact no 'personality' or role in myth and seldom appeared as independent figures; rather they were used as a collective group of male and female (and often the sexually ambiguous 'fecundity figures') who together represented Egypt in its constituent parts.

These nome deities can appear in statuary accompanying the king, the best example being the series of triad statues from the pyramid complex of Menkaure at Giza, each showing the king flanked by the goddess Hathor and one of the nome gods, shown as a male or female figure: although now far from complete, it is reasonable to assume that the original series of figures represented the king with all the nomes of Egypt in turn.

More frequently, nome gods are found represented in two dimensions: rows of these figures were often placed around the lower parts of walls of temples, particularly in the New

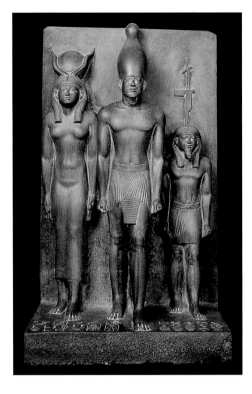

A triad statue depicting King Menkaure accompanied by the goddess Hathor and a nome deity representing the 4th Upper Egyptian nome (that of Thebes).

Kingdom and Graeco-Roman Period. They are usually shown bearing agricultural produce from all the regions of Egypt as offerings to the god of the temple. These processions of nome deities could be expanded to include representations of towns and distinct regions that were not part of the canonical nome lists, so that contemporary

Below A relief showing a series of regional deities from the cenotaph-temple of Ramesses II at Abydos.

important towns could be included as contributing to the offering-bearing. It is doubtful that these nome gods would have been of much interest to the population of the nomes themselves, serving instead as a representative of the nome in the greater assemblage of Egypt as the sum of its individual parts for the benefit of the king and the god(s) in whose temple they appeared and to whom their offerings were directed.

Gods of the City

Unlike the characterless nome deities, who were probably of not much interest to the general population, much more important representatives of regional identity were those individualized, active gods who were particularly associated with the nome and its urban centres. These were deities who had names, identifying visual characteristics and divine families. They appeared in myths and, certainly by the New Kingdom, were often known beyond the nome or city with which they were particularly associated. Indeed, the evidence suggests that we should think of these deities as city-gods rather than nome gods, since it is their association with cities rather than regions that is best attested. This is not surprising, since we come across these gods in contexts associated with an urban elite, whom we might think of as the 'scribal class' or 'participants in hieroglyphic culture'. These contexts include inscribed objects (and statues) from significant temples, texts within tombs in elite cemeteries and scribal literature. Most importantly, these gods had temples, which made them very much residents of the town or city, and making it natural for an Egyptian to think of the god, the god's temple and the city in which it was located, as deeply integrated. This can be seen clearly in the Ramesside literary genre of 'Longing for the City' hymns, which stress the close association in the mind of the writer between the city and its patron deity:

> 'My heart has stolen away, hurrying to a place it knows. It travels south to see Hwt-Ka-Ptah [Memphis].... Come O Ptah, take me to Memphis and let me see you at my leisure.'
>
> Papyrus Anastasi IV

> 'O Thoth put me in Khmunu [Hermopolis Magna], your town, which is sweet to live in.'
>
> Papyrus Sallier I

It is noticeable that, in both these cases, the name of the town or district directly refers to one or more of the gods with whom it is associated. Hwt-Ka-Ptah, or 'Mansion of the *ka* of Ptah', refers to the temple area at Memphis sacred to Ptah, but was also used as a name for Memphis more generally (and, ultimately, was the source of the word 'Egypt'). Khmunu, or 'Eight-Town', refers to the eight primordial gods who appear in the local version of the creation myth: the toponym Hermopolis Magna is the name for the city in the Graeco-Roman Period, deriving from a perceived identification between the Egyptian god Thoth and the Greek god Hermes.

The King and Local Gods

Of course the most important member of the elite 'scribal class' was the king himself. He was in the best position to make manifest the position of a deity within the city by creating monuments for him or her. The vast majority of all surviving temples from ancient Egypt is the work of kings, either in embellishing or replacing 'local' structures with more impressive buildings, which only royal resources could create, or in the initiation of immense building projects. Whatever the scale, the intention was the same: by providing for a local god, the king was displaying his concern for local religious practices and bringing royal resources in materials and skills to a regional centre, but he was also making manifest the unique relationship between the king and all the gods of Egypt. Only the king could have this special connection with the gods, only the king was depicted approaching the gods and only the king could be regarded divine himself.

Of course, it may be that our evidence is skewed. We do not have any surviving examples of what a temple in a small town in ancient Egypt would have looked like any more than we know what that small town itself would have looked like. It may be that, away from significant centres of local political and economic power, temples were indeed built by local people to worship local gods and were made from local materials (i.e. mudbrick rather than stone) and would have looked similar to the 'preformal' temple at Medamud, but one might suspect that the regularization of form that went along with royal involvement in the Middle Kingdom and later, if not before (again Medamud is the most telling example), was the norm in any town of any size anywhere in the Nile Valley or Delta.

Gods in their Temples

However, this question of royal involvement must not distract us from what temples were actually for, and how they might have contributed to the life of the towns and cities within which they were built.

The first thing to note is that gods were thought of as literally inhabiting the temples built for them. The most common words for temple, *pr-nṯr* (per-netjer) or *ḥwt-nṯr* (hwt-netjer), refer to a 'house' for the god in the same terms as a 'house' for any other person. The god's presence was located in the image – usually a statue – that was housed in the innermost part of the temple, the sanctuary. Divine worship consisted of rituals – the regular offerings of food, drink and incense, together with a change of clothing – performed by priests on and for the divine image. This was very much in parallel with the service provided to a member of the elite by their servants, indeed the most common term for a priest was *ḥm-nṯr* (hem-netjer), literally 'god's servant'. Congregational worship was not the norm, since temples were built as houses for gods, not places where worshippers came together for divine service in which priests directed the congregation in praise of an invisible god.

Therefore Egyptian temples were not primarily structures by which a distant god was contacted by a local population (although they could, as we shall see, have that function too), but real houses. Huge, magnificent, heavily decorated stone houses in many cases, but houses nonetheless, located in towns and cities alongside the houses of the other local residents. Moreover, as the most important resident of the town, the house of the god often had a central location. Indeed in major cities, certainly in the New Kingdom, the temple was the core around which the city

The texts above the heads of these regional deities identify them as personifications of the towns of Dendera (left) and Medamud (right).

grew. Although it is common to speak of places like Amarna, Pr-Ramesses and (to a lesser extent) Thebes and Memphis as 'royal cities' based on the main influence on their building, it would also be accurate to speak of them as 'divine cities' since the god(s) within them were the most important resident and their dwellings the most important structures.

The exclusive nature of major New Kingdom temples, usually only accessible to the king and his nominated proxies, the professional priesthood, might suggest that these structures, although the dominating architectural presence in a city, were essentially isolated from it. This is only partially true, for two main reasons. First, these major temples were hidden behind the massive mudbrick walls of the temple enclosure – an 'urban citadel' that was not simply sacred space, but also contained a series of other important structures requiring regular access, such as palaces, workshops, storage facilities and, sometimes, housing. Secondly, while the great doors of these temples were usually firmly closed, they could be opened to a wider public, most notably on special occasions when divine festivals offered the opportunity for centrally organized events in which the whole community could participate. The most public aspect of these festivals would be procession, when the divine

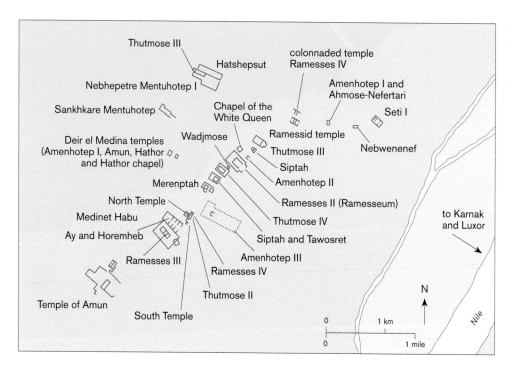

The landscape of the Theban West Bank during the New Kingdom was dominated by royal mortuary temples.

image was taken out of the temple and brought into the sphere of the city-dwellers as a whole.

The specific nature of the procession and events connected with it would depend on the town in which they were carried out. Those at Thebes are the best known, with the images of the god Amun and his family leaving their 'home' at Karnak in order to process southwards to the satellite temple of Luxor (the 'Southern Harem' of the god) in the annual Opet Festival, or to travel across to the West Bank of the Nile to visit royal mortuary temples in the 'Beautiful Festival of the Western Valley'. Both of these festivals involved processional routes that crossed or travelled along the Nile, and also went overland. For the latter, the overland processional route between Karnak and Luxor temples was provided with a paved road, lined with sphinxes and regular barque-chapels where the processional boats of the gods could rest. An additional effect of the creation of this avenue was to provide a physical 'spine' for Thebes – the fixed elements (certainly from the late 18th Dynasty onwards) were the Karnak complex in the north, Luxor Temple in the south and the processional avenue linking the two. Everything else had to fit around this 'spine' and it became increasingly substantial as successive kings sought to display their devotion to Amun

by adding to his 'house' at Karnak and, to a lesser extent (but notably under Amenhotep III and Ramesses II), to the Luxor Temple.

The West Bank of New Kingdom Thebes was also dominated by a series of massive temples linked to the river by a series of canals. These were royal mortuary establishments, built by individual kings to celebrate their divine kingship and their relationship with Amun and the gods of the afterlife. For other major cities, the dominating role of temples and temple-

Below An important part of the monumental 'skeleton' of New Kingdom Thebes was the processional route linking Karnak with Luxor Temple.

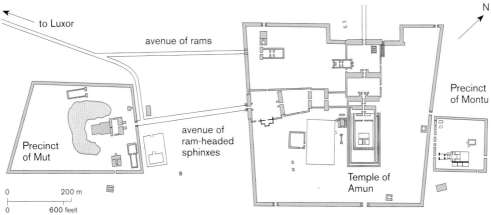

to Luxor

avenue of rams

N

Precinct
of Montu

Precinct
of Mut

avenue of
ram-headed
sphinxes

Temple of
Amun

0   200 m

0   600 feet

enclosures as physical features is clear, although more difficult to define precisely than that at Thebes. Our understanding of the great cities of Memphis, Amarna, Hermopolis Magna, Sais and Pr-Ramesses is that their temples were central to the town-planning that took place there.

Having described the royal, defensive and divine aspects of Egyptian cities, we shall now turn to consider them from the perspectives of their most numerous inhabitants: the people who built the cities, lived in them and recorded them for posterity in models and texts, and also in the remains they left behind to be found by archaeologists. For these were, above all, cities for – and of – people.

Above Aerial view of Karnak (top) from the southeast showing the beginning of processional routes to Luxor Temple and to the temple complex of the goddess Mut, with (below) a plan showing the relationship between the Amun and Mut temples.

PART III

Cities for People

City Government

The administration of towns and cities in dynastic Egypt was part of a complex pattern of central and regional government whose functions, and officials, often overlapped. The three most important institutions involved in this process were the state/crown administration (broadly the same thing), provincial administration and temple administration. It is not really possible to provide a clear division of responsibilities for these three administrative systems, not least because of their relative shifts during the dynastic period, most dramatically during the First and Third Intermediate Periods when, at times of no central state/royal administration, regional and temple functionaries effectively took control of their localities throughout Egypt. It is worth noting, too, that other institutions were also administratively and economically significant at different periods, especially the military, not least in their administration of fortress-towns. It will, however, be useful to sketch out here the roles and duties of the court, temple and provincial officials as the backbone of the Egyptian administration.

Royal Administration

The main source of power was the king, and the most powerful officials were those attached to the royal administration. The physical location of that administration is less easy to identify, not least because of the rather mobile nature of the court (as expressed in the person of the king and his retinue), especially after the Old Kingdom. The royal residence (ẖnw, see p. 37) may have been a more static feature in the Old Kingdom, but it is unclear whether this was one residence (at Memphis) or several (associated with each king's Memphite pyramid complex?).

Early in the Middle Kingdom, the establishment of a royal residence at Itj-tawy near Lisht by Amenemhat I seems to have led to a doubling of some royal officials: those who were 'following the king' and those who were 'in the palace'. In the New Kingdom, the royal administration was split into two complementary bureaucracies, each under a vizier, one for Upper Egypt (based at Thebes) and one for Lower Egypt (based at Memphis or Pr-Ramesses). But although these nominal 'capitals' existed, the official duties of the royal administration were

Previous pages This scene on a wall from the First Intermediate Period tomb of Ity (from Gebelein in Southern Egypt) shows the filling of a granary.

Below The great granaries attached to the major Theban temples, like the Ramesseum pictured here, were capable of storing hundreds of tons of grain and have been described as being as much a national bank as a food reserve.

invested in the officials themselves, who travelled between cities, independently of the king or in his retinue.

Temple Administration

The gods of Egypt were wealthy, some extraordinarily so, partly as a result of donations of land and other assets. The officials in charge of these assets thus wielded considerable economic power. However, the division between divine and secular income was not always a clear one, with provincial governors also often acting as controllers of provincial temples, institutions that were major local landowners in their own right. At the level of the state, the huge donations to major temples made by the king, partly as a result of Egypt's imperial conquests during the New Kingdom, created important economic institutions, with vast landholdings throughout Egypt, which could nonetheless be used by the state if needed. It is no coincidence that a major institution such as the Ramesseum at Thebes had a huge series of storerooms – principally granaries – safe within its enclosure walls. Together, the granaries of the Domain of Amun at Thebes have been referred to as New Kingdom Egypt's 'national bank', the control of which gave massive resources to anyone who held it.

Provincial Administration

Nomes

The most significant unit for provincial administration throughout the dynastic period was the nome (see maps right and above). The modern word 'nome' derives from the Greek *nomos*, although the ancient Egyptian term was *sp3t* (sepat). The Egyptian writing of *sp3t* was usually in the form of a hieroglyphic symbol (▦) which used to be regarded by Egyptologists as a plot of land criss-crossed by irrigation channels, although many scholars now believe it to be an area of land subdivided into individual plots. Whatever the derivation of the sign, the *sp3t*/nome was a remarkably resilient geographical unit, comprising a regional administrative area, somewhat similar to (although usually rather smaller in area than) an English county or a French *département*.

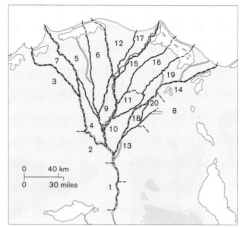

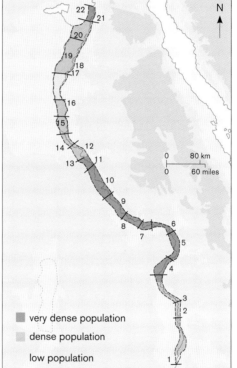
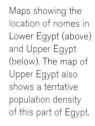

Maps showing the location of nomes in Lower Egypt (above) and Upper Egypt (below). The map of Upper Egypt also shows a tentative population density of this part of Egypt.

very dense population

dense population

low population

The exact number of nomes was subject to some variation over 3,000 years, partly when marginal land (including the Mediterranean shoreline) was made productive and therefore capable of being considered part of the 'real' Egypt, but also because of boundary changes, not least in the Delta where Nile branches often formed nome boundaries and these would inevitably change as those branches altered their courses (see pp. 181–82). However, there was no significant overhaul of the system, which seems to have been in place by the 3rd Dynasty and continued with remarkable consistency (especially in Upper Egypt) until the Graeco-Roman Period.

Upper Egypt was divided into 22 nomes and these were broadly established by the end of the Old Kingdom. Lower Egypt had 20 nomes, though because of the dynamic geography of the Delta mentioned above, this number was only fixed in the Graeco-Roman Period.

The origin of individual nome divisions is not clear. Some may have been influenced by the zones of control of Predynastic proto-kingdoms; some had an obvious geographical unity to them. Most consisted of seemingly arbitrary units of roughly equal size along the Nile Valley (where division along the linear river was usually fairly easy) and in the Nile Delta (which was somewhat more problematic, given the shifting Nile branches and fluctuating Mediterranean coastline). It has been suggested that differences in territorial size between nomes (e.g. the southernmost nomes of Upper Egypt have a significantly greater area than those a little further north around the Qena bend) may be to do with the agricultural potential of individual nomes and the desire on the part of the state to create nomes that had a roughly equal productive capacity (and therefore roughly equal levels of tax revenues to the state).

Mayors and Nomarchs

By the later part of the Old Kingdom, our understanding of the organization of provincial administration is clearer. The ideal situation seems to have been that each nome would be overseen by its own 'Great Overlord' ($ḥry-tp$ '3, hery-tep aa), sometimes referred to in modern literature as a nomarch. These local leaders seem to have commonly held two offices: that of 'Great Overlord of the Nome' plus 'Overseer of Priests' ($ỉmỉ-r$ $ḥmw-nṯr$, imi-r hemu-netjer) of the patron deity of the most important town of the nome; this latter role would give the nomarch control over the income from land owned by the temple. This dual role is often expressed in titles of the Old and Middle Kingdoms, as in the cemetery of Meir where a nomarch could be referred to as 'Overseer of Priests of Hathor, lady of [the town

of] Kis, Great Overlord of Nedjfet Pehtet [the 14th Upper Egyptian Nome]'. The combining of offices in this way, which gave provincial administrators access to temple property, could be a problem, however, especially if there was a local dynastic succession among nomarchs, and for this reason we see a series of royal decrees (most famously from Coptos) protecting temple property from local interference.

During the Middle Kingdom, the title $ḥ3ty-ʿ$ (haty-a) is more commonly used for the main official of a nome. This has a variety of possible translations, from 'hereditary prince' to 'mayor'. The latter translation suggests that, when compared with the Old Kingdom, towns or 'city districts' were more important in the Middle Kingdom and later. This is probably true to some extent, and there is more evidence for each nome having a central-place urban centre for the administration of the nome, elite residences and specialist economic functions. However, it would probably be a mistake to over-emphasize the size and importance of these towns (especially before the New Kingdom) since provincial Egypt was essentially rural and the typical experience for most Egyptians would have been the small/medium-sized village rather than the large town.

As far as the state was concerned, the role of the nome (and its leaders) was to provide revenue for the state. This was most obviously expressed in the form of agricultural products, especially grain, although some nomes were responsible for other economically important activities depending on their location, such as provision of stone in the 15th Upper Egyptian nome, which contained the alabaster (travertine) quarries at Hatnub. The assessment of rent and taxation of crops from agricultural land was centrally organized and would most sensibly have taken place on an annual basis. The 'time of the count of cattle and people' was most often a biennial event (though not necessarily so), which allowed the assessment of the numbers of the most economically valuable movable assets of a nome. The cattle count was obviously a major event as it features on the walls of the tombs of many provincial officials.

The organization of corvée labour for state activities (such as pyramid building?) was another way in which the nome was expected

Scenes of harvest, especially the grain harvest, are frequently depicted on the walls of New Kingdom tombs. A ubiquitous accompaniment to that harvest is its recording and assessment for tax purposes by teams of inspectors.

to contribute to royal activity. State officials might be appointed to oversee the activities of nomarchs, but this was primarily to ensure that resources flowed smoothly from the regions to the centre; as far as local administration itself was concerned, the state was probably uninterested in how each nomarch ran his nome on a daily basis.

The physical location for administration at a national and local level is less easy to identify, and not only because of the poor archaeological survival of the most likely locations such as central Memphis. Even in relatively well-preserved administrative centres such as the royal city of Amarna or a well-populated regional centre (with royal connections) like Kahun, purpose-built administrative districts are not easy to find. Instead, the evidence from both locations suggests that the distinction between home and office was not an important one for relatively high-ranking Egyptian officials and that the ḫ3 (kha, 'office, bureau') often mentioned in administrative texts may refer to one of the public rooms in the large house of a well-to-do official.

The cattle count was an important occasion of economic assessment, when these valuable animals would be tallied by the regional authorities, as illustrated here in a wooden model from the Middle Kingdom tomb of Meketre.

Towns and Houses of the Middle Kingdom

A small number of sites, especially from the Middle and New Kingdoms, provide us with extraordinary amounts of evidence for the settlement archaeology of ancient Egypt. This evidence includes both the detailed archaeological recovery of the architecture of the settlement itself, of the houses within it, their contents and, if we are very lucky, textual material that describes the lives of their inhabitants. In the two following sections we shall consider this evidence.

Kahun – 'Senwosret is Satisfied'

The most important surviving settlement of the Middle Kingdom is the town that was probably called Hetep-Senwosret ('King Senwosret is satisfied/at peace'). The name of the town reflects both its function and its founder – it was part of the pyramid complex built by King Senwosret II near the mouth of the Faiyum at a site now known as Kahun (after Petrie's original usage to distinguish it from the nearby pyramid site, which he designated Lahun/Illahun). The town was located immediately adjacent to the now-destroyed Valley Building of the pyramid complex; the pyramid itself is over 1 kilometre (⅔ miles) further to the west. It is clear from this positioning, and from documents recovered from Kahun, that at least part of the town was designed to be the residence of the priests who served the mortuary cult of Senwosret II. However, the size of the town makes it likely that it was a significant settlement, which had functions beyond that of being an elaborate Middle Kingdom version of the pyramid temples of the Old Kingdom. Documentary evidence from the site indicates that an office of the vizier was located here, and that at least some of the building work on the later pyramid of Amenemhat III at nearby Hawara was directed from Kahun. The town was occupied until the 13th Dynasty – at least 100 years after its foundation.

Discovering Kahun

Kahun was principally excavated by Flinders Petrie in two major seasons of work, from April to May 1889 and October 1889 to January 1890. He 'cleared' a large proportion of the town with a speed quite astonishing by today's standards, but his excavation reports and plan of the site (opposite) remain the most substantial body of evidence for Middle Kingdom towns, their houses and the contents of those houses.

The Layout of Kahun

Kahun was centrally planned on the same sort of orthogonal layout that is typical of known royal projects of the Middle Kingdom. Its external wall was roughly square, 384 by 335 m (1,260 by 1,100 ft). Today it is located at the interface between desert and cultivated land; as a result a substantial portion of the south and southeastern parts of the town have been lost.

Texts and Toys

Kahun is important not just because of its architectural remains, but also because of the wealth of small finds recovered by Petrie. These include the most important set of Middle Kingdom papyri, which cover a wide range of topics from the administration of local temples as well as personal letters and medical texts. From these sources we know that Kahun was an important seat of regional

The survival of many objects from ancient Egyptian sites – especially desert cemeteries – has preserved a substantial number of items of everyday life, even organic materials like this basket.

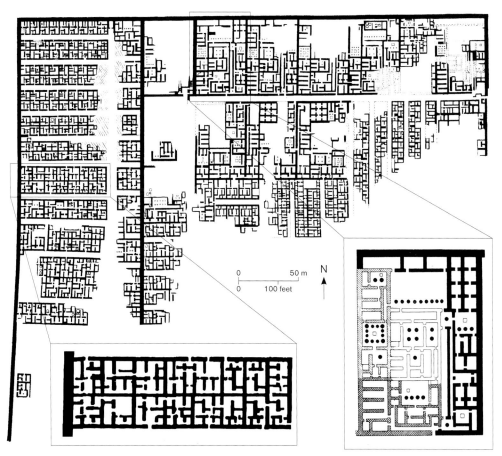

The map of Kahun produced by its excavator, Flinders Petrie, together with plans of two very different types of housing, back-to-back terraces (left) and large mansions (right).

government and that it possessed a prison – perhaps in the now-lost part of the site. Just as important were the objects of everyday life that were left behind when the town was abandoned at some point in the 13th Dynasty. These also give a strong impression of a real and vibrant community, and include tools, items of personal religion, children's toys and even a rat-trap.

The Western Quarter

On the western side of the town, a broad strip containing rows of back-to-back houses was divided from the rest of the settlement by a mudbrick wall. The disappearance of the southern part of this locality and the dividing wall here means that it is not clear whether there was any means of communication between this quarter and the rest of the town, nor is it obvious why this strict division was present. Earlier suggestions that this part of the town was used to house a community of non-Egyptians have

now been largely discounted, although there clearly were *aamu*-asiatics present at Kahun, just as there were in many locations in Middle Kingdom Egypt. American Egyptologist David O'Connor has suggested that the Western Quarter might have been designed to house the priests who served in the adjacent Valley Temple of Senwosret II, perhaps on a temporary, part-time basis, while the Eastern Quarter was the 'real' town of Kahun, which was home to a permanent resident population, and which had its own religious focus in a temple dedicated to the god Soped. That 'real' town may have been partly supported by the farming of the floodplain that was close to the town, and has since encroached on the southeastern sector of Kahun. However, the Western Quarter of Kahun is important for our understanding of domestic architecture of the Middle Kingdom because it contains the period's largest group of planned and organized 'small houses'.

Back-to-back Terraces

Most of the inhabitants of Kahun lived in small houses, over 200 of which were excavated by Petrie. These houses were made up of small numbers of rooms, many relatively narrow and corridor-like, and roofed with barrel-vaults. These seem to have begun life as individual units with a common ground plan, creating standardized blocks of back-to-back terraces, as part of the centrally planned, highly regularized official origins of Kahun.

Among these small houses a number of variants can be detected. The smallest are no more than 8 by 7.5 m (26 by 24 ft) and this roughly square ground plan is just enough for two main rooms, plus two smaller ones, along with the connecting space between them. A variation of this type is 8.5 by 5.25 m (28 by 17 ft), with the entrance on the broad side, and with only three rooms, all opening from a small entrance hall. The largest version of this type of house has either 7 or 8 rooms, which either opened off a central room (or rooms) or had a more complicated (and perhaps more private) internal arrangement.

However, the plan produced by Petrie shows considerable variation within these houses, as internal walls were added or demolished to adapt to the particular circumstances of the families and individuals who actually lived within them. In some cases, even the rectangular box of the house itself did not limit the inhabitants' desire for space, as neighbouring houses could be knocked together to form larger dwellings.

The Eastern Quarter

The northern part of the Eastern Quarter is dominated by a series of large (42 by 60 m, or 138 by 197 ft) multi-roomed structures, which all seem to have been built to a similar design. Six of these structures lie side-by-side, immediately to the north of the main east–west street of the town, while three lie on the southern side of the street. These nine buildings have generally been considered to be large residential houses, for the community leaders of Kahun, but they are so extraordinarily bigger than any other non-royal housing from ancient Egypt – apart from the spacious villas of Amarna – that there has been a good deal of scholarly debate about their exact function(s).

Although each of these large Kahun houses has a different level of completeness, owing to varied archaeological survival, they are likely to have had a standard plan, the different elements of which, and their interpretation, can be summarized as:

1   Small rooms at the entrance to the house, immediately after entering the house from the street, which are most likely to be a Porter's Lodge.
2   A set of large rooms, which have been described as stables, but which would also be suitable for a group activity such as weaving.

A cut-away line drawing of the wooden model from the tomb of Meketre showing a villa and its enclosed garden. Note that the villa itself has been severely 'compressed' in order to give emphasis to the garden.

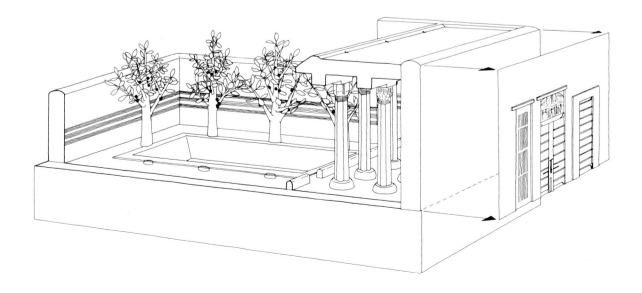

3 A set of small, square interconnected rooms, which are generally accepted to be a granary.

4 A series of open spaces close to the granary, which would be suitable for baking, brewing and other food-production activities.

5 A set of rooms close to the granary, which would be a suitable location for an administrative office if close attention was being paid to deposits and withdrawals of grain from the granary.

6 A large central courtyard.

7 Two integrated sets of rooms, which open onto the central courtyard. These have been identified as residential units (each one has an identifiable bedroom, with a raised bed platform), but who exactly occupied these units is not agreed.

The 'Core House' at Kahun

It seems most likely that the real heart of this complex is a 'core house', whose entrance is behind the north-facing colonnade on the south side of the large courtyard. This is an entrance that is some distance away from the street-entrance to the complex as a whole, and suggests privacy – the workshops and offices can be visited without entering the core house. The core house has enough rooms to provide a comfortable living space for a family, and there is little doubt that this is where the head of the household resided. However, the presence of a second residential unit within the complex is more of a puzzle. Suggestions put forward to explain the presence of this second house include the idea that it was to provide accommodation for servants or a steward. Alternatively, it may have been the main residence of female members of the household, where infant children were brought up. Another suggestion is that it may have been the place where an adult eldest son of the family lived, with his own nuclear family, before taking over the main core house on his father's death or retirement. This last suggestion is based on the idea that these complexes at Kahun were not designed primarily for comfortable, elite residence, but as administrative and economic institutions with an importance for the community as a whole.

'Urban Estates'?

Barry Kemp has made the intriguing suggestion that the large houses at Kahun should be considered as 'urban estates' whose similarity to Amarna villas is not primarily in their size, but in the complexity of their functions. Just as Amarna villas seem to have had the important role of acting as economic and administrative 'hubs' for city districts at Amarna (see p. 90), so the complexes at Kahun had functions well beyond the servicing of the needs of the family (or families?) that lived in them.

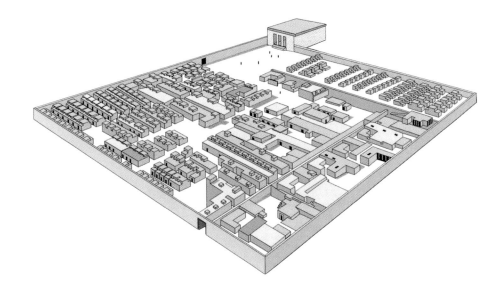

A possible reconstruction of the town of Kahun, based on the plan on p. 65.

Part of the evidence for this is the presence of a large granary in each of the Kahun elite houses where the level of archaeological survival has been sufficient to identify these structures. These granaries could each hold over 300 cubic metres (10,594 cubic feet) of grain, and therefore had a total aggregate capacity of over 2,700 cubic metres (95,350 cubic feet). If each of these granaries were filled to capacity at harvest time, the grain within them is estimated to be enough to feed a population of between 5,000 and 9,000 people – a figure that is close to, or exceeds, most estimates of the total population of Kahun.

This suggests that the most important asset of the Kahun community – its grain – was not stored in a centralized granary area, but was distributed within the urban estates of its community leaders. This emphasizes the role of these large houses as administrative centres overseen by community leaders who had immediate control over communal assets. The same is also likely to be true of other centralized production and distribution activities, including weaving.

Wah-Sut – An Enduring Place

Although remarkable, Kahun is not entirely unique. In 1902–3, Canadian archaeologist Charles Currelly began the excavation of a Middle Kingdom town at Abydos; the dig was later continued from 1994 by a team from the University of Pennsylvania led by American archaeologist Josef Wegner. A series of clay sealing impressions from the town gave its name, 'Enduring are the Places of Khakaure True of Voice in Abydos', the first part of which is Wah-Sut. Like Kahun, Wah-Sut was a royal foundation whose function was primarily to service a royal mortuary foundation, in this case the mortuary complex of Senwosret III (which some scholars believe is his tomb, and others a dummy 'cenotaph' tomb). Also like Kahun, Wah-Sut grew to a size and level of population that went well beyond what was needed for the servicing of even a royal temple.

The Elite Houses

Although the town has not yet been completely excavated, it was at least 4.5–6 hectares (11–15 acres) in area. Most of what has been

The administrative gatehouse, behind the mayor's residence, giving access to the town of Wah-Sut.

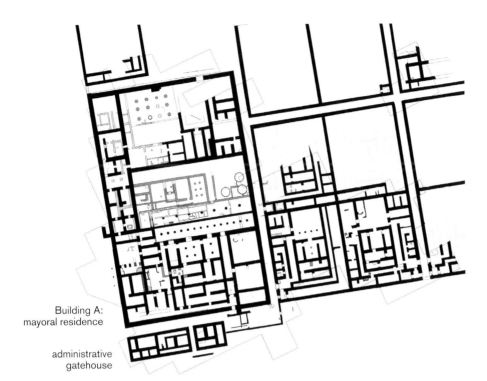

Plan of the town of Wah-Sut, after the excavations at the site up to 2012.

Building A: mayoral residence

administrative gatehouse

excavated to date has consisted of an area filled with elite mansions, very reminiscent of the 'urban estates' at Kahun, although rather smaller. They were planned in typical orthogonal style, each house 27.5 by 31.5 m (90 by 103 ft), and each part of a block of four houses. The layout of the internal rooms is also remarkably similar to Kahun, consisting of a core house fronted by a colonnaded courtyard and an entrance some distance from the street, a suite identified by the excavators as a 'secondary residential unit' and a series of rooms that parallel the Kahun house's production and storage areas, but on a significantly smaller scale, suggesting that they did not have the same core supply and administration function as the mansions at Kahun.

The Mayor's Residence

That centralized function was probably served by the largest elite dwelling to be discovered at Wah-Sut, the residence of the Mayor, which the excavators called Building A. This was a huge structure – at 82 by 52 m (269 by 171 ft) it was larger than any of the four-house blocks that were built nearby. It consisted of a series of

distinct units, most of which were accessed from a large entrance court containing 12 sycamore fig trees in neat 4 by 3 rows. The core residential house stood on a raised platform and had a very impressive entrance consisting of an 8-columned

Below Ongoing excavation in the area behind the mayor's residence at Wah-Sut.

portico 42 metres (138 ft) wide immediately followed by a shallow hall 38-metres (125-ft) long containing 14 columns. Other areas within the Mayor's residence included storage and production areas (including a large granary) and, once again, a separate residential unit, which was at one time occupied by the 'King's Daughter' Reniseneb, as suggested by many seal impressions naming her.

Although the town of Wah-Sut was a deliberate royal foundation, the titles held by its community leader were similar to those of other 'normal' settlements of Middle Kingdom Egypt in that they brought together in one person two offices: Mayor (*ḥ3ty-ꜥ*, haty-a) of the town of Wah-Sut and Overseer of the Temple (*imi-r ḥmw-nṯr*, imi-r hemu-netjer) of the most important local deity – Senwosret III himself.

Qasr es-Sagha and Avaris

Although Kahun is the best-known example of a town that provided basic, standardized housing for its working population, it is not the only Middle Kingdom site to have produced this type of small house.

Snail Houses at Avaris

Middle Kingdom Avaris in the Eastern Delta was also the result of centralized planning on the orthogonal model and here, too, back-to-back terraces were built. These were in blocks 12 houses wide (i.e. 24 back-to-back houses) separated by streets over 2.5 m (8 ft) wide. In contrast to these relatively wide streets the houses themselves were tiny at only 5 by 5 m (16 by 16 ft). They also, unsurprisingly, contain only a small number of rooms, arranged in a basic, spiral layout, which leads their excavator – Austrian archaeologist Manfred Bietak – to call them 'snail houses'. However, although the smallest Kahun houses were not much bigger than the Avaris examples, it has been suggested that the latter were so small that they may have been designed for temporary occupation (perhaps for the workforce on a specific project?) rather than for permanent residence.

Quarrymen at Qasr es-Sagha

The site of Qasr es-Sagha is located in the desert north of the Faiyum. It is one of a number of sites in Egypt's deserts (see also p. 215) designed to house miners or quarrymen involved in the acquisition of stones, metals and minerals for the Egyptian state. Most of the settlements set up for these workers were very basic in nature – essentially campsites for short-term, seasonal occupation. Qasr es-Sagha was rather different. For one thing, it possessed a stone temple of strikingly unusual form, but whose very existence suggests an intention for permanent residence rather than occasional camping. The settlement built by the Middle Kingdom state to house their workers in this distant and desolate place also indicates a serious intent for urban development, and once more demonstrates the love of town planners of that period for regularity and the right-angle.

The settlement consisted of a rectangle 114 metres broad and 80 metres deep (374 by 262 ft), orientated north–south and with an enclosure wall. A central street running north–south, with a gateway through the enclosure wall at each end, divided the settlement in half. Although the site

Reconstucted plan of the workers' town at Qasr es-Sagha, with a detailed plan of one of the individual housing units.

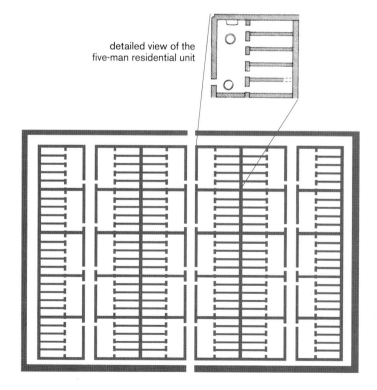

detailed view of the five-man residential unit

has suffered from erosion on its eastern side, it seems likely that the internal parts of the town were a mirror image on either side of the main street. The internal division of the town was into four blocks running north–south; the two central blocks consisted of 10 back-to-back houses, while the two outer blocks consisted of a row of five houses each. The entrances to all these houses therefore looked across the street to another house opposite them.

The 30 houses all seem to have been the same size and layout. Each had an entrance from the street giving access to a court 13 metres wide by 5.25 metres deep (42 by 17 ft). This court was used for a variety of communal, domestic activities, as indicated by the presence of ovens in some of them. At the rear of the court, five doorways gave access to five long, narrow rooms of approximately 8 by 2 metres (26 by 6 ft) each. It is tempting to see these as individual bedrooms. Although it is difficult to be certain, the evidence suggests that each of these houses was home to five individuals, who shared a certain amount of communal activity, perhaps mainly cooking and eating together. Given the nature of the site, it is difficult to think of these households as families, and they are more likely to have been five-man teams within the organization of workgangs at Qasr es-Sagha.

Big Houses and Small Houses in the Middle Kingdom?

An overview of Middle Kingdom housing strongly suggests that there was a huge disparity between large elite residences and tiny non-elite residences (including those at Avaris and Qasr es-Sagha), with not much in between. Against this it might be argued that the elite houses at Wah-Sut are not nearly so large as those at Kahun, but this is in part because of the way the large Kahun houses (and mayoral residence at Wah-Sut) had such an important role to play in administration, production and distribution at the site. However, even the basic core house at Kahun and Wah-Sut is significantly larger than any of the small houses at Avaris and Qasr es-Sagha ('small houses' at Wah-Sut have not yet been discovered and excavated) and this seems to suggest a stark, non-graduated distinction between the haves

and have-nots in Middle Kingdom Egypt, which is not what the evidence of cemeteries of this period suggests (see pp. 120–21). Perhaps the important fact is that the towns we have been looking at are all 'official' foundations and may have reflected a rather rigid view of society by the state, rather than the reality of social diversity that can be reflected in housing in 'organic' towns of the period. This diversity is reflected in the few 'organic' towns to have survived from Middle Kingdom Egypt.

Model Houses

The relationship between the living and the dead, their tombs and their houses, will be discussed below (see pp. 120–21), for cemeteries were important and active parts of ancient Egyptian towns. An important aspect of this relationship was the need for the living to provide the dead with food offerings so that the *ka*-spirits of the deceased ancestors would not go hungry in their tombs. However, although this ongoing relationship between the living and the dead was an ideal, it was soon recognized that tombs, the houses of the dead, needed to be self-sufficient in the generation (using magic if need be) of everything the dead might need, especially food and drink, avoiding a reliance on living relatives to visit the tomb. A by-product of this need for self-sufficiency was the representation of parts of the city within the tomb, which provide us with a picture of urban life.

Little Boxes – Wooden Models of the Middle Kingdom

For elite tombs of the Old Kingdom, these representations took the form of an increasing level of decoration on the walls of the tomb, with scenes of food offering and, later, food production and, later still, the production of other types of goods. In the Middle Kingdom, while elite tombs with decorated walls continued, an increasingly important aspect of provincial cemeteries was the appearance of less-elaborate tombs, usually of the shaft-and-chamber type, which belonged to people – doctors, professional soldiers, middle-ranking administrators – whom we might call middle class. These tombs had little in the way of elaborate superstructures or decorated walls, but the burial chamber was usually big enough to contain both a wooden coffin and a selection of objects.

Some of these objects were wooden models that were more modest alternatives to extensive scenes painted on rock-cut tombs. Their basic repertoire included groups of little wooden figures carrying out everyday tasks: brewers and bakers are especially common, as are butchers and cow-herders, textile workers and potters. Not only are the figures themselves shown going about their daily business (as servants for the benefit of the tombowner), but they are shown with the equipment needed to carry out their occupations, and often also the premises in which they worked. Granaries are often shown, with little figures carrying sacks of grain and little wooden scribes shown recording this activity.

These models also included boats, which had a religious symbolism – allowing the deceased to journey to and from the pilgrimage town of Abydos (home of the most important cult centre of Osiris, lord of the afterlife) – but which also emphasize river travel as the prime means of long-distance communication in dynastic Egypt.

It is unclear to what extent most of the owners of these models were employers of servants when alive, but some clearly were. The most famous set of wooden models from the Middle Kingdom come from the Theban tomb of the administrator Meketre. These include modelled scenes of boats fishing with nets, and scenes of the counting of cattle, but most are standardized wooden boxes each containing a workshop of a particular activity, including baking and brewing, spinning and weaving, butchery and carpentry. Another of these boxes represents a much-abbreviated residential house with a more lovingly modelled colonnade and tree-filled courtyard. It is tempting to see in the Meketre models the component parts of an 'urban estate' much like those at Kahun.

Soul Houses

When Petrie was excavating the Middle Kingdom cemetery of Deir Rifeh in Upper Egypt in 1907, he recovered over 150 examples of a class of object that had only occasionally been found before. These were elaborate ceramic trays, designed to receive offerings for the dead. They

Models of granaries are often found among the range of wooden models from Middle Kingdom tombs – they were to be a source of grain for the tombowner. They might also be shown being filled with carefully accounted-for grain (below right) or having the grain turned into flour (below left).

were placed above ground next to fairly simple graves. Because these trays had been modelled to give them a house-like appearance, Petrie called them 'soul houses' and the name has stuck. The extent to which they actually resemble contemporary houses is a matter of debate. On the one hand, they needed to serve as trays in which the offering could be placed, but they do also seem to have been poorer substitutes for the large offering chapels of elite tombs of the same period, which certainly had house-like aspects to them. The tomb was, after all, the house of the *ka*. The need to produce a functional ceramic tray encouraged the depiction of external aspects of the house, particularly any courtyard or open area in front of it, while the internal aspects of the house would tend to be ignored or simplified. The emphasis on an external courtyard would be especially relevant if this was where food preparation generally took place, as the 'soul houses' themselves were especially concerned with the provision of food.

The surviving 'soul houses' show different levels of attempts to emulate houses. Some emphasize the courtyard, with perhaps a sunshade supported by a set of pillars. Others depict the front of the house, especially the columned portico that also provided a shaded area at the front of the house. Some seem to indicate that houses could have two storeys, while the roofs of many 'soul houses' are provided with a *mulqaf*, a hood-like structure over a hole in the roof designed to channel any cool breezes down into the house. Some examples move away from the open tray format and look much more like real houses, with walls, windows and a door, although the need to make these 'soul houses' capable of carrying offerings means that the roof is in these cases removed.

Although the value of 'soul houses' as accurate depictions of Middle Kingdom domestic housing might be questioned, they are extremely useful in depicting features that were, presumably, common in 'ordinary' Middle Kingdom houses (temporary shaded structures, *mulqaf*s), but that do not survive in the archaeological remains of the lower parts of largely 'official' constructions of the period such as at Kahun and Wah-Sut.

Models of houses found within Middle Kingdom tombs could vary from large, detailed wooden models like that from the tomb of Meketre (bottom left) or elaborations of simple ceramic offering trays (bottom right).

Towns and Houses of the New Kingdom

It is perhaps unsurprising that the evidence for life and work in the New Kingdom comes from two settlements that are unique – the workers' village of Deir el-Medina (which provides the best evidence, both archaeological and textual, of any period from anywhere in Egypt) and the new-build foundation of Akhenaten at Amarna – because the special reasons for their creation are the same reasons that their evidence has been preserved: their less fertile locations away from the majority of settlement. The city of Amarna will be described in the Gazetteer (pp. 155–63), but in this section that follows its Workmen's Village will briefly be compared with the vast array of evidence from Deir el-Medina.

The Village – Deir el-Medina

The village of Deir el-Medina is far and away the most important source of evidence for towns and villages in ancient Egypt. It provides the best evidence for the physical layout of a town/village, for the size and nature of individual houses, and for the lives of the people who lived in that town and those houses.

Evidence from the village comes in the form of the architectural remains of the houses and the village they comprise, other structures around the village (including cemeteries and shrines), physical objects from the houses and the tombs, and texts written by the villagers themselves that reflect on their everyday lives. This rich collection of varied types of evidence means that we can build a coherent picture of life in the village and of the lives of individual villagers. Nowhere else in ancient Egypt – or perhaps the ancient world – can we take a named, non-royal individual and examine their house, their tomb and their relationships with other named individuals.

Excavation History

Because of this range of high-quality archaeological evidence, Deir el-Medina has been the focus of archaeological work for a series of excavators. The Italian archaeologist Ernesto Schiaparelli's 1905–9 work in the village's cemeteries has resulted in Turin Museum now containing some of the best examples of New Kingdom burial goods, including those from the intact 18th-Dynasty tomb of Kha and Merit. The Ramesside tomb of Sennedjem provided a similar range of goods and had the bonus of being painted – presumably by its owner and his colleagues – in dazzling colours. The 1913 work of German linguist Georg Möller for Berlin Museum was the first to recover in significant quantities the ostraca (fragments of limestone (or pottery), which were the scrap paper of ancient Egypt) whose texts are such an important aspect for the reconstruction of the lives and activities of Deir el-Medina villagers. Most importantly, the extensive excavations of French archaeologist Bernard Bruyère for the French Institute during 1922–40 and 1945–51 concentrated on the excavation of the core village itself, and structures in its environs such as the chapels.

This scene from the tomb of Sennedjem at Deir el-Medina shows him and his wife enjoying a bucolic afterlife in an agricultural landscape not dissimilar to that of Egypt itself.

A Royal Town for Royal Tombs

The paradox of Deir el-Medina is that, although it is the closest we can come to seeing the lives of 'ordinary' Egyptians, it is unique. Founded to house the skilled craftsmen (and their families) who dug and decorated the royal tombs in the Valley of the Kings, it was in some ways the descendant of the Old and Middle Kingdom pyramid towns. However, it was neither a barracks to house a substantial, transient labour force, nor was it a town whose inhabitants had an official role in the perpetuation of cults of dead kings; its function was to keep together a set of people with particular skills. Furthermore, those skills would be required by every king who wanted a tomb in the Valley of the Kings, and so Deir el-Medina and the Valley of the Kings developed a relationship of mutual dependency that lasted over 400 years.

Unlike the significantly dispersed pyramid complexes that preceded them as royal tombs, the Valley of the Kings tombs were both much smaller and very close together. The tomb of (probably) the earliest king to be buried in the Valley, Thutmose I, is only 200 m (656 ft) away from the abandoned tomb of Ramesses XI. A single settlement, close by but not too close, was all that was required as living quarters for the workforce for every Valley of the Kings tomb. So, despite its unusual origins, Deir el-Medina was a settlement that had a real longevity. The date of its foundation is not certain: by the Ramesside Period the workmen regarded King Amenhotep I and his mother Ahmose-Nefertari as their royal patron-deities, although the stamped bricks in the earliest phase of the enclosure wall give the name of Amenhotep's successor, Thutmose I.

A Community of Workmen

Deir el-Medina's stability in location, and the norms of Egyptian social (im)mobility, were also ideally suited for the transmission of the specialist skills required for royal tomb-cutting and decorating. Deir el-Medina was just like any 'real' settlement in Egypt in the sense that it was essentially made up of families for whom it was their home. Workers for the royal tomb were not made: they were, quite literally, born, as succeeding generations at Deir el-Medina passed their specific skills down from father to son.

Although the village might suddenly be increased in size to cope with a major step-change in royal demand (as seems to have happened during the reigns of Horemheb and Ramesses IV), most Deir el-Medina workmen had been born in the village, and so too had most people they knew. The title of the most important summary of the written evidence from Deir el-Medina by one of the most important figures in scholarship on the village, the Czech Egyptologist Jaroslav Černý, has the telling title 'A Community of Workmen at Thebes in the Ramesside Period'; Deir el-Medina was indeed a community, and one with a shared communal memory and a web of interpersonal relationships that could stretch back many generations.

A view across the remains of Deir el-Medina. In the foreground are the walls of some of the village houses while in the background, at the foot of the cliffs of the Theban mountain, are tombs from the Western Cemetery.

Food and Drink

If the self-reproducing character of the village makes it look like any 'normal' settlement, other features emphasize its unusual character. The most obvious of these is its inability to support itself. Left to their own devices, most settlements were perfectly capable of surviving, indeed flourishing, without the external interference of the state. Most settlements were, of course, primarily agricultural and could comfortably exist on the food they grew – the tax-collecting state was probably seen as a burden rather than a supportive institution.

Deir el-Medina was different. Owing to the need for easy access to the Valley of the Kings, it was located somewhere no sensible Egyptian would live – not just on the edge of, but effectively in, the desert. Although the 'hidden' and 'secluded' aspects of Deir el-Medina are often over-emphasized (a relatively gentle stroll of less than an hour would take a Deir el-Medina villager of the Ramesside Period from his/her home to the bank of the Nile, passing the great temple of Amenhotep III along the way), it was isolated from self-sufficiency in two specific ways.

The first is the range of skills the villagers possessed. The able-bodied male workforce was trained for work in the royal tomb, not food production; although Deir el-Medina villagers obviously engaged in auxiliary economic activities, this would not be enough to keep themselves in the necessities of life. Secondly, although the location of the village was not so distant as to isolate the villagers from interaction with the rest of the West Bank (or, indeed, Thebes in general), the transport to the village of the major quantities of foodstuffs required to support the village was another matter. This is especially noticeable in the problem of making sure there was enough water.

The village could therefore only survive with a large, well-organized and expensive support system. The umbilical cord that fed Deir el-Medina was supplied by the state as one of the costs of royal tomb-construction. When that umbilical cord was removed *c.* 1070 BC, because the Valley of the Kings ceased to be the place for royal burial, Deir el-Medina became unviable as a self-supporting settlement and the villagers did what any sensible person would have done in the same situation. They packed their bags and left.

The 'Village de Repos', high above Deir el-Medina on the path to the Valley of the Kings, seems to have served as temporary accommodation for villagers working on the royal tomb project.

The Village and its Environs

In its final and largest form, the village occupied an area of 6,400 square metres (1.6 acres), though for most of its life it was somewhat smaller at 5,600 square metres (1.4 acres) (see fig. below). It contained 68 houses (although more were built outside the core village), enclosed by a perimeter wall. The main entrance to the village was on its north side, which gave access to the main street that ran down the centre of the village.

The same combination of the 'real' and the 'artificial' settlement that can be seen in

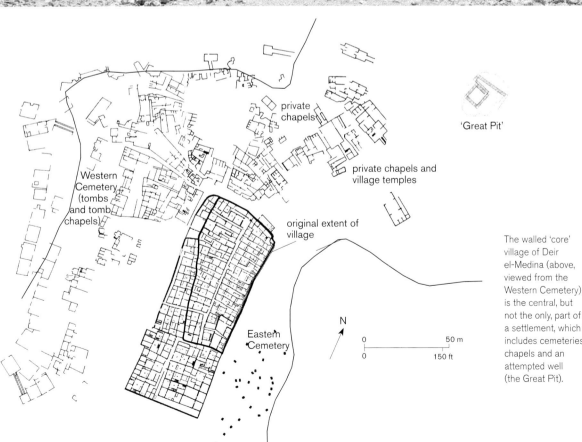

'Great Pit'

private chapels

private chapels and village temples

Western Cemetery (tombs and tomb chapels)

original extent of village

Eastern Cemetery

N

0   50 m
0   150 ft

The walled 'core' village of Deir el-Medina (above, viewed from the Western Cemetery) is the central, but not the only, part of a settlement, which includes cemeteries, chapels and an attempted well (the Great Pit).

the multi-generational, externally supported community at Deir el-Medina is also present in the physical appearance of the village itself. Although Deir el-Medina was essentially a planned settlement, it was not designed around the orthogonal grid-plan of typified Middle Kingdom planned settlements, such as Kahun. Instead, and unlike the grid-planned Workmen's Village at Amarna with which it is often compared (see pp. 86–87), Deir el-Medina nestles comfortably in the valley selected for its location.

The Typical House

Because Deir el-Medina was a 'real' village that evolved over time, no two houses are exactly the same, since each had to adapt to the needs of 'real' families who lived within them. However, as at Kahun, the houses were so closely packed together that opportunities for expanding the basic footprint of the building were limited – really, extra space might be obtained only by going down (for which there is evidence) or going up (for which there is much debate), but not sideways. As in the Amarna Workmen's Village (see below), the basic house seems to have been constructed by the state, with later additions and changes to the basic design the responsibility of individual householders. It would also appear that there was little change in the basic house plan from the early 18th-Dynasty foundation to the later Ramesside additions and, because of this, it is possible to speak of a standard Deir el-Medina house plan, while appreciating the potential for variation from this basic model.

The basic house had stone rubble foundations and stone lower courses, but with upper courses of mudbrick. The walls were then covered with mud plaster, forming a smooth, flat surface that could be decorated. The extent of that painted decoration is debated, owing to the partial survival of the walls. The exterior walls were whitewashed, presumably in part to reflect the unremitting summer sun of southern Egypt, particularly in the reflective desert bowl of the little valley in which Deir el-Medina was located.

The average Deir el-Medina house was consistent in its long, narrow shape, although with some variability in size – they might be as long as 27 m (89 ft) or as short as 13 m (43 ft), with the average around 20 m (66 ft), but there

A House Census at Deir el-Medina

A fragmentary papyrus in Turin Museum lists two sets of houses and their occupants at Deir el-Medina. It gives a good impression of the range of family-groups in the village, although the number of houses that appear to be occupied by single men is puzzling.

List I
1 The House of Amennakht (plus his wife Tenetpaip, his mother Tarekhan and his sister Kaytmehty)
2 The House of Paankha
3 The House of Djehutymose
4 The House of Penpare
5 The House of Inherkhau
6 The House of Pawaamen
7 The House of Pennesuttway
8 The House of Montuhatef

List II
1 The House of Qedakhetef (plus his wife Merutmut, his son Paankheriautef and his daughter Wenher)
2 The House of Amennakht (plus his wife Tahefnu)
3 The House of Aapatjau (plus his wife Wabet and his daughter Meresger)
4 The House of Hornefer (plus his wife Hutiyt and his son Qenna)
5 The House of Ipuy (plus his wife Henutmire and his daughters Henutnetjeru, Duanofet and Hathor)

was much less variability in width: between 4 and 6 m (13–20 ft). Unsurprisingly, the larger houses belonged to the Foreman and the 'Scribe of the Gang', and these were located close to the entrance to the village.

Typically, the front door opened directly from one of the main streets of the village, while the back wall of the semi-open kitchen area at the rear of the house was the perimeter wall of the village. Surviving evidence suggests that the main door was made of wood, set in a wooden or limestone frame, which could be inscribed with the name of the householder. At least some of these doors were painted red – this combination of red doors in white walls must have given the exterior of Deir el-Medina houses an appearance not dissimilar to Middle Kingdom house models (see fig. p. 72). The main door was not in the centre of the front elevation of the house, but to one side, and it was in line with the internal doors that gave access to the four main sequential spaces in the house. These rooms, as described by Bruyère in his 1939 publication of the village were:

Room 1: 'Front Room'/'Parlour'/*Vorhof/Salle du Lit Clos*

This room was entered directly from the street, by stepping down two or three steps into a roughly square room. The lower parts of the walls, up to about 1 metre (3 ft) from the floor, were whitewashed. The most striking element of this room was a construction made of mudbrick in the form of a rectangular block built against one of the walls, averaging 1.7 metres long by 0.8 m wide by 0.75 m tall (5 ft 7 in. by 2 ft 7 in.

by 2ft 5 in.), with screen walls protruding above the edge of the platform on all sides, but with an opening on the long side that was accessed by a short flight of steps. This structure was plastered, whitewashed and painted with images that suggest it was used for female activities, especially childbirth (representations include the protective deity Bes) and female grooming. Some 28 of the 68 houses at Deir el-Medina contained these structures, which Bruyère called '*lits clos*' – enclosed beds (or 'box beds').

The function of these 'beds' is one of the great puzzles of Deir el-Medina, with some scholars proposing that they were used during childbirth, others arguing that they would be eminently impractical for such a procedure.

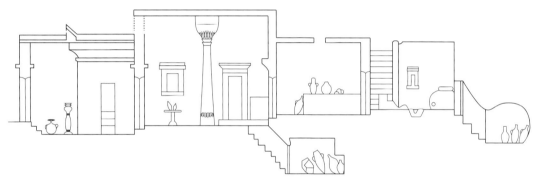

Although it might vary in detail from house to house, it is possible to describe a standard plan Deir el-Medina house (cross-section above) based on the substantial architectural remains at the site (below).

The counter-suggestions are that they may have acted as normal beds (with the images providing a generalized protective rather than specifically female-protective aura) or that they may simply have acted as substantial bench-altars for household deities. Given the need for flexible use of space within these small houses, it is probably best to regard the 'box beds' as structures that had several layers of function and meaning, each one of which might be given greater or lesser importance by the particular families who owned them (see box opposite).

Room 2: 'Living Room'/*Wohnraum*/*Salle du Divan*

This room was entered by stepping up two or three steps from the first room so that the floor level was the same as that of the street. This room often had a central wooden column (sometimes two) on a stone base, which supported a roof higher than in any other part of the house. The difference in height between the ceiling of this room and that of the rooms in front of and behind it might have been to enable window grilles for clerestory lighting and ventilation to be put in – perhaps necessary given how little opportunity there was for windows in these terraced houses. Inbuilt 'furniture' included a low platform ('divan') made of mudbrick, which would have been equally suitable for sitting or lying on. In the northern part of the village the houses were founded directly on limestone bedrock and in some of those houses a cellar was dug out underneath this platform, which was used for additional storage for items such as large pottery vessels.

The walls of this room often contained a series of niches and/or false doors, which were used to house objects connected with the religious life of the household, especially figures of household deities and 'ancestor busts'. The latter suggest there was a thriving ancestor cult that connected the living family members of the household with their dead ancestors, often buried close by in one of the Deir el-Medina cemeteries.

Rooms 3 and 4: Transitional Space

At the rear of the main central room of the house was what might be called a transitional zone that separated the main space (Room 2) from the kitchen at the very rear of the house.

Typically this zone contained two main elements, which divided the width of the house between them. The first was a relatively small room of undistinguished character (it did not have any obvious standard fixtures or fittings, unlike Rooms 1 and 2). The second, and narrower, element was a corridor, but one that had a door at each end and often a bench along one wall.

Room 5: The Kitchen/*Wirtschaftshof*/*Cuisine*

The kitchen was the easiest part of the Deir el-Medina house for the excavators to identify because of the food-preparation equipment often still in place. Typically this equipment consisted of a round brick oven; a limestone mortar set into the floor, which would have mainly been used for the processing of grain; and a kneading trough. This part of the house did not have a solid roof, but a shelter of light matting, which would allow smoke and cooking smells to escape while providing a welcome shade from the sun. As with Room 2, additional storage in the kitchen was provided by digging out a subterranean storage area, which often went underneath the perimeter wall.

'Room' 6: The Roof

The remains of the lower courses of a flight of stairs in many of these houses indicate a well-established route to one of the most intriguing part of the house: the roof.

However, unlike for houses at the Workmen's Village at Amarna, there is no evidence that Deir el-Medina houses had a second storey, and indeed several scholars have commented that the walls at Deir el-Medina are too thin to support such a structure. Nevertheless, perhaps equipped with a simple reed shelter, the roof would have been a valuable work and storage area, as is obvious from comparisons with modern village houses (figure p. 93).

House Use at Deir el-Medina

This account of the standard house plan at Deir el-Medina raises a number of interesting questions. Perhaps the first is, 'Where did the residents sleep?' It is likely that the answer lies within the flexibility in the use of space already noted with regard, for example, to the smaller Middle Kingdom houses at Kahun. At Deir

Gendering Space

One of the most difficult problems in archaeology is interpreting the social meaning of space. In the case of Egyptian settlement archaeology one of the biggest questions of this type is the extent to which the space within houses can be 'gendered' – are there areas used mainly or exclusively by men or women and, if so, what does this tell us about Egyptian society?

Those lucky enough to be invited into the house of a well-to-do modern villager in Egypt will usually be taken into a room that is specifically set aside for entertaining visitors. More particularly, these will be male visitors of male members of the household. The only women the visitor is likely to see are those bringing in food and drink to the male guests before quickly disappearing to the rear of the house – the bedrooms and especially the kitchen – which are the domain of the women of the house. It would be very inappropriate indeed for male visitors to enter this part of the house.

Deir el-Medina houses present us with a collection of evidence that seems to have potential for similar types of 'gendering', but this brings its own problems. The most obviously functionally 'female' part of the house is the kitchen at the rear. This might suggest the seclusion of the women of the household in the innermost parts of the house. The other area that seems to have a specific connection with female concerns is the first room, the room of the 'enclosed bed', whose decoration and (possibly) function as we have seen suggest a concern with fertility and childbirth. Some commentators therefore argue that the first

room of the house was where the women of the house gathered, while the central room was the gathering-place for males of the family.

However, if this is the case, then a room that seems to be connected to the intimate concerns of the females of the house is the most public of the entire house: every visitor to any part of the house would have to pass through it.

In addition, it is clear that, for most of the week, adult males were absent from the village, working at the Valley of the Kings and living on site or at the 'Col' settlement (see fig. p. 76). It is therefore likely that, for 8 days out of 10, Deir el-Medina was very much a village of women.

Figured ostraca (fragments of limestone or pottery with drawings on them) can give an informal and informative insight into the lives of villagers who drew them, as with this fine example of a breast-feeding New Kingdom lady.

el-Medina, variations from the basic house layout are minor, but it is clear that the size and composition of the families who lived within these houses was subject to a good deal of variability.

Most of the houses we are used to today are self-limiting by the large and difficult-to-move furniture put in them. A smallish bedroom with a large double-bed in it cannot become a very different room without a good deal of effort. However, one might compare studio flats in crowded cities that have fold-up beds in order to make a more efficient use of space and convert a daytime living area to a bedroom for the night. While elite Egyptians with large multi-roomed villas might have been able to designate a specific room as a bedroom (see pp. 67, 161), and keep it for that sole use, a Deir el-Medina villager would not necessarily have had that luxury. But nor would they have had the luxurious but limiting set of furniture that made the switch of room-use a chore.

Although it is difficult to be precise, it is likely that most of a Deir el-Medina house could become a bedroom at night, having had a quite different function during the day. Equally, anyone who has lived in a flat-roofed house in the Egyptian countryside knows how attractive the open air on the roof becomes during the hot Egyptian summer (mosquitoes notwithstanding), while an indoor room, perhaps with a small brazier in the corner, is much more comfortable on cool winter nights. But there is a more fundamental issue here, because the question of the occupation of individual houses cannot be taken on its own: the Deir el-Medina villagers did not live in isolation, their houses were within the village, within the environs of the village and within the landscape of western Thebes. Deir el-Medina does not just give us an example of what a typical New Kingdom house might have been like, it also suggests how a community interacted with its local environment.

Tombs

The cemeteries at Deir el-Medina are perhaps the best example of the physical integration of the dwellings of the living and the dead in any individual community of ancient Egypt. The presence of the village cemeteries is perhaps the most obvious evidence that Deir el-Medina was not a temporary residence for transient workers, but a community that had put down roots – those roots were the community's dead.

Because of the location of Deir el-Medina within what was effectively an extended desert cemetery, a physically close relationship developed in a way that would have been difficult in most other Nile Valley sites. The eastern and western slopes of the valley, at the bottom of which sat Deir el-Medina, were used for the village cemetery: the Eastern Cemetery mainly during the 18th Dynasty and the more extensive Western Cemetery in the Ramesside Period. The strikingly visible, often pyramidal, superstructures of the Ramesside tombs (see fig. opposite), erected in some cases only a few metres from the perimeter wall of the village, are an obvious indicator of the way in which the cemetery was very much part of everyday life at Deir el-Medina, as the living interacted with the dead through offering and ancestor cults.

House Contents

Although a number of New Kingdom sites have provided the architectural remains of houses, it is usually difficult to imagine how these houses would have been filled with the possessions of their owners. A rare exception to this is Ostracon Cairo 26670. This valuable document comes from Deir el-Medina and appears to be an inventory of the contents of a house that has been left unoccupied for some reason.

it is clear that houses could contain a variety of different types of boxes and other storage items. It is noticeable that no small personal items, clothes or very cheap items such as pottery are mentioned, presumably because these were so disposable that the owner felt no need to record their existence.

List of items left behind by me in the village:

3 khar-*sacks of barley*	2 *footstools*
1½ khar-*sacks of emmer*	2 *folding stools of wood*
26 *bundles of onions*	1 *sack of* lubya-*beans*
2 *beds*	12 *bricks of natron-salt*
1 sheqer-*box*	2 *pieces of* iker-*furniture*
2 *couches for a man*	
2 *folding stools*	1 *door*
1 pedes-*box*	2 seterti *of sawn wood*
1 *inlaid* (?) tjay-*box*	2 hetep-*containers*
1 harit-*furniture*	1 *mortar*
2 *griddle-stones*	2 medjay-*containers*
1 gatit-*box*	

The list of items is not by category – furniture is mixed in with foodstuffs – but is roughly by order of value. The meanings of some of the words used for these objects remain obscure, although

A range of simple household objects – a stool, a basket and a hand-brush – from the New Kingdom tomb of Kha at Deir el-Medina.

More generally, the evidence from ostraca suggests that the possession of a house and a tomb was the core of the property portfolio of a resident of Deir el-Medina – ultimately it would be the tomb (some of which were multi-generational) that would guarantee permanent residence at Deir el-Medina.

Chapels

The area to the north of the Western Cemetery, on the path to the 'Great Pit' (see map p. 77) was the location for a series of small home-made chapels. These were used for a variety of purposes, most obviously for the worship of local deities, but also as social clubs or community centres (see p. 92) for groups of like-minded individuals from the village, referred to by Bruyère as *confréries*. Like the cemeteries, the chapel area was an obvious extension of Deir el-Medina, spreading in an unconfined way beyond the rigid boundaries of the core village itself. Within this same categorization of extra-

mural activity we can include the rock-cut 'Sanctuary of Ptah' (patron-deity of craftsmen) on the path from Deir el-Medina to the Valley of the Queens, and a series of smaller chapels built high above the village on the path to the Valley of the Kings.

Daily Life at Deir el-Medina

The physical remains of Deir el-Medina give us a strong impression of the houses, streets and ancillary buildings of a real ancient Egyptian village. The ostraca recovered from the site, written to and from the villagers themselves, give an equally strong impression of those physical remains having once been populated by a vibrant community. They are perhaps the most vivid reminder that the ancient Egyptians were real people with everyday concerns not so different from our own. All of the quotations below come from ostraca or papyri of the Ramesside Period, from Deir el-Medina.

The tombs at Deir el-Medina – built by the villagers themselves using their specialist skills – were intended to be as visible as those of more high-status Egyptians, including superstructures composed of chapels topped with small mudbrick pyramids.

A Community at Work

The central reason for the existence of Deir el-Medina was the excavation and decoration of royal tombs in the Valley of the Kings, and the tombs of members of the royal family in the Valley of the Queens. It is not surprising that a good deal of the documentation from the village refers to this work.

> To the Fanbearer on the right of the King, Mayor, Vizier Ta. The scribe Neferhotep greets his lord in life, prosperity and health....
>
> Another communication for my lord, to wit, I am working in the tombs of the royal children which my lord ordered to be constructed. I am working very well and very efficiently, with good work and efficient work. My lord should not worry about it. I am working extremely well and I am not tired at all.

Some of the ostraca are notes asking for tools or materials to be brought:

> The scribe Nebneteru addresses the scribe Ramose.... Please pay attention and bring me some ink, because my chief has told me that the good ink has gone bad.
>
> To the scribe Huy: Please tell Khaemtore, 'You must send to me your jug, the adze, the double-edged knife and the two awls.'

The copper chisels used by the workmen were valuable in their own right as substantial pieces of expensive metal. They therefore needed to be carefully accounted for:

> Fourth month of Winter, Day 21. The Day of [issuing] chisels to the gang.
> Chisels, 68: 34 on the right side,
>   34 on the left side.

The evidence suggests that there was a rather relaxed attitude towards attendance at the worksite. The following extracts from the attendance register of workers at the royal tomb list individuals who were absent on a particular day, and some of the reasons for that absence:

> Second month of Inundation, Day 23.
> Those who were with the scribe Pashed working for the vizier – Ipuy and Nakhtemmut.

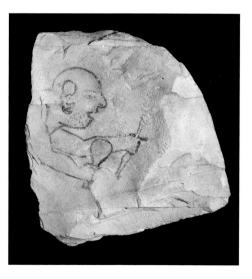

Another ostracon from Deir el-Medina shows a workman with mallet and chisel in hand – perhaps a quick sketch by one workman of a colleague.

> Those who were with the chief workman Khay – Khamu, Sawadjyt and Kaha (who was ill).
>
> Those who were with the chief workman Paneb – Kasa (his wife being in childbirth he had three days absent), Kasa son of Ramose (who was ill) and Raweben (who was ill).
>
> Fourth month of Winter, Day 6.
>
> Sawadjyt was absent from work, making a box for Hay.
>
> Khamu was absent from work making a statue for Hay, and Khaemseba was absent from work with him.
>
> Nakhtsu was ill and Rahotep was ill.

Along with food rations, the state provided a range of services to the villagers:

> Year 1, third month of Winter, Day 15. Giving clothes to the washermen today.
>
> What came from him in the third month of Winter, Day 16, what was given to them to launder at the riverbank – 10 kilts, 8 loincloths and 5 sanitary towels.

Labour Relations

The workmen of Deir el-Medina had a far from reverent attitude towards their superiors and they were quick to complain about, and to, each other:

The draughtsman Prehotep communicates to his chief, the scribe of the Place of Truth Qenhirkhopeshef. What is the meaning of this negative attitude that you are taking towards me? I am like a donkey to you. If there is work bring the donkey and if there is fodder bring the ox. If there is beer you never ask for me, you only ask for me if there is work!

The scribe Pabaky addresses his father the draughtsman Maaninakhtef…. I listened to what you said to me – 'Let Ib work with you.' But look, he spends every day bringing the jar of water. There is no other job for him every day … the sun has set and he is still far away with the jar of water.

Making Things for Each Other

The skills that the craftsmen of Deir el-Medina acquired could be put to good use in making and selling products to each other.

The workman Hay greets the scribe Imiseba…. I am busy making the bed. It will be beautiful. Send the ebony so there will be no delay, and also the webbing material … and you should send me some pigments.

Year 3, third month of Summer, Day 16. What the workman Paneb gave to the draughtsman […] for the construction work he did in my house: a workroom and a wall makes 1½ sacks [of grain].

One loincloth, two pairs of sandals, another loincloth, three bundles of vegetables, 2½ shaaty-worth of pigment, one mat, wood, two baskets of grain, two irkes baskets, making a total of 6½ shaaty. This is what Aanakht gave Merysekhmet in return for the painting of his burial chamber.

Please send this to me today … a depiction of the god Montu seated on a throne and a depiction of the scribe Pentawere kissing the ground in front of him in adoration of him, as an outline drawing.

Please make for me a weret-amulet, because the one you made for me has been stolen.

Not all of these transactions went smoothly. The use of barter and the exchange of goods rather than a negotiable currency (the common

extension of credit for purchases), not to mention a common reluctance to pay, gave rise to many situations like the one described below:

A statement by the workman Mose…. Your husband, the scribe Amennakht, took a coffin from me. He said, 'I shall give a calf in exchange for it.' But he has not yet given it to me. I said this to Paakhet who replied, 'Give me a bed in addition, and I will bring you the calf when it is mature.' I gave him the bed…. If you are going to give the ox, send it, but if there is no ox return the bed and the coffin.

Dishonesty

Within a comparatively rich community like Deir el-Medina, and with the constant flow of goods, theft was almost inevitable:

I am informing you of the property which was stolen from the house of Ipuy: one mat, 50 pieces of wood veneer, one pair of men's sandals, one deben of incense, three necklaces and three signet rings.

As for the fish which you sent … only 13 fish were delivered to us. Five of them had been removed. Demand them from the person you sent with them!

Marital Disharmony and Family Solidarity

Despite a sometimes difficult relationship with their employers, the Egyptian state (represented by the vizier and his officials), most of the problems faced by the villagers were caused by themselves. Specifically, these were the inter-personal and family problems perhaps typical of a small community. The first quotation below is part of a long-running, almost soap-opera style drama, concerning the notorious Paneb:

He said, 'Paneb slept with the lady Tuy when she was the wife of the workman Kenna. He slept with the lady Hel when she was with Pendua. He slept with the lady Hel when she was with Hesysunebef … and when he had slept with Hel he slept with Webkhet her daughter. Moreover, Aapekhty, his son, also slept with Webkhet!'

The workman Horemwia addresses his daughter Tanetdjesere. You are my good daughter. If the workman Baki throws you out of the house I will take action. The house itself belongs to Pharaoh, but you can live in the anteroom to my storehouse because I built it and nobody in the world can throw you out of there.

Takhentyshepse addresses her sister Iy…. I shall send you the barley for you to have it ground for me and add emmer wheat to it. You shall make bread with it for me because I have been quarrelling with Merymaat [her husband]. He keeps telling me 'I will divorce you' because of my mother and questioning the amount of barley needed for the bread.

Isis addresses her sister Nubemnu…. Please pay attention and weave for me that shawl … because I am really naked!

Having a Laugh

Nothing gives a greater sense of the humanity of long-dead people than evidence that they had a sense of humour. The Deir el-Medina ostraca include this joke, which can still raise a smile:

> You are like the story about a woman, blind in one eye, who was married to a man for 20 years. When he found another [wife] he said to her, 'I am divorcing you because you are blind in one eye' and she said to him, 'Have you just discovered this after the 20 years I have spent in your house?'

The Workmen's Village at Amarna

Deir el-Medina is unique as a settlement whose surviving physical remains are matched, if not surpassed, by the quality of the textual evidence of the lives of its inhabitants, but it is not the only settlement that can be categorized as a 'workmen's town' or 'workmen's village'. As in the Old and Middle Kingdom, the construction of royal monuments, and their continued operation, relied on groups of specialized workers who were housed at the site as part of the royal project. The New Kingdom has provided us with other examples of such settlements, such as the town built by King Ahmose at the beginning of the

18th Dynasty to service the monumental sacred complex built at Abydos.

Perhaps the closest parallel we have to Deir el-Medina is the so-called 'Workmen's Village' at Amarna. The isolation of this village from the main urban centre at Amarna – it is possibly on the way to the royal tomb – suggests that this settlement may have been built to house the Deir el-Medina tombmakers themselves, transferred from Thebes to Amarna in order to deploy their skills on the creation of royal tombs at the new capital. Unfortunately this is speculation, as the Amarna Workmen's Village has not (yet) provided any documentary evidence as to its function or the lives of its inhabitants, unlike Deir el-Medina.

That this village was a centrally planned project is clear from the rigid layout of the settlement: a brick-walled 69 m (226 ft) square containing 72 almost identically sized houses arranged in six parallel rows (see fig. opposite). The ground plan of each house was divided into three sections, and at first sight they seem to be rather smaller and more compact than the Deir el-Medina houses. However, the careful excavation of parts of the Workmen's Village by Barry Kemp for the

A plan and adjacent reconstruction of one of the houses in the Workmen's Village at Amarna, Gate Street 8. Note that the stairs lead not to the roof, but to an upper storey.

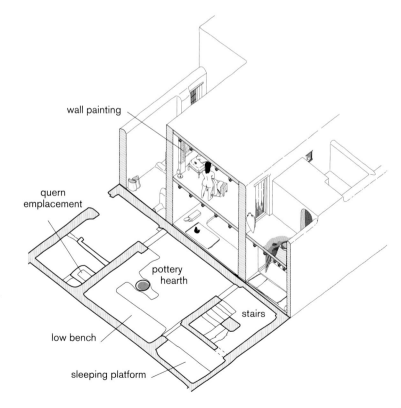

wall painting

quern emplacement

pottery hearth

low bench

stairs

sleeping platform

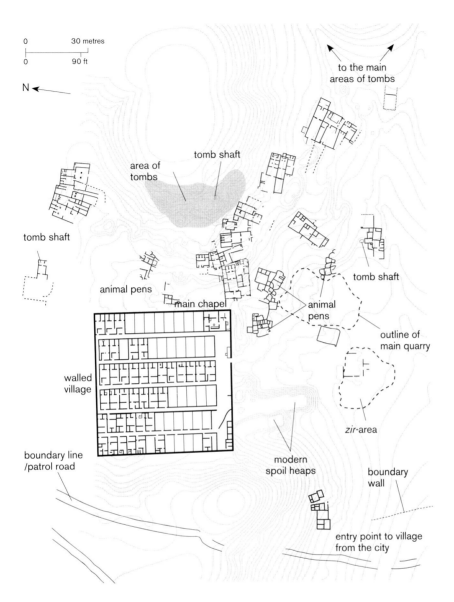

0   30 metres

0   90 ft

N ←

to the main
areas of tombs

tomb shaft

area of
tombs

tomb shaft

animal pens

main chapel

animal
pens

tomb shaft

outline of
main quarry

walled
village

zir-area

boundary line
/patrol road

modern
spoil heaps

boundary
wall

entry point to village
from the city

Like Deir el-Medina, the Workmen's Village at Amarna consisted of a 'core' walled residential area surrounded by a series of chapels and tombs, and also a number of animal pens.

Egypt Exploration Society, has revealed that the basic plan of these houses seems to have been adapted by individual householders to suit their individual needs. The central room of the house was probably a family living area with brick-built benches surrounding a low hearth for warmth during the winter. The front room of the house, perhaps surprisingly, was a working area for food preparation and 'cottage industries' such as weaving. The room(s) at the rear of the house were quite small, perhaps for storage, and at the back was a small kitchen and a staircase that gave access to an upper storey, which is where the room(s) used as bedrooms were located.

Outside the walled village itself were a series of structures used by the villagers. These include a series of small private chapels, animal pens and a space (the *zir*-area) that was probably used for the reception of supplies from the main city to support the villagers.

The Amarna Workmen's Village therefore offers a variation on both individual houses and integrated settlements made available to (one assumes) valued state employees during the New Kingdom. But it is also striking that, while the specific configuration of both houses and village may vary, the total amount of space, and facilities available, are actually very similar.

Country Houses

Although, with exceptions at Amarna, there are few surviving traces of noble villas from the New Kingdom, we have some idea of how they must have looked from images preserved upon tomb walls and from some texts. In both these sources we are given a vivid impression of how a rich Egyptian treasured a vision of restful country living, much like an English gentleman of the 18th century might have sought refuge from the hurley-burley of London in his country estate. The following description comes from a New Kingdom document, Papyrus Lansing. It describes the amenities and comforts of the country villa belonging to a man called Raia:

Raia has built a splendid villa which is opposite the city of Edjo. He built it on the [river]-bank … as a work of eternity, planted with trees on every side of it. A water-channel has been dug in front of it and one's sleep is only disturbed by the splash of a wave. No one can tire of looking at it, happy at its gate and giddy in its halls. Fine door-posts of limestone are inscribed and carved, doors newly hewn and walls inlaid with lapis-lazuli.

Its granaries are well stocked and filled with plenty. [There is] a fowl-yard and an aviary with geese, byres full of oxen, a breeding bird-pool with geese and horses in the stable. There are *skty*-boats, ferry-boats and cattle-boats moored at its quay.

You stroll around new islands and endless pasture whose grain is more plentiful than the standing water [of the inundation] which was there before. Boat-crews have landed at its quay to gladden the granaries [with] many endless heaps for the lord of Thebes.

At its west is a pond for hunting *ro*-geese of all sorts, a hunting-resort from the very beginning. Another one of its ponds is full of fish, more than in a lake. Its *ah*-bird is like a bird of the marshes.

Joy dwells within it and no one wishes for anything else for it.

Many animal-stalls are around it and a grazing-field for oxen, goats, capering kids and many lowing short-horned cattle.

It has many cool places with green grass in both summer and winter. Within the irrigation-basins are many *wd*-fish, *bulti*-fish, *sna*-fish and *dss*-fish; fish are more numerous than the sands on the river bank and there is no end of them!

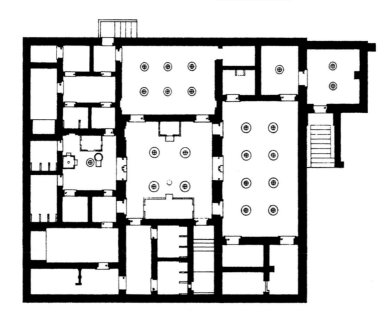

At the heart of every elite estate was the core house. This multi-roomed example from Amarna, belonging to the vizier Nakht, has a square ground plan of 30 m (almost 100 ft) along each side.

The god Amun founded [this place]; truly it is his place.

You sit in the shade of its trees and vines, eating their fruit, wearing wreaths of their branches and intoxicated with their wine.

Skty-boats are built for you from the wood of their fir-trees and a chariot from the wood of the *tjaga*-trees.

Here you are healthy and contented every day, the blessings of Amun are with you O Raia, Chief Overseer of the Cattle of Amun.

Two things are being stressed in the encomium of Papyrus Lansing. First is the degree of comfort (Raia is woken by nothing noisier than a gentle river-wave splashing against the shore) and leisure (hunting and fishing) the villa provides. But it is also noticeable how much emphasis is placed on its economic endowments. Raia's villa is notably well-stocked in being able to produce food (and high-quality food at that) for Raia and his family, but its self-sufficiency even extends to chariot-production!

Although this seems to be an idyll of isolated, peaceful country living, there is one section of this reverie omitted from the quotation above, because it deserves to be considered further.

The poor, the old and the young have all come to live in its neighbourhood. Your sustenance is established and a flood-bearing fowl is for whomsoever has come to you.

What does this mean? It appears to describe the opposite of what most people would want in a country residence: near-neighbours of a clearly disadvantaged and seemingly dependent social class. However this is exactly the situation

Depictions of the villas of elite Egyptians on the walls of their tombs often reflect the description of Papyrus Lansing, stressing the abundance of their gardens and storerooms.

we find at Amarna, with large villas surrounded by small residences in what can be regarded as 'mixed' neighbourhoods. This pattern of 'mixed' neighbourhoods seems to be something of a common occurrence in Egyptian cities, possibly thanks to the notion of patronage by the villa of the dependencies as an aspect of local government, at least as far as acquisition of basic staples of life might be concerned.

It answers some of the questions of city (as opposed to village) living – how do the specialized craftsmen of big industrial cities acquire their agricultural requirements (most obviously food and drink, but also clothing, etc.) if they are now carrying out specialized tasks and do not directly (unlike the peasantry) actually produce anything that can be eaten and drunk? For specialized communities of great importance to the state (such as Deir el-Medina), provision could be made from the state apparatus, but the direct provision to all the dwellers within a large city would require a huge command economy. Instead, it seems that the mechanism for distribution to the city-dwellers of Amarna, and perhaps elsewhere, was based on delegated patronage. The king gave land to the elite of Amarna, who lived in large villas, which also had productive capacity in them. These elite, as part of their public duty, themselves redistributed agricultural goods and other manufactured goods to their clients.

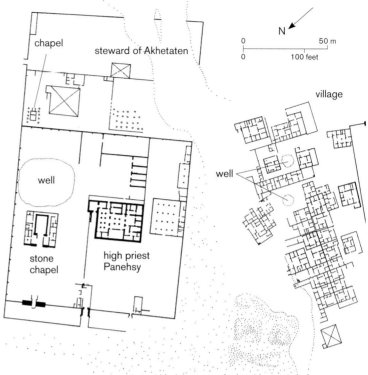

The house of the high priest Panehsy at Amarna is a good example of an elite villa, set in its own spacious grounds. It had a cluster of much smaller houses built next to it, which may have been satellite dependencies of the elite residence.

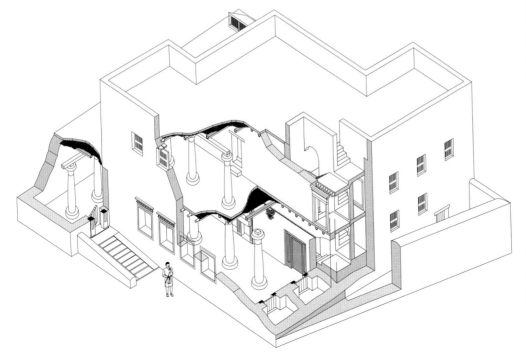

Reconstruction drawing of the multi-storey house of the chariot officer Ranefer at Amarna.

Community Centres

Our overview of Egyptian houses during the dynastic period has revealed a number of interesting patterns. One of these is the way in which elite members of society could expect to live in spacious dwellings, although a good proportion of that spaciousness was not directly to do with their domestic comfort, but instead it existed to provide areas where they could carry out their administrative and other functions as community leaders. This seems to be the case in places as different as Middle Kingdom Kahun and New Kingdom Amarna, and we should imagine this as a pattern for most of the dynastic period. Even on a sub-elite level, any house with internal space greater than the bare minimum is often associated with some sort of specific employment-related activity, for example the house of the sculptor Thutmose at Amarna whose function as a workshop was made clear by the discovery of part-finished sculpture (including the famous Berlin bust of Nefertiti) within it.

In contrast, non-elite housing is typified by its striking lack of space. Even if we assume an upper floor, the houses at Deir el-Medina, Amarna's Workmen's Village and the small houses at Kahun are very far from most modern, Western individuals' ideas of adequately spacious. This might be partly mitigated by the idea of flexible use of space within the house, as discussed above (pp. 66–67). A broader answer might be provided by the idea that houses were only rarely fully occupied by the family groups associated with them. The adult menfolk of Deir el-Medina, for instance, spent most of their 10-day week at the royal tomb in the Valley of the Kings, and they would have lived there or in the 'Col' village part way between the Valley and Deir el-Medina itself (see fig. p. 76). Although this work pattern may well be peculiar to Deir el-Medina, with its unique employment opportunities, the idea that life – either work or leisure – was lived outside the house, indeed outside the village, is an important one.

It is easy to imagine what most Egyptians were doing for most of the day in an agricultural economy where fields and animals needed to be tended (although inundation time is an interesting exception). But although the evidence from the houses themselves and the working lives of their occupants provides a coherent pattern, it does not explain where communal activities took

This reconstruction of part of the city of Amarna is centred on a 'middle-ranking' residence/workshop, belonging to the sculptor Thutmose.

place, especially when these might involve groups of people whose relationships were not family-based, including, potentially, the entire village.

The 'Enclosure of the Tomb'

The best example of a physically defined area that could function as a 'community centre' was the 'Enclosure of the Tomb' at Deir el-Medina. This structure seems to have been located a slight distance away from the village on the path to the Ramesseum (i.e. towards the more heavily populated banks of the Nile). It acted as a reception point for deliveries (especially foodstuffs) made to the villagers, and was looked after by one or more watchmen assisted by a doorkeeper. Ostraca from Deir el-Medina give a good sense of other activities carried out in the 'Enclosure of the Tomb': an interesting mixture of community-based enterprises, including private transactions and beer-drinking. It was most typically a place for

community gatherings and for the reception of external officials, for example the assembly of the work gang to hear the news of the accession of Ramesses VI (and to be given a variety of gifts to mark the occasion). It also seems to have been the place where the *kenbet* – a court made up of local officials who administered village-level justice in local disputes – met.

Such community centres undoubtedly existed in other villages and small towns. One of these seems to be the so-called *zir*-area at Amarna (see fig. p. 87). About 50 m (164 ft) in front of the Workmen's Village was a brick enclosure 11 m (36 ft) square, which was later replaced by a series of large storage jars in rough stone/rubble emplacements. This area, like the 'Enclosure of the Tomb' at Deir el-Medina, seems to be an interface between a workmen's village and the outside world that would provide it with supplies. Though of course its location outside settlement walls could just be because a convenient open area outside a tightly packed village was needed for communal activities.

Aerial photograph of the Workmen's Village at Amarna, viewed to the south, in 1993. The ancient trackways on the desert in the foreground are particularly clear.

Open Spaces in 'Normal' Towns and Villages

However, this raises a set of problems. The most obvious is the atypical nature of the settlements concerned – both Deir el-Medina and the Workmen's Village at Amarna were purpose-built villages for a specific set of state employees, who are supplied by the state with a substantial proportion of their requirements. The vast majority of small settlements in ancient Egypt would not have been like this, and would not have required a place where bulk supplies would be delivered for redistribution, because those villages would be self-sufficient in their major requirements. Nonetheless it is difficult to imagine that most ancient Egyptian villages would not have had some form of communal area, either outside the village itself or, perhaps more likely, a space or spaces in the form of external shared courtyards created by densely packed housing. It is easy to imagine these spaces being used for a variety of communal activities, from local courts to specific leisure activities to simply being a cool shaded space on a warm summer evening where friends and neighbours could gather.

As far as larger towns are concerned, there was potential for use of space associated with more substantial semi-public buildings – courtyards in front of temples or the residences of important local officials might have provided areas for public activities.

However, it must be admitted that, apart from assuming anthropological parallels with modern Egyptian villages, the evidence for this conclusion is slight. There is no indication that such internal spaces existed at Kahun, with its unremitting rows of back-to-back terraced houses, but the difference here, as at Deir el-Medina and Amarna, is the state-sponsored nature of the settlement and, perhaps even more relevantly, its desert-edge location. A settlement built immediately next to the desert edge would clearly have significantly fewer space problems – and more opportunities for the creation of specific community spaces outside the core settlement – than a floodplain site that would become an island during the inundation. It is worth noting that, although we know a good deal about what

went on at the 'Enclosure of the Tomb' at Deir el-Medina through the written evidence of the ostraca, the 'Enclosure' has not been detected archaeologically, probably because it was – like the *zir*-area at Amarna – a poorly built structure of local materials that could easily disappear back into the surrounding desert landscape.

Aerial view of a modern rural village in Egypt, illustrating a range of building materials and techniques.

93

Feeding and Supplying the City

Like all major settlements, the towns and cities of ancient Egypt required a constant supply of agricultural products to feed and (in the case of flax and linen) clothe their urban population. Some of this food could be produced locally in and around the city itself, for example by river-fishing and small-scale market gardening, but the necessary large-scale agriculture – especially the production of grain – took place elsewhere. The evidence from Amarna (see p. 162) suggests that the work of processing this grain to produce the dietary staples of bread and beer was carried out both in state production facilities and at a domestic level. In both cases, national and local government took a great interest and were involved in making sure that the huge quantities of grain required were collected, transported and safely stored. The production of this grain – and a variety of other foodstuffs from vegetables to fine cuts of beef – was carried out in the agricultural hinterland that made up the vast majority of Egypt.

In addition to agricultural products to feed its population, a city required other things, not least the materials that would allow it to grow. Although the basic building material – mudbrick – was always easy to obtain locally (see pp. 31–32), the great monumental hearts of many Egyptian cities from the New Kingdom onwards required specialist materials, especially stone from specific quarries, which were often hundreds of miles away from the city that required their sandstone, granite, quartzite or alabaster.

The Wilbour Papyrus

One of the most informative documents for the pattern of land-tenure, and therefore food-production, in ancient Egypt, at least for the Ramesside Period, is the Wilbour Papyrus. This dates from Year 4 of Ramesses V (i.e. 1147 BC) and is a record of the measurement of land and assessment of tax for the northern part of an

Although bread was the main staple of the Egyptian diet, the prominence given to the butchery of cattle in tomb scenes, like this example from the Old Kingdom, indicate the prestige value of beef as a food.

area sometimes referred to as 'Middle Egypt' (the Nile Valley between Herakleopolis Magna and Asyut). The document is unique in its size (over 10 m or 33 ft long) and scope as a surviving papyrus, but was part of an extensive tradition of land ownership and taxation surveys of ancient Egypt – other papyri, from other periods simply have not survived in the fortunate way that the Wilbour Papyrus has. It is a record of a survey as it was actually carried out by a team working during the summer months.

The picture that emerges from this document is an extremely complex one. It falls into two sections. One part ('Wilbour Text A') is concerned with land located in four distinct but adjacent zones in an area that corresponds to Middle Egypt and the mouth of the Faiyum from Atfih to el-Minya, most of which is owned by major temples from outside the region (although some is owned by temples within the region itself) and worked and administered for those temples by local officials. The second part ('Wilbour Text B') is concerned with broadly the same region, but with land owned by the crown, but again administered by local officials. It should be noted that the amount of land listed in both documents is less than 10 per cent of the probable available total for the whole region. Since this is a tax-collection document, the identification of the location, size and estimated yield of individual plots of land is of paramount importance. Location is provided by reference to 416 named settlements in the region.

The Places of the Wilbour Papyrus

The three largest places in the papyrus are well known. The southern part of the region (on the border between Zones 3 and 4) contains Hardai, capital of the 17th nome of Upper Egypt, located close to the modern city of el-Minya. Towards the northern limit of the region (Zone 2) is Tpehu, capital of the 22nd nome of Upper Egypt. Zone 1 is an enclave in the western part of Zone 2 and containing Ninsu (Herakleopolis Magna), capital of the 20th Upper Egyptian nome. Zone 1 includes Mer-Wer, the Harem Palace of Medinet el-Gurob (see p. 48). Zones 1 and 4 are significantly smaller in area than Zones 2 and 3.

Other significant administrative centres in the region (because they also had ḥ3ty-ʿ (haty-a)

Ancient Egyptian cooking methods appear to be quite uncomplicated and largely consisted of grilling, baking and boiling.

mayors) were Shede and She (both close to Mer-Wer), Onayna (close to Ninsu) and Spermeru (capital of the 19th Upper Egyptian nome, approximately halfway between Ninsu and Hardai). It is noticeable that the capitals of Upper Egyptian nomes 18 (H-nesu) and 21 (Smen-Hor) are not mentioned.

The names of most of the 416 individual locations within this region had some sort of descriptor added to them, especially ỉ3t (iat, mound), ʿt (at, house), wḥyt (wehyt, village), bḫn (bekhen, villa) and p3 sg (pa seg, fortress) – for further discussion of the first four terms, see p. 37. Of those plots that can be located within specific zones, 123 are in Zone 1, 22 in Zone 2, 46 in Zone 3 and 102 in Zone 4 – i.e. there is a clustering of settlements around the significant centres of Hardai and Ninsu. Moreover, although there is a fairly even distribution of 'villages' and 'mounds' (i.e. established minor settlements) in all four zones, the 'villas' and the 'fortresses' are definitely concentrated in Zones 1 and 4.

The People of the Wilbour Papyrus

A further insight into the information about settlement distribution in the Wilbour Papyrus comes from the occupations of some of the tenants within the different zones. The most useful of these are 'cultivator/farmer' (ỉḥwty, ihuty), 'herdsman' and 'stablemaster', because each of these suggests a type of economic activity based on land-use. It should be noted that the term ỉḥwty is a contested one – while the conventional translation is 'cultivator/farmer', it has been argued that it means something like 'Agent of the State Treasury'. 'Cultivators' are found in high numbers in Zone 1, but in low numbers in Zone 3, while 'herdsmen' are only common in Zone 3. 'Stablemasters' are found in Zones 2, 3 and 4. This suggests a concentration of agriculturalists around the main population centres of Ninsu and Mer-Wer. This is probably a result of a combination of factors: major centres of population would organically develop in areas of rich agricultural land, while the reduction in transport costs for moving cereal crops into large population centres would also be an attraction. By contrast, less-productive agricultural areas (either because they were naturally so, or because human activity had made them so) between major population centres could be used for the pasturing of animals, which would be more flexible in their ability to be moved around for grazing or to be taken on their own legs to market.

A further feature worth noting in the distribution of tenants' occupations is the significant numbers of 'soldiers' and 'Sherden' (foreign mercenary soldiers) in Zones 3 and 4, suggesting both military establishments in this area and the settlement of veterans. This in itself suggests that the (re-)settlement of parts of the Nile Valley – particularly at times of political crisis – may have been more dynamic than we might suspect.

Distribution and Transportation

Boats

There were two ways of moving people and goods in ancient Egypt, by land and by water, and the latter was much to be preferred. Egypt – a country dominated by the Nile river and criss-crossed by canals was ideally suited to riverine transport. The river flowed from south to north, while the prevailing wind blew from north to south, so transport was facilitated in both directions and gave the Egyptians their hieroglyphic determinatives for travelling north (a boat with its sail furled (⛵) and south (a boat under full sail ⛵). If anything the Egyptians were nervous sea-goers, but river travel must have been natural to them, particularly during the inundation, when the volume of the river and the area of land it covered increased dramatically.

Unsurprisingly, boats came in a variety of shapes and sizes, from small 'domestic' craft to vessels owned by the crown and other state institutions. Availability of raw materials was paramount; on a local level the papyrus marshes furnished all that was needed for a simple canoe or skiff, while the wherewithal to create large-scale vessels, from the boat buried close to the pyramid of King Khufu to state barges to transport vessels, was a more significant undertaking, often requiring the acquisition of timber from external sources, especially cedar from Byblos on the Lebanese coast.

Once the waters of the annual inundation had subsided, teams of draught animals ploughing fields, as seen in this wooden model from the Middle Kingdom, would have been a familiar sight in the Egyptian countryside.

A heavily laden river-craft transports a mixed cargo of goods in this Old Kingdom tomb scene at Saqqara.

Moving Stone

Large-scale river transport allowed two major things to happen that were vital for the development of ancient Egypt. First, it facilitated the establishment of a centrally controlled, unified state by affording the ability to move substantial quantities of agricultural surpluses – especially grain – around the country with relative ease. This meant that major urban centres with substantial populations could be supplied even from well beyond their immediate hinterland. Secondly, the movement of large quantities of building stone – to say nothing of massive monoliths – from their quarries to distant building sites allowed the emergence of Egypt as a state that found expression through monumental construction.

The Old Kingdom pyramids may well have been largely constructed from local stone from nearby quarries, but the fine-quality limestone that cased these monuments needed to be brought across the river, while the significant quantities – and large blocks – of granite had to be brought over 800 km (500 miles) from Aswan. The temples of New Kingdom Thebes similarly could not have been built on such a scale without the supply of riverborne stone from sandstone quarries such as Gebel Silsila, while obelisks and colossal statues would have been an impossibility without river travel.

A good indication of the large-scale movement of stone comes from a group of ostraca found at the Ramesseum at Thebes, which refers to the construction of the mortuary temple of Ramesses II. These documents indicate that the supply of building-stone was effected by a flotilla of 10 ships carrying sandstone from the Gebel Silsila quarries. These documents indicate that stone blocks came in standard sizes (most common were 2.5 by 2 by 1.5 cubits, or c. 1.25 by 1 by 0.75 m, 4 by 3¼ by 2½ ft), each ship carrying between 5 and 7 blocks, with a total load somewhere between 12 and 20 tons each. The ships themselves were probably 3–4 m (10–13 ft) wide by 9–13 m (20–43 ft) long. This flotilla of relatively small craft was probably one of a series that was used to ensure a constant supply of stone to this long-term building project, and its size presumably minimized the loading facilities required at the quarry and those for unloading at the building site (including travelling along canals). Bigger projects included a fleet of 44 ships and 3,000 men plus 500 masons sent to extract stone for the Medinet Habu complex of Ramesses III. One-off projects required something bigger. To transport the obelisks of Thutmose I from Aswan to Thebes, Ineni used a transport barge 120 cubits long by 40 cubits wide (i.e. 63 by 21 m, 207–70 ft). A similar barge is illustrated by Hatshepsut at Deir el-Bahri.

The movement of grain-ships at harvest time would have filled the Nile with these craft: here one is being loaded in a scene from the New Kingdom tomb of Wenensu.

Moving Grain

The skills that the Egyptians developed for long-distance transport of stone were also used for the movement of other bulk cargoes, especially grain. The ability to move huge amounts of this basic foodstuff around Egypt was critical to the ability of the state to organize its redistributive systems. These systems included the collection of grain revenues owed to major state temples of the New Kingdom from tenants on temple land all over Egypt and their transportation to the great storerooms at sites such as the Ramesseum, before redistribution to the populace.

The most informative document for this process is the Ramesside Papyrus Amiens, which refers to a flotilla of 21 ships bringing in the grain harvest in the 20th Dynasty for the Estate of Amun-Re at Medinet Habu. Papyrus Amiens, and similar grain transportation documents, suggests that the ships involved could be as impressively large as all but the largest stone-shifting ships. Boats that were used to carry 900 bushels of grain would have been faced with a cargo of *c.* 33 cubic metres (1,165 cubic feet), and would therefore have needed to have been as large as 20 m (66 ft) in length by 7 m (23 ft) wide.

The quaysides where such cargoes were unloaded would need to have been able to cope with a rapid movement of the grain to the storerooms for which they were intended. They would also have been a natural location for other types of commercial activity, especially markets.

Markets and Traders in the Old Kingdom

We have already seen that illustrations of the production of food and other goods were regularly shown in the range of topics depicted in the 'scenes of everyday life' in elite tombs of the Old Kingdom. Among other types of genre-scene, illustrations of markets were not common, but did appear in a sufficient number of tombs that it would be incorrect to speak of them as being rare. What these scenes cannot do is inform us as to what extent markets were significant economic features during the Old Kingdom, although they stand as a counter to the notion that Old Kingdom Egypt was an economically monolithic state whose resources were all channelled towards the building of megalithic monuments.

Indeed the range of goods being bought and sold in these Old Kingdom market scenes is remarkable. Some seem to show what one might expect – foodstuffs produced and sold on a small scale, perhaps through the deliberate over-production of basic staples (e.g. bread, beer and vegetables), as well as more specialist food-production; markets such as these may have been the most common venue at which fishermen traded their catch. However, what is perhaps more surprising is the depiction of trading activity involving luxury goods and specialist services, such as jewelry, domestic furniture and seal-engraving. Unfortunately, these scenes do not give much clue as to where these markets were held; the New Kingdom evidence is more helpful.

Markets and Harbours in the New Kingdom

One of the terms often found in connection with markets in texts of the New Kingdom (especially Deir el-Medina ostraca) is the *meryt*. This was the place where markets were held, but more specifically it refers to a place on the riverbank, one at which ships could moor: a quayside. As noted above, the riverbank is the logical place for a market – boats could pick up and unload goods, and local traders could cluster around the normal outlet for long-distance traders. Moreover, as the natural location for a ferry, the *meryt* was a crossroads, the place where east bank and west bank could come together, because of the inevitable dependence on the river for the transport of goods.

A ship's log documented in Papyrus Turin 2008+2016 records that the ship was moored 'at the quay' of such-and-such a place on its travels along the river. For major settlements the *meryt* was probably a harbour, for smaller riverbank settlements it was probably something much more modest, perhaps a makeshift mooring-place at the river's edge. In addition, the riverbank terminus of any ferry provided an obvious place where individuals from the east and west bank of the Nile could meet to exchange their specific types of surplus produce. These *meryt*-markets are well known from two New Kingdom Theban

sources, depictions in Theban tombs and in ostraca from Deir el-Medina.

Unlike Old Kingdom market scenes, depictions of local trading activity at New Kingdom Thebes are careful to show the physical context of the local market. In the tomb of Ipuy from Deir el-Medina, women traders are shown exchanging goods with sailors, as also seems to be the case in the tomb of Khaemhet. Most remarkable of all, the tomb of Kenamun shows stalls set up by individual traders on the quayside in order to carry out the sale of small-scale goods – sandals, scarves and food – to foreign traders who have arrived in their substantial merchant vessels. The Kenamun scene seems to show different levels of trading activity at a busy quayside, possibly one primarily associated with institutional-level trading activity (a major temple?): small-scale traders come along to exchange small-scale goods with the individual sailors from the ships. The location of this scene has been disputed (it may be Thebes or Memphis, given the international character of the major trading activity being carried out).

This idea of the *meryt* as a trading centre with some sort of physical structures is given support by references to the *meryt* in ostraca from Deir el-Medina. The use of the town-sign determinative in some examples of the word suggests that there was some sort of physical settlement there, and this idea finds further support in references to members of the Deir el-Medina workforce owning property there. For example, the workman Nekhemmut owned a so-called *at* there, while in Ostracon BM 5637 an *at* of the *meryt* is mentioned, from which some loaves and oil were stolen – in this context an *at* was probably some sort of storeroom/ place of business on the quayside, perhaps even one of the booths depicted in the scenes from Kenamun and Ipuy.

Market-traders – both men and women – exchange goods from little booths on the riverbank, as illustrated in the New Kingdom tombs of Kenamun (below) and Ipuy (below left).

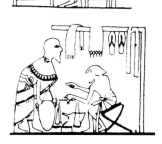

Working Life

For most Egyptians, work essentially meant one thing – agricultural labour. The Wilbour Papyrus (see pp. 94–96) suggests that the pattern of landholding in the Ramesside Period at least was quite complex, but the people at the bottom of that system would have experienced a working life, governed by the seasons of the agricultural year, that would have been hardly different from that of their ancestors. While small settlements would certainly have contained a number of craft-specialists who had the skills and equipment to serve local needs – a village potter for instance – it is larger settlements that would have provided most opportunities for skilled craftsmen, as demonstrated in the list of occupations of the inhabitants of Maiunehes at Thebes (see pp. 40–41). Indeed we have already noted that the concentration of skills, materials and specialized equipment, in part to serve the demands of urban residents, is one of the defining characteristics of a city. In ancient Egypt many of these craftsmen and their workshops would have come under the direct or indirect control of major institutions, such as the crown or major temples.

Looking at Work: Words and Pictures

Our ability to assess the nature of work in ancient Egypt is limited by our sources of evidence. Administrative documents are an important source, but these are very much directed towards state enterprises – the settlement from ancient Egypt that has provided most evidence for the lives of its workers is perhaps the most consistently state-sponsored: Deir el-Medina. For non-administrative evidence, the lens through which we see the work of non-literate, non-elite Egyptians are the texts created by literate Egyptians and the illustrations on the tomb walls of elite Egyptians.

The Satire on the Trades

The superiority of the scribe is a major theme in Egyptian literature; this is hardly surprising since many of these compositions were written, at least in part, as texts for the instruction of young scribal trainees. One of the best known of these instructive compositions presents itself as the

A modern potter's workshop, in Deir el-Gharbi, where this trade is the main industry today.

OCCUPATIONS OF THE
SATIRE ON THE TRADES

Sculptor/Stoneworker	Field-worker
Goldsmith	Mat-maker/Weaver
Coppersmith	Arrow-maker
Carpenter	Messenger
Jeweller	Furnace-tender
Barber	Sandal-maker
Reed-cutter	Laundryman
Potter	Fowler
Bricklayer	Fisherman
Gardener	

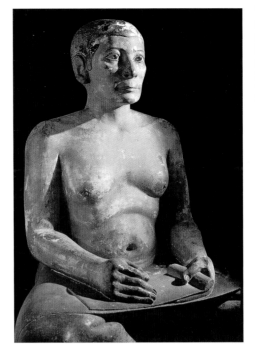

This Old Kingdom statue of a squatting scribe from Saqqara is notable because it shows an older man, rather than a youth at the beginning of his bureaucratic career.

wise words of a man named Dua-Khety to his son, Pepi, but the nature of this advice has given it the modern title of *The Satire on the Trades*. Composed in the Middle Kingdom, it continued to be copied into the Ramesside Period.

The basic premise of the *Satire* is that the occupation of the scribe is not just more prestigious, but also more comfortable than any other, and Dua-Khety provides a list of jobs and the disadvantages attached to them to prove the point. Scholars are divided as to whether the vision of non-scribal work is meant to be taken seriously or is an exaggeration for comic effect, but in either case the attitude is very far from one of the dignity of labour.

The life of the peasants was an obvious target for the scorn and horror of the educated elite, not just because of the nature of their basic daily toil,

Wooden models found in Middle Kingdom tombs can provide important three-dimensional information on the organization of different crafts, like this wonderful example from the tomb of Meketre showing the process of linen production by spinners and weavers with their looms.

The Trades in Egyptian Tombs and Texts

The vignettes included here connect – and contrast – tomb scenes that show images of working life with the sharp commentary on these various activities found in *The Satire on the Trades*. Together, the evidence from these sources provides a fascinating snapshot of working life in ancient Egypt.

The **sandalmaker** is utterly wretched among his tubs of oil. He is well – if it is well to be with corpses – and he chews on hides.

The **laundryman** washes at the riverbank in the vicinity of the crocodile…. His food is mixed with filth and there is no part of him which is clean. He cleans the clothes of menstruating women. He weeps as he spends all day there with a washing-board and washing-stone.

The **weaver** inside the weaving-shed is more wretched than a woman. His knees are drawn up against his belly. He cannot breathe the air. If he wastes a day without weaving he is beaten with 50 lashes. He has to bribe the doorkeeper with food to allow him to come out into the daylight.

The Sandal-maker

Every **carpenter** who grasps the adze is wearier than a field-worker. His field is his wood, his hoe is the adze. Here is no end to his work … at night-time he must light his lamp.

The **reed-cutter** goes north to the Delta to get arrows for himself. he has done more than his arms can do. The mosquitoes have killed him and the sandflies have butchered him, so that he is cut to pieces.

I have seen the **metalworker** at his labour at the mouth of his furnace. His fingers are like a crocodile's and he stinks more than fish roe.

The **potter** is covered with earth, although his lifetime is among the living. He digs in the fields more than swine to fire his pottery. His clothes are stiff with mud and his loincloth is made of rags. The air which comes from his burning furnace enters his nose.

Tomb scenes showing a selection of the trades in ancient Egypt. Clockwise from above: sandalmakers from the tomb of Rekhmire, carpenters from the tomb of Rekhmire, reed-cutters from the tomb of Puyemre, and laundrymen from the tomb of Ipuy.

The Laundryman

The Carpenter

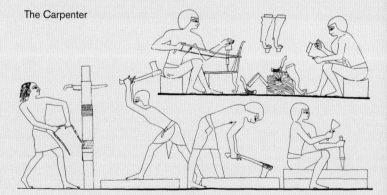

The Reed-cutter

The types of workers depicted on the walls of private tombs could vary from producers of low value, high quantity items like mudbricks, to those of high-value materials, like these jewellers.

but also their vulnerability to be conscripted by the state to be used as forced labour:

> The field-worker wails more than the guinea fowl, his voice louder than that of a raven. His fingers have swollen and stink to excess. He is weary, having been taken away to work in the Delta, and so he is always in rags.

Other jobs also provide targets for Dua-Khety's scorn, including skilled craftsmen (e.g. stoneworkers, carpenters, jewellers, reed-cutters, bricklayers, weavers, arrow-makers and sandalmakers), exponents of pyrotechnology (e.g. goldsmiths, coppersmiths, potters and furnace-tenders), food providers (e.g. wine-makers, fowlers and fishermen) and those involved in service industries (e.g. barbers, laundrymen and messengers).

Although many of the dismissive descriptions of non-scribal occupations are rather vague, some are curiously specific, such as that of the carpenter's lot, which has an odd extra section giving an example of the work involved in roofing a room whose dimensions are slightly less than 5 by 3 metres (16 by 10 ft):

> It is miserable for the carpenter when he works on a ceiling. It is the roof of a chamber 10 by 6 cubits. A month goes by in laying the beams and spreading the matting. All the work is accomplished, but as for the food which should be given to his household [while he is working], there is no one who will provide for his children.

An unshaven carpenter works with his hand-held adze on scaffolding for a building project, in a tomb-scene from the New Kingdom.

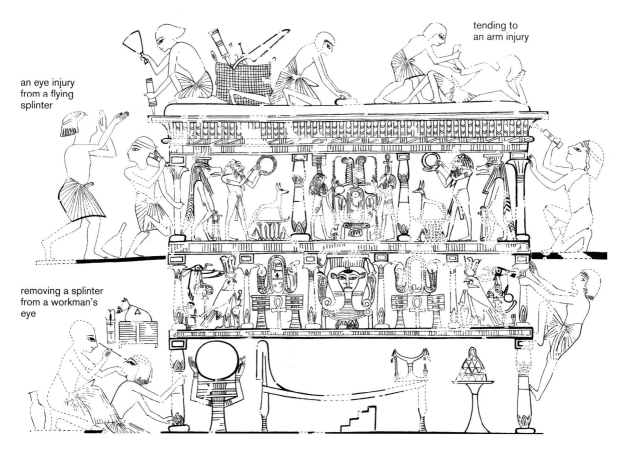

tending to
an arm injury

an eye injury
from a flying
splinter

removing a splinter
from a workman's
eye

Although this shows a knowledge of the process of roofing a house, which is still practised in Egyptian villages today – wooden roofbeams on which reeds/matting are laid at right-angles, then covered with a layer of mud plaster – the speed with which the job is accomplished is hardly impressive.

Work on Tomb Walls

This rather jaundiced view of non-scribal work is, however, not entirely supported by another elite viewpoint, that provided by images of workers engaged in a variety of tasks that are consistently depicted on the walls of elite tombs from the Old Kingdom until the Graeco-Roman Period. In the view of Miriam Lichtheim these images 'breathe joy and pride in the accomplishments of labor' in a way that is quite at odds with the vision presented in the *Satire on the Trades*.

However, it should be noted that depictions of craftsmen and labourers found in tombs – either as two-dimensional images on walls or as three-dimensional models – are most often

shown in order to demonstrate the abilities of the tombowner in organizing such activities for the king, or to provide a magically available world that could supply the tombowner with all they required in the next life. Although some scenes on tomb walls of the New Kingdom depict the tombowner undertaking agricultural work for the lord of the afterlife, Osiris, in the 'Field of Reeds', this is obviously intended to be participation of a limited kind, as demonstrated by the presence in tombs of the same period of *shabti* figures – small statuettes equipped with agricultural tools that were designed to act as magical substitutes for their owner for any obligation to manual work in the afterlife.

Interestingly, the most obvious example of a private tomb showing the dangerous and uncomfortable aspects of the working life are from the Deir el-Medina tomb of Ipuy, where the 'scenes of daily life' seem to be taken directly from Ipuy's observed experience of life and work.

The tomb of Ipuy at Deir el-Medina contains this depiction of magnificently ornate funerary furniture, although the main theme of the scene seems to be the industrial injuries that might be suffered by the artisans involved in the production of that furniture. The annotations suggest what may be depicted.

Water and Sanitation

Intuitively one might think that access to water was not a problem for most ancient Egyptians who lived in close proximity to the Nile or a canal running from it. Indeed the visitor to Egypt today who sees the country while cruising up or down the river will often see children swimming in the Nile or women washing clothes on its banks. However, the immediate availability of this extraordinarily rich water source did not, and indeed does not, solve the requirements for water of either an ancient or modern population, especially when it comes to water for human consumption. One reason for this is the use of the Nile, not only as a source of water and major transport artery, but also as the channel for human (and animal) waste, and so major settlements with the greatest requirement for water also produced the most immediate pollutants of that water. In addition, although tasks that required heavy use of water below drinking quality would have been carried out on or close to the banks of the Nile, this was not without additional risks; as the *Satire on the Trades* notes: 'The washerman washes on the riverbank with the crocodile as a neighbour.'

Collecting Water

We have some idea about how much water would be required. The practicalities for water consumption for humans in a tropical climate today, as suggested by the United Nations Refugee Agency, indicate a minimum survival ration of 7 litres (1½ gallons) per day, more typically 15–20 litres (*c.* 3½–4½ gallons) per day as a minimum allocation for a refugee in a refugee camp. Animals are more water-greedy: every day, cattle need 25–30 litres (*c.* 5½–6½ gallons), goats and sheep 15–20 litres (*c.* 3½–4½ gallons) and pigs 10–15 litres (*c.* 2½–3½ gallons). Therefore access to substantial quantities of clean water was crucial for all Egyptian settlements.

The answer was to sink a well. In the cultivated areas of the Nile Valley and Delta this could be achieved by sinking a stone-lined shaft well, which essentially consisted of a 'tube' formed by small limestone blocks (the small *talatat* blocks favoured for rapid building work at Amarna were ideal). The gap between the outside of this tube and the surrounding soil could be filled in with clean sand. The sand and the gaps between the blocks would filter the water, which could be drawn from the well using a leather bucket on a

Although an obvious source of water, the banks of the Nile were not always the safest place to drink, as illustrated on this New Kingdom papyrus.

Although unsuitable for large-scale agricultural irrigation, the *shaduf* was a useful device for lifting limited quantities of water, for example to water a garden in an elite residence, as in this New Kingdom tomb scene.

rope. Such wells must have been very common in dynastic Egypt, but, because of the nature of their construction, few of them have been discovered and excavated. Rare examples, both from the reign of Ramesses II, come from Tell el-Abqa'in in the West Delta (p. 185), Samana near Qantir in the East Delta and Amarna (see below). A later variant of this type, attested at Sais, had a lining of ceramic 'rings'. In the Nile Valley and Delta, apart from times of very low Nile inundations, subsoil water levels were high and wells easy to sink. Paradoxically, the time when usable water would have been most difficult to come by was when the floods of the inundation covered the land.

In some desert or desert-edge sites it was necessary to cut through rock in order to reach a good water source. Such effort was usually only attempted as part of a royal enterprise that required the provisioning of an expedition in extreme conditions. Textual references to such wells in the gold-bearing regions of Nubia and the Eastern Desert can be found at Kanais (near Edfu) where Seti I notes:

How painful is a way that has no water! What are travellers to do to relieve the parching of their throats? … Woe to the man who thirsts in the wilderness! Now, I will plan for them. I will make for them the means to sustain them so that they may bless my name.

The temple built by Seti I, along with a well, at the mining site of Kanais in the Eastern Desert.

Ramesses II boasts of surpassing his father's achievement in digging wells for gold-miners in his stela from Quban, which talks about a well in 'the desert land of Akuyata' that had been abandoned at 120 cubits (about 60 m, 197 ft) during the reign of Seti I, but when Ramesses chose the nearby spot to sink a well, water was struck at only 12 cubits. This well, like many of these important facilities, was given a name: 'The Well [which is called] Ramesses, Beloved of Amun, is Valiant in….' Although these early Ramesside wells have not yet been discovered, a set of similar, contemporary wells was sunk into the soft limestone under the site of Zawiyet Umm el-Rakham (pp. 221) to reach an aquifer containing fresh water 4 m (13 ft) below the surface.

Wells in the Archaeological Record

However, despite these examples of actual wells and reports of well-construction, water supply is an aspect of settlement archaeology that seems to be vastly under-represented. Although partial archaeological survival is a major issue, the fact that we have no idea how, for instance, the substantial community at Kahun acquired its water is remarkable. The only site with a large ancient population to have produced relatively extensive evidence of well-use is Amarna. These are attested archaeologically in the city, and from illustrations of them in private tombs of the Amarna elite.

The particular conditions of Amarna (subsoil water is reached 9 m (30 ft) below current ground level) required that wells be constructed in two stages, firstly a large, square pit, with an access stairway running down its interior sides. At the base of this pit a narrower shaft was sunk to reach water. A large well was a standard element of the equipment of the large Amarna villas, where they probably served not just the immediate household but a wider neighbourhood. This would create the ideal situation of not moving water further than necessary – since a litre of water weighs 1 kg (2.2 lb), a family of four with water needs of 15 litres (3½ gallons) each per day, had a total daily requirement weighing more than 60 kg (132 lb).

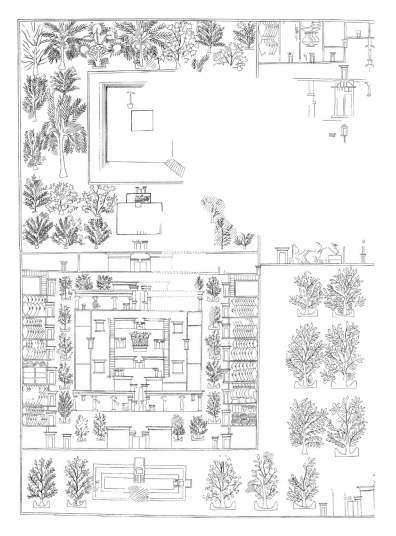

In addition, the social aspects of a well as a focal point for a small settlement, or a neighbourhood within a larger one, may also have been more widely important. As Edward Lane-Poole, writing about village life in Upper Egypt in 1895, noted:

> In the neighbourhood of every village there is a well, shaded by a clump of palm-trees. Here the men often collect for gossip, and hither the women come to fetch their water, their tall, upright, well-formed figures moving gracefully under the weight of the large pitchers they carry on their heads.

Scene from the tomb of Meryre at Amarna, showing the royal gardens. The most striking feature is the detailed depiction of a well (top left), which, for emphasis, is actually carved slightly deeper into the wall of the tomb.

Schools

For a society whose elite were literate bureaucrats, education was obviously very important. The *Satire on the Trades* (see pp. 100–3) is only the best-known example from many texts designed for the training of young scribes, and whose message was the superiority of the life of the literate and in particular the duties of the scribe over any other occupation. Locating exactly where such training took place is rather more of a problem.

There were many situations where a formal location created specifically for group learning was not required, such as where an individual pupil visited a private tutor or a student learned through 'on-the-job' training. It might also be the case that a convenient space that could be used for a variety of purposes might be pressed into use for group teaching on a regular or occasional basis. All of these situations occurred in ancient Egypt.

Ostraca

Our most important source of evidence for educational activity in Egypt comes from the student exercises written on discarded ostraca. Ostraca, especially the important collection from Deir el-Medina, are a key source of documentation for the lives of ordinary Egyptians. They allow us an insight into the day-to-day community and its individual concerns that would otherwise be lost to us. The vast majority of these ostraca come from the New Kingdom, and especially from the Theban area, so it is dangerous to make broader assumptions from this evidence for formal education throughout Egypt and throughout Egyptian history. However, although some aspects of this evidence might relate to special cases (the villagers of Deir el-Medina and the officials of the great Theban temples), the picture that emerges does fit rather well into the pattern of what we know from other periods and places.

Temple Schools

Evidence for actual schools – places where groups of children could be brought together for organized education – is rather scarce. The term usually used for such places – *'t sb3* (at seba) 'Place of Instruction' – to describe a physical location is not very common. Where such evidence does exist, it comes mainly from major temple institutions of the New Kingdom in Thebes. This is not surprising since one of the most obvious groups of people who would need to be trained to read and write were the priests and administrators of the great temples of New Kingdom Egypt, and so it is from these major institutions that we find the most compelling evidence for specific areas being used for group teaching.

The best-known example is the Ramesseum at Thebes, where a large collection of ostraca was excavated in an area behind the main temple in the vicinity of the massive storerooms (see pp. 60–61). These particular ostraca were not,

Ostracon from Deir el-Medina containing a poem written by the scribe Amennakht in praise of his city, Thebes.

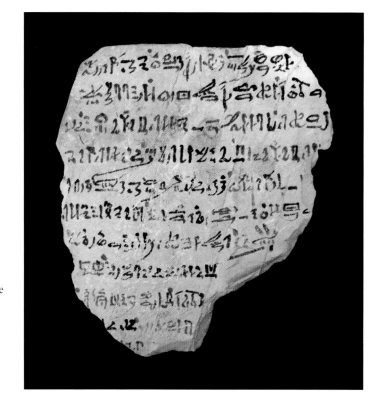

as one might expect in this area, primarily administrative, recording the coming and going of goods from the storerooms themselves, but discarded school texts. It is tempting to think of this part of the temple enclosure at the Ramesseum as being a quiet place where young temple recruits could be trained.

This picture of temple education is supported by the autobiography of Bakenkhonsu, High Priest of Amun under Ramesses II, where he speaks of his childhood saying that:

> I was a man of Thebes from my father and my mother, the son of the second priest of Amun in Karnak. I came out from the room of writing in the temple of the lady of the sky [i.e. the goddess Mut] as an excellent youngster.

> I was taught to be a *wab*-priest in the domain of Amun, as a son under the guidance of [his] father.

This suggests that, in the Ramesside Period at least, major temples arranged for the education of the children of their officials, presumably with a view to their succession in those offices. The Bakenkhonsu text further suggests that major temples also had specific designated areas within them where such teaching was organized, perhaps rather like the area in the Ramesseum.

Palace Schools

The other place one would expect to find education taking place is at court, where royal princes and the children of high-ranking Egyptian families would be trained in the governing skills they would need. Such activities would certainly have been carried out at the *Kap* in 'Harem Palaces' (see p. 48). The use of the royal Residence as a place for the training of the children of the ruling elite of Egypt, including the provinces, is suggested in the introduction to the *Satire on the Trades*, which begins:

> Beginning of the Instruction by the man of Tjaru, whose name is Dua-Khety, for his son called Pepi, as he journeyed south to the Residence, to place him in the school for scribes, among the sons of officials and the elite of the Residence.

It is easy to imagine that education at the Residence was a valued privilege, not only for the education it would bring, but also for the useful contacts that would be gained.

Deir el-Medina

The Deir el-Medina ostraca (see opposite) are especially important as a means of understanding how education was organized in New Kingdom Egypt, since a significant proportion of the workforce there – those who inscribed the walls of the royal tombs they worked on – had a particular need to be able to read and write. This is an unusual situation in a population where literacy rates were probably no more than 5 per cent.

Ostraca from Ramesside Deir el-Medina reflect a variety of educational setups. These include students who produced written exercises in their own time, which were then sent to a tutor to be marked and corrected. However, the only specific reference to a school within the ostraca themselves comes at the end of the 20th Dynasty,

Wooden models of scribes often accompany Middle Kingdom tomb models showing the filling of granaries, indicating the importance of proper accounting.

at which time the villagers had decamped to the temple-complex of Medinet Habu.

However, there is archaeological evidence from Deir el-Medina for specific places that could have been used as a school. One of these is the 'chapels', which, as we have seen (p. 83), were not just used for private and small-scale religious worship, but provided a flexible space for a variety of social usages just outside the village. A group of about five 'chapels' at Deir el-Medina, referred to as area K2, produced a cache of 102 ostraca. Of this collection 90 were literary (rather than letters or administrative) in content, and many had significant corrections made to them, suggesting they were written by trainee scribes; 34 were sections of the prime educational texts *Instruction of King Amenemhat, Satire on the Trades* or the *Kemyt*.

Educational Excursions

The earliest reference to the *'t sb3* (at seba) 'Place of Instruction' comes from the First Intermediate Period tomb of Khety at Asyut. Another tomb from a little later in the same period, that of Iti-ib-iker is particularly interesting: it was clearly visited often in the early New Kingdom as evidenced by more than 140 graffiti on its walls, most of which come from this period. These graffiti are not random scribbling – a significant number are copies of the sort of literary texts used in scribal training. The excavator of these tombs, German Egyptologist Jochem Kahl, has suggested that this tomb was used as 'a destination for school excursions', and it is clearly the case that a large ancient tomb would provide an ideal quiet place for teaching a class, while its walls would carry images that could act as teaching aids in their own right.

Although partly destroyed by the building of a temple to Hathor in the Ptolemaic Period (far left), the area to the north of the village of Deir el-Medina still contains a series of small temples and chapels, which were used for a variety of community activities.

Crime in the City

The opportunities for criminal activity provided by the concentration of wealth and property in towns and cities were seized upon wholeheartedly by some ancient Egyptians, just as they have been within all societies. Equally, significant centres of population and administration provided places where justice could be done and punishments meted out. However, the picture we get from ancient Egypt is that the administration of justice was pushed as far down to local level as possible. Villagers were expected to regulate their own affairs, and while appeals could be made to higher courts including – in theory at least – the king, the state did not go out of its way to interfere in the lives of ordinary Egyptians.

The exception to this was when state property itself was concerned. The evidence from Ramesside Thebes – in the ostraca from Deir el-Medina and the records of the 'Tomb Robbery Papyri' – shows this pattern. Deir el-Medina villagers dealt with their own disputes, including minor criminal offences. They, and others, only fell foul of the state – in the form of the vizier and his officials – when thefts from royal temples and tombs were involved. In the latter case, the state not only became involved in prosecuting offenders, but in dealing out the severest of punishments.

Judgment and Judges

Justice, as an aspect of *maat* – the maintenance of cosmic order – was ultimately the responsibility of the king. However, as with other offices that were theoretically a royal responsibility but in practice needed many individuals to be properly dispensed – such as priestly duty in major temples – delegation was necessary. In the first instance, in the New Kingdom at least, that delegation was to the two viziers. The New Kingdom *Duties of the Vizier* texts specifically refer to this responsibility and how it might be further sub-delegated. Interestingly, the place where vizieral justice is meted out is specifically mentioned: the 'judgment hall'. It is likely that the judgment hall was not a separate structure used only for this

activity, but referred to that part of the vizier's 'palace' where members of the public were admitted with their petitions and supplications or dragged to face justice.

In rural districts, a similar situation was also the case, with justice residing in the hands of local officials. When the Middle Kingdom fictional character Khunanup, the so-called 'eloquent peasant' of the *Tale* named after him, goes to the city of Ninsu (Herakleopolis Magna) to take his legal complaint to the High Steward Rensi, he tracks him down and pesters him in a variety of locations. On the first occasion, Khunanup finds Rensi coming out of the door of his house and about to board his official

The highest-ranking civil servants could 'collect' a series of important offices. Paser, who served under Seti I and Ramesses II, was both Southern Vizier and High Priest of Amun at Karnak, where this statue was found.

Both supplicating petitioners and the criminally accused assumed an appropriately grovelling posture when approaching civil authorities, as illustrated here in the tomb of the Old Kingdom vizier Mereruka.

barge. On a later occasion, Khunanup gives his speech to Rensi at the entrance of the judgment hall. This turns out to be an unsuccessful tactic since Khunanup is ordered to be beaten by functionaries of the judgment hall who have whips for just such a purpose. On another occasion, Khunanup appeals to Rensi as he is coming out of the door of the temple of Herishef (the chief deity of Herakleopolis).

Although this story is fictional, it is likely that it was set against a background that would have been realistic and familiar to the listener. This suggests that although there were places where (criminal?) cases were normally dealt with – the judgment hall – a high official could in fact be petitioned in any of the places he frequented. There were three normal 'business places' of a high-ranking provincial official: his 'house' (presumably both dwelling and offices), the local temple (for cultic or religious tasks?) and the 'judgment hall' (where summary justice in the form of corporal punishment was meted out).

Local Justice

At Deir el-Medina two processes can be seen operating for the generation of a verdict in civil or criminal cases. The first of these was the *kenbet*, a local court made up of community leaders, who would hear pleas and pass judgment on villagers who were in dispute with each other or who had been reported for a misdemeanour. This court seems to have assembled as and when it was necessary; the physical location for this court, as noted above, was the 'Enclosure of the Tomb' at Deir el-Medina. Presumably other *kenbet* courts met in similar places and to judge similar cases throughout New Kingdom Egypt.

The second process attested at Deir el-Medina was oracular judgment – a public performance, which fused justice with religious performance. The oracle was the image of the god carried in procession. Normally this would be one of the manifestations of the god Amun. The evidence from Deir el-Medina suggests that the oracle could be consulted at a variety of locations, including the forecourt of the temple as the god emerged, at various points along the processional route and in the village itself, possibly including on-the-spot consultations next to the property that was the subject of the original dispute. The means by which the oracle gave its judgment is not clear (on some occasions it was a forward or backwards movement). The *kenbet* court and the judgment by the oracle should not, however, be considered as two completely separate strands of justice, and appealing the judgment of one before the other was a common occurrence.

Punishment

Punishments tended to be as immediate as possible. Corporal punishment or a fine was the most usual consequence of a guilty verdict for a relatively minor offence. Incarceration for its own sake was not the norm – this would have been unworkable for village-level punishment, and the Egyptian state had little interest in holding individuals as prisoners in purpose-built facilities. Instead, imprisonment was connected to forced labour, whether in Egypt itself or (in the New Kingdom) in the mines and quarries of Nubia. This form of transportation to work-camps, sometimes combined with brutal physical punishment, was the standard sentence meted out by the Egyptian state to the guilty during the New Kingdom. The sort of punishment that might be expected for a serious offence is neatly summed up in the common oath, 'If I speak falsehood then let my nose and ears be cut off and let me be transported to Nubia.'

The extent to which the death sentence was applied is disputed. Death by impalement seems to have been the standard mode of capital punishment in the New Kingdom. A Ramesside example of the punishment decreed in the case of someone stealing temple property was that the offender should be 'placed on top of the wood next to the temple from which he shall have stolen'. It is likely that the sentence was carried out close to the institution from which the property had been stolen, presumably as a dreadful warning to others. There is some debatable evidence that ritual burning of particularly serious criminals – those who had desecrated temples or tombs – may have taken place, particularly from the Late Period, but possibly as early as the Middle Kingdom.

The 'Great Prison'

One of the most intriguing institutions referred to in relation to punishment is the 'Great Prison' at Thebes, whose workings are partly described in Papyrus Brooklyn 35.1446. This institution, which came under the direct supervision of the vizier, had a number of functions. Elements of the 'Great Prison' included a record-office for the register of those convicted of criminal offences, an area where trials could be held, prison cells for holding prisoners awaiting trial or punishment and the facilities for carrying out those punishments. Additionally it served as a barracks for those sentenced to a labour-based punishment, or for the use of the corvée – a form of forced labour that was a form of taxation rather than a punishment, but one which nonetheless required an element of compulsion.

Casual beatings seem to have been an accepted practice when lower-status individuals came up against the authority of the state or its agents.

This hieroglyphic determinative gives a gruesome suggestion of the method by which execution 'on top of the wood' was carried out.

Leisure

The cities of dynastic Egypt did not really have public buildings in the way that seems normal in cities of the 21st century or even the Classical world. The only partial exception to this lack of deliberately constructed public space in ancient Egyptian cities is the institution of the temple, but these structures, as we have seen, were subject to a series of restrictions on access and use. Indeed it can be said that major Egyptian cities ('royal cities') were not built for the convenience of the vast majority of their inhabitants, especially in the range of facilities provided by the central authorities. For instance, unlike Greek or Roman cities they did not have a forum or agora where citizens and non-citizens could meet and do business. Still less did they have civic amenities built for the comfort or entertainment of the cultured elite or the masses – only in the Graeco-Roman Period did Egypt have public baths, theatres, hippodromes or amphitheatres, where the populace could be entertained.

Public Entertainment

It is, moreover, difficult to find activities in ancient Egypt that involved public gatherings. There do not seem to have been significant mass-audience sporting events or other forms of public entertainment. Amusements seem to have been conducted at a domestic or village level – perhaps listening to the village storyteller was the closest most Egyptians would have come to public entertainment.

Moreover, as well as in the obvious lack of physical remains of purpose-built spaces, this absence of a public arena for entertainment is striking in literature. The largest audiences referred to seem to be those involved in royal amusement, be it a story told (or a magician performing) at the royal court to entertain a bored king, or the same king displaying great feats of hunting in the number of lions, bulls or ostriches he could slaughter.

Fishing and fowling in the Nile marshes seems to have been a popular pursuit of elite Egyptians from the Old to the New Kingdoms, if depictions in their tombs are to be believed. This New Kingdom tomb scene of Nebamun shows him enjoying a day's hunting with his family on an improbably small canoe.

Sport

This lack of specific sports-based architecture also strongly suggests that there were no organized individual or team-based sports. Broadly speaking, this was probably true, although activities that can be broadly characterized as 'sporting' for which we have evidence include elite pastimes such as hunting (including in chariots), fishing and fowling. These activities used as their venue the great outdoors, more specifically the places where the objects of hunting – fish, birds, antelopes etc. – might be found, notably the marshes of the Nile fringes and the rather more distant deserts. Elite participation in these pasttimes, which mirrored similar royal hunting achievements, is depicted on the walls of tombs from the Old Kingdom onwards, but can hardly be thought of as involving spectators or any changes to the urban environment.

The same might also be said about other outdoor sports for which tomb scenes are the only real evidence. The 'boat jousting' (in which poles were used to knock opponents from the decks of their boats) of the Old Kingdom might have had non-elite participants and (probably) spectators, but it took place on the Nile. The range of outdoor games depicted on the walls of the Middle Kingdom tombs at Beni Hasan, which include team catching-games and what appears to be an early form of hockey, were most likely to have been carried out by groups of villagers or townsfolk in any convenient open area, very similar to the ubiquitous space for playing football (soccer) in modern Egyptian villages.

Royal Occasions

The only significant evidence we have for gatherings of people at specifically built structures is in royal contexts. The 'Windows of Appearance', which seem to be an important aspect of palace/temple architecture in the New Kingdom were designed so that the king (and sometimes whole royal family) could be presented in an elevated position above an assembled multitude. The occasions when such presentations took place included the ceremonial rewarding of officials, as is sometimes depicted in their tombs. It is also possible that the area in

The Middle Kingdom tombs at Beni Hasan depict an unusually wide range of leisure activities including gymnastics and, possibly, hockey.

front of major New Kingdom temples was the suitably impressive venue for the ritual execution of selected prisoners of war after a successful military campaign or the impalement of those convicted of capital crimes, presumably before a suitably appreciative audience of loyal Egyptians. It is unlikely that other purpose-built arenas for royal activity – notably the *heb-sed* courts in which the king's thirty-year jubilee (and regular subsequent jubilees) were celebrated by a royal run to demonstrate his physical fitness – had an audience beyond a closely defined elite.

Houses of Ill-Repute?

There is no ancient Egyptian equivalent of the brothels of Pompeii – or at least not of buildings whose function as such can be readily recognized in the archaeological record. That is not to say they did not exist, but none has been convincingly identified at any of the town sites excavated to date. The evidence for prostitution in ancient Egypt is rather slim, especially before the Late Period. However, some scholars have argued that the scenes of erotic activity depicted in the famous Papyrus Turin 55001 can most easily be interpreted as taking place between prostitutes and their clients in a brothel.

Taverns, inns and public houses also seem remarkably absent. The reason for this is likely to be that recreational drinking and partying took place at household or neighbourhood level. This seems to be the situation at Deir el-Medina where workmen were given time off work to brew beer that would be consumed at particular festivals. This was perhaps natural for communities where the direct provision of the materials to make beer – as well as beer itself – was part of the regular wages of the workmen. It would therefore only remain for us to find an appropriately convivial context in which this consumption could take place – the 'Enclosure of the Tomb' at Deir el-Medina (see p. 92) may have been such a place.

For the elite, the scenes on tomb walls of the New Kingdom suggest that providing banquets

The depiction of scantily clad female musicians and dancers was a regular addition to scenes of banqueting in private tombs of the New Kingdom.

for significant numbers of guests, with food (and wine) from one's own resources as well as musicians and dancers seems to have been the main means of partying and providing hospitality.

The production of beer, which was a natural extension to the baking of bread, provided both a nutritious liquid and, for those who could not afford wine, an obvious social lubricant for festive occasions.

Tourism

The advent of large-scale foreign tourism to see the monuments of ancient Egypt is often dated to the efforts of Thomas Cook and Son who, by 1898, were conducting 50,000 visitors down the Nile. Since then the flow of ordinary visitors – not including savants, scholars or archaeologists – wishing to see these ancient marvels has continued to expand so that, in 2008, over 12 million foreign tourists visited Egypt.

However, even by 1898, the viewing of ancient Egyptian monuments by foreign visitors had already had an illustrious history: Greek and Roman tourists marvelled at these great and strange works of antiquity. In some cases – most notably Herodotus – these visitors left written accounts of what they saw, which was often much more complete and varied than the remains that have survived to the 21st century, making these travellers' tales of real archaeological value.

More remarkable still is what might be called ancient domestic tourism – the visiting of already-venerable monuments by individuals who lived during the dynastic period, most notably the New Kingdom. The places where this tourism is most obvious are the royal cemeteries close to Memphis. Here the combination of the most populous city of New Kingdom Egypt existing in close proximity with the most spectacular of ancient monuments – the royal pyramids of the Old Kingdom, already by the 18th dynasty over a thousand years old – provided an environment where an appreciation of the physical remains of the distant past could flourish. For a literate Egyptian living during the reign of Ramesses II, though the greatest of the royal pyramids at Giza had been built a millennium earlier, they were part of a culture that could readily be understood. For this literate elite, Old Kingdom pyramids could be easily visited, their owners identified and their relevance to contemporary cultural life easily recognized.

The full extent of this ancient tourism is unknown, but it seems to have been a significant feature of cultural life, at least in the Memphite area, during the New Kingdom. Our knowledge of these visits comes from something that we would today consider essentially destructive – graffiti scrawled upon the monuments themselves. That these ancient notes are usually in black ink suggests that the graffiti-writers went prepared. Clusters of these graffiti are known from around major Old Kingdom monuments at Saqqara, Abusir, Abu Ghurob and Meidum. Giza is distinctly and oddly lacking in these graffiti, although the pattern of the commemoration of ancient visits may have been rather different there (see box overleaf). The major themes referred to in the graffiti are the wonder and respect due to these magnificent monuments of great kings of the past, but also the wish that the reverence shown by these tourists will itself be rewarded by gaining the favour of the dead king and gods.

Below Graffiti – the informal texts put on monuments and the natural landscape by non-royal Egyptians – come in different forms, from (top) this ink scribbling marking a New Kingdom visit to the Old Kingdom pyramid complex of Djoser, to elaborately carved inscriptions like this (bottom) set from the Late Old Kingdom on a sandstone outcrop at el-Kab.

Ancient Visitors at Ancient Sites

Tourists at Giza?

In 1936–37 the Egyptian archaeologist Selim Hassan carried out a major clearance around the Great Sphinx at Giza. His work uncovered a group of over 50 stelae, dating to the New Kingdom, which had as their subject private individuals' homages to the Sphinx as embodiment of the god Horemakhet. Among these stelae one is especially striking: it depicts two New Kingdom officials who seem to be identified by the accompanying inscriptions as the scribes Montuher and Kamutnakht. The stela has a typical Ramesside format, showing worshippers in the bottom half of the stela and the object of worship in the top half. The two scribes have their arms raised in devotion, though Kamutnakht's right hand holds a writing palette – perhaps in readiness for an opportunity to write an appropriate graffito – and he balances a bag over his right shoulder, which it is tempting to think of as a picnic lunch for the pair's visit to the Giza plateau. Most striking of all is the depiction of the sphinx and two pyramids (shown overlapping in an unusual attempt at perspective), which, apart from the unrealistically steep angle of the Khufu and Khafre pyramids, is a view not dissimilar to one which a visitor standing on the roof of Khafre's valley temple can enjoy today.

Two views of the pyramids of Giza: from the New Kingdom stela of Montuher and Kamutnakht (left), and as they appear to modern visitors (below).

The scribe Aakheperkaresonb visits the mortuary temple of the pyramid of Sneferu at Meidum

Year 41, under the Majesty of Horus-king [Thutmose III]. The scribe Aakheperkaresonb, son of Amenmensu, the scribe and lector-priest of [Thutmose I]), true of voice, came here to see the beautiful temple of the Horus-king Sneferu.

He found it like heaven within when the sun-god is rising in it and he exclaimed, 'Heaven rains with fresh frankincense and drops incense upon the roof of the temple of the Horus king Sneferu'.

The rest of the text continues with Aakheperkaresonb urging future visitors to say the offering-prayer for the benefit of Sneferu.

The scribe Nashuyu visits the pyramids at Saqqara

Nashuyu's visit is recorded by a graffito at the pyramid of Khendjer at Saqqara. His trip – which seems to have been combined with a festival celebrating the emergence of the god Ptah from

Although ownership of the pyramid at Meidum is still disputed, graffiti from the New Kingdom make it clear that visitors of that period considered it to be the work of King Snefru.

his temple – was partly to seek the favour of the Old Kingdom kings Teti and Djoser:

Do good, do good O Teti-beloved-of-Ptah, do good to the scribe Nashuyu, the servant of your servant, Nedjemmerut. Do good, do good O Djoser-discoverer-of-stoneworking. Do good, do good to the scribe Nashuyu….

Year 34, 4th month of Summer, Day 24. The Day of the festival of Ptah, Lord of Memphis, when he appears outside the temple in the evening….

The scribe Hednakht visits the Step Pyramid complex of Djoser

As well as the practical benefits that Hednakht sought from the gods, the theme of a jolly family day out among the pyramids is also mentioned:

Year 47, 2nd month of Winter, Day 25. The treasury-scribe Hednakht, son of Tjenro and Twosret, came to take a stroll and enjoy himself in the West of Memphis, along with his brother Panakht, scribe of the vizier.

He said, 'O [all] you gods of the West of Memphis and glorified dead, may you grant a full lifetime in serving your good pleasure, with a goodly burial after a happy old age, like yourself.'

The Old Kingdom royal tombs at Saqqara seem to have been the most visited ancient sites during the New Kingdom, especially the Step Pyramid complex of King Djoser.

Death in the City

There is one part of many towns and cities from ancient Egypt that survives much better than the rest: the cemetery. This is largely down to its location, because, while the houses for the living needed to be near the Nile and its canals, with the flooding that it brings, houses for the dead needed to be placed well above the rising waters of the Nile, either on the desert edge of Upper Egypt or the 'turtlebacks' of the Delta.

Houses of Eternity

As we have seen, houses for the living were made from sturdy yet essentially disposable materials. Mudbrick was the building material of choice for the vast majority of structures, with some additional wooden or stone elements (see p. 31). However, while cheap, easily made and easily replaceable building materials were used for the houses of the living, houses for the dead – which were designed for eternity – were ideally constructed from the most durable materials possible and, moreover, materials that displayed the wealth and status of the tombowner. Although, for many, a tomb-superstructure made from mudbrick might be expected to last a considerable time in an Egyptian desert cemetery, for the very richest members of the elite, this wealth and status meant stone.

Exactly how stone was deployed depended on the fashions of the period and the geographical location of the tomb. In the Memphite cemeteries of the Old Kingdom, squat, rectangular superstructures now referred to as *mastaba*s were constructed (at least as far as their external faces and internal rooms were concerned) from locally quarried limestone blocks. In New Kingdom Thebes or central Egyptian sites such as Beni Hasan in the Middle Kingdom, the local cliff-faces provided the ideal locations for rock-cut tombs. Moreover, the latter, constructed high above the cultivation, were often capable of being seen from great distances, making them an obvious and permanent part of a landscape that, because of the actions of the Nile, might have a very changeable and dynamic floodplain settlement.

Houses for the Ka

The cemetery was a very important part of the town that it served, indeed it was clearly considered to be an integral element of the physical space inhabited by the community of that town. This is due to the specific beliefs regarding the afterlife held by the Egyptians. Among the variety of possible (and not mutually exclusive) afterlives believed available to a non-royal Egyptian, the concept of the *ka* was the longest-lasting and most influential factor in the development of the cemetery as an active part of the town. The *ka*-spirit was separated from the body by death, but rather than journeying to 'another place', was limited to its tomb. It also continued to require several important things that it had needed in life – a place to dwell (the preserved body within the tomb), together with food and drink. This meant that the tomb was regarded in the same way as an ordinary house – a place where a person dwelt – and the tomb was often referred to as the 'House (*pr*) of the *Ka*'.

This equivalence of house and tomb extended to architectural details, such as porticoed entrances, derived from 'real' houses. It also involved the creation of physical space, within the tomb, that could be used by the living. Larger private tombs could have multiple rooms forming cool, comfortable interiors in marked contrast to the hot sun-baked exteriors of the Egyptian summer – much like houses themselves. The burial chamber itself would be inaccessible to the living – perhaps a little like the private rooms at the rear of a normal house – while more accessible, decorated parts of the tomb could include (at least in Old Kingdom *mastaba* tombs) an inner court.

The connection between the living and the dead in ancient Egypt was most obviously expressed in the regular provision of food for the deceased, especially offerings of bread and beer.

The necessity for access to the tomb by the living was driven in part by the *ka*'s need for food, which, ideally, would come in the form of offerings supplied by the tombowner's descendants, priests who were paid from endowments to the tomb or pious visitors – collectively, individuals who were part of the same community as the tombowner. The bond between the living and the dead, expressed by food offerings from the former to the latter – and the possible reciprocal protection of the living from evil spirits by the deceased – was one of the reasons that the dead and the living together made up a single, active community. Tombs, and the cemeteries that contained them, were therefore not marginal structures with little regular relevance to the living, but part of the town.

Towns for the Dead

This relationship meant that ancient Egyptian cemeteries were places of regular activity. Cemeteries could be referred to by the term *niwt* (which, as we have seen (pp. 35–36), is a common word for 'town'), for example on an inscription from the 'town' of tombs around the pyramid of Khufu at Giza on which the tombowner states 'I have made this tomb in this town (*niwt*) of my Lord [i.e. the king].' Cemeteries could also mirror the social stratification of the parts of towns inhabited by the living. Beni Hasan is a good example again, for here the large tombs of the local elite – nomarchs and governors – formed a terrace cut into the face of the cliffs of the eastern mountain, while the sloping ground beneath this elite cemetery contained shaft-tombs in which were buried, not the poorest inhabitants of this nome, but a well-to-do town-dwelling population who had what one might think of as 'professional' occupations. It is tempting to think of the cemetery at Beni Hasan, which served the nearby local nome capital of Menat-Khufu, as reflecting the dichotomy of a few large mansions and many small houses, and this seems to be typical of the few well-preserved Middle Kingdom towns we know of, such as Kahun or Wah-Sut at Abydos.

The columned halls of elite provincial tombs of the Middle Kingdom, like this example from Beni Hasan, seem to be based on the architecture of contemporary elite residences for the living.

PART IV

Graeco-Roman Egypt

The Classical City in Egypt

When Egypt became a Hellenistic kingdom, following Alexander's invasion of 332 BC and the subsequent installation of the Ptolemaic dynasty, significant changes took place in the urban geography of Egypt. The later absorption of Egypt within the Roman imperial system after the death of Cleopatra VII in 31 BC ushered in a further period of major adjustment. This section will examine the evidence for continuity and change in the towns and cities of the Graeco-Roman Period, which had two major phases, each roughly 300 years long: Ptolemaic Egypt (332–31 BC) and 'early' Roman Egypt (31 BC–AD 395. 'Late' Roman Egypt, from AD 395 to 641, is the period when Egypt came under the control of the Byzantine Empire). Because of the significant differences between cities of the Classical Period in Egypt and what went before, it is worth considering urban developments of this era in their own right.

The evidence for this period is, in many ways, superior to that of the much longer dynastic period. In archaeological terms it is self-evident that later structures will normally have a higher survival rate than earlier ones built in the same locale. However, the propensity for the use of fired red brick and lime mortar, rather than unbaked mudbrick, in the Roman Period means that even relatively modest buildings of this period have a greater chance of surviving both water and diggers for *sebbakh* (the rich fertiliser composed of degraded mudbrick). The result of this is that the sight of a red-topped mound of fired brick (and pottery) sitting on top of an even more ancient pile of mudbrick is a common sight, especially in the Nile Delta, at sites such as Tell Mutubis. It should be noted, however, that the remains of Graeco-Roman sites have not always been treated with much interest by archaeologists keen to dig down to the dynastic layers below. Moreover, even these sites are not immune from pillaging and the phenomenon of even more modern sites sitting on top of them.

The Polis

The Hellenistic ideal for settlement was based on the Greek conception of a city: the *polis*. Ideally the polis would be a self-governing urban centre with its own extensive (Greek

Previous pages
The mosaic floor that gives the name of the Alexandrian house in which it was found, the 'Villa of the Birds'.

This striking mosaic of a woman with a headdress in the form of a ship's prow, found at Thmuis in the Delta, has been claimed to be a personification of the city of Alexandria, although another possibility is that it is a portrait of the Ptolemaic queen Berenike II.

This reconstruction of Alexandria looks westwards along Canopus Street. The Heptastadion leading to Pharos Island, flanked by the Eastern and Western Harbours, can be seen on the right, with Lake Mareotis visible on the left.

style) institutions. It would be supported by a network of smaller settlements that existed within its agricultural hinterland (*chora*). The Ptolemies found one existing city in Egypt that fitted the bill – Naukratis in the Eastern Delta, which was essentially a city of Greek settlers that had developed *polis*-like institutions with which the Ptolemies could identify. In Alexandria, the Ptolemies inherited, in its early stages, a city that would certainly develop *polis* institutions, and they later founded another one: Ptolemais Hermiou 16 km (10 miles) south of Akhmim in southern Egypt.

Technically these were the only three 'cities' (in so far as they could be defined as a *polis*) in Ptolemaic Egypt. However, there were more than three 'functional' cities in Ptolemaic Egypt, even if only three were termed *polis*. There were also, of course, existing major population centres, which became equally, or even more, important during the Ptolemaic Period and there were new settlements, which, even if they were not

termed *polis*, were substantial and important nevertheless. It was also common to (re-)name these settlements after members of the Ptolemaic royal family, hence a profusion of Ptolemy-, Arsinoe- or Berenike-compounded toponyms.

The Ptolemies exercised a light touch when it came to the organization of the administration and physical appearance of Egyptian cities, but the same was certainly not true of the Romans. Their reorganization of their newly acquired province was radical and far-reaching, affecting both the social structure of Roman Egypt and its physical reflection in its settlements. The Romans established a clear hierarchy of settlements. First were the 'Greek' cities, of which Alexandria was the largest and most obvious example. On the next level down were the metropolis cities of the *chora* (nome), which were often longstanding nome-capitals. On the third and lowest level were villages.

These distinctions were not just based on the size of settlements, but were also reflected in the status of their inhabitants, particularly their social status and – perhaps most important of all – their tax obligations. Alexandrians and Roman citizens were exempt from the poll tax. *Metropolites* – the inhabitants of the metropolis cities – paid at a reduced rate, but villagers were assessed at a full rate. The consequence of this policy was to privilege cities and city-dwellers, by placing the burden of poll tax firmly on the agricultural population. Internally, major towns were divided into a series of administrative districts or *amphoda*. These were identified by a simple numbering system (including the adjacent Delta cities of Thmuis and Mendes which had 20 and 9 districts respectively, and Memphis which had only 5).

Public Facilities

Perhaps the most distinctive physical change in Graeco-Roman cities compared with their dynastic predecessors was the appearance of public buildings that serviced activities unknown in the Egypt of Khufu or Ramesses II. Associations based on social-relatedness and shared pursuits such as the *gymnasia* of the Graeco-Roman world might be seen as

distantly connected to the *confréries* of Deir el-Medina (and, presumably, other dynastic towns and cities), but the institution of the public baths was entirely new. Perhaps even more striking were mass-audience sports and other forms of entertainment that required large and specialized buildings in which they could take place. Examples of such structures include the 11,000-seat theatre at Oxyrhynchus and the extraordinary Hippodrome at Antinoöpolis. Because of the size of these buildings, shoe-horning them into existing dynastic settlements was not usually a feasible proposition, and the enthusiasm by which they were greeted by the population of such town might be doubted. However, provision of such places was an inherent part of the planning of Classical cities so new foundations would have had these facilities incorporated to service a more cosmopolitan local population.

In both archaeological remains and texts, the cities of Graeco-Roman Egypt provide us with evidence of their distinctive character. Alexandria is the obvious, dominant example, but other cities – some new foundations, some radically changed in the Graeco-Roman Period – allow us to see this.

The most significant excavated part of Alexandria, apart from its cemeteries, is the area now known as Kom el-Dikka, which contained, among other things, this theatre, part of the civic centre of the 4th century AD.

Alexandria *ad Aegyptum*

The patriarch of Antioch Michael bar Elias, writing in the 12th century AD, but probably quoting a source from the 4th century AD, enumerates the different buildings within the 5 districts of Alexandria, which total 2,478 temples, 6,152 courts, 24,296 houses, 1,561 bath-houses, 845 taverns and 456 porticoes; bar Elias concludes his summary by noting that 'Alexandria is the greatest of the cities of the inhabited world'.

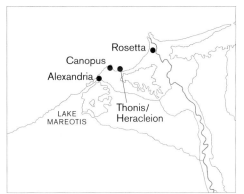

A New Maritime City

Famously, Alexandria was founded by Alexander the Great himself. An existing small settlement called Rakotis was chosen to become the site of a great city on account of its advantageous location. Its selection was driven not by the desire to found a new city in a place that would make sense for the government of the Nile Valley and Delta (such as Memphis), nor to create a city in a place with no existing associations (as Amarna had been), and certainly not in a location with long-standing family connections (like Pr-Ramesses), but by the desire for a maritime city. The combination of a Mediterranean location with two good, natural harbours, and inland communications (not to mention a supply of fresh water) served by a branch of the Nile flowing into the nearby Lake Mareotis, made Alexandria perfectly fit for purpose.

Top An aerial view of the Eastern Harbour at Alexandria, looking eastwards. The mediaeval Qaitbay Fort in the foreground occupies a position close to where the Pharos lighthouse would have stood.

That purpose was to be a Hellenistic city to rival any of those of the other *Diadochoi* (successor-kings of the Macedonian empire) or indeed any existing city of the Mediterranean. It was to be the capital of a Ptolemaic empire whose heartland was Egypt, but which also extended across the eastern Mediterranean and which embraced something the dynastic Egyptians were always wary of – the sea. In these terms, Alexandria was brilliantly successful and for half a millennium its only rival in the claim to be the greatest city of the ancient world was its eventual political and military nemesis, Rome.

Other Western Delta sites

However, Alexandria was not the first city to be built on the Mediterranean coast of the Western Delta. Immediately to the east of Alexandria in Abukir Bay were the ports of **Canopus** and **Thonis-Heracleion**, strategically located close to the point where the Canopic Branch of the Nile met the Mediterranean and provided an important point of entry into Egypt for foreign, especially Greek, sailors. Both cities had developed an urban character that was part Egyptian and part Greek (the main temple at Thonis-Heracleion seems to have been dedicated to the Greek hero Heracles) in a manner that was very much the model for Alexandria itself.

Though we do not know exactly when Canopus and Thonis-Heracleion were founded, both benefited from major works carried out during the reign of Nectanebo I (380–362 BC). His additions to the temple at Thonis-Heracleion were among the latest major building work in the city, for although it was Egypt's main port during the Late Period, it declined during the 4th century BC. Canopus's importance seems to have continued into the Graeco-Roman Period, however: a temple to Osiris was built by Ptolemy III and excavations in the city have yielded many Ptolemaic stelae. References in the works of Roman writers suggest Canopus was in decline during the first centuries AD, but the area has remained inhabited through to the modern day.

The dynamic nature of the Mediterranean coastline has meant that much of Canopus and all of Thonis-Herakelion, like a significant portion of Alexandria itself, are now submerged

beneath the sea. A programme of underwater archaeology initiated by French archaeologist Franck Goddio has done much to develop our understanding of both cities.

The People of Alexandria

One of Alexandria's most striking elements as a city was its cosmopolitan character. Being a new city, it needed to be populated. The population that was drawn to the city consisted, logically enough, of a Macedonian ruling elite, but also a range of people from around the Mediterranean who were attracted by the opportunities provided by this new, exciting venture. Native Egyptians could also potentially be enticed to this new city, and so it developed a character that reflected

The torso of a queen represented as Isis, carved from black stone and with inlaid eyes, at the site of its discovery in Heracleion. The statue is thought to represent Cleopatra II or Cleopatra III. Other fragments completing this piece were found scattered over an area of 350 m (1,148 ft).

the Ptolemaic empire itself – a mixture of the Egyptian and the wider eastern Mediterranean. Because of this curiously hybrid character, at its location on the edge of the traditional area of Egyptian settlement in the Western Delta, it became known as Alexandria *ad Aegyptum* – 'Alexandria, next to Egypt'.

The influx of immigrants, especially Greek-speaking, within large cities seems to have led in many cases to the development of distinct districts with an ethnic character, although the extent of this (including the status of Jewish groups in different cities, especially Alexandria) is still a matter of controversy.

The Layout of the City

Alexandria was a *polis*, a city whose physical layout and institutions were derived from the Greek world from where its rulers came. Classical tradition gives the main credit for the specific planning of the city to the architect Dinocrates of Rhodes. Hardly any of ancient Alexandria is visible today and our knowledge of the layout of the city and the buildings it contained is primarily based on the accounts of contemporary visitors, such as Strabo, together with a relatively limited amount of archaeological work.

Alexandria was divided into five districts, each of which was identified by one of the first five

Founding Alexandria – the Satrap Stela

This stela was set up in the city of Buto by Ptolemy I in 316 BC, when he was Satrap (Governor) of Egypt for Alexander's son, Alexander IV. Its purpose was to re-establish order – Ptolemy confirms the claim of the temple of the goddess Wadjet in Buto to an area of land in the Delta, and claims that he returned to their temples those statues of the gods that had been seized by the Persians. But all was not traditional:

He made as his Residence 'The Fortress of the King of Upper and Lower Egypt Mery-Amun Setep-n-Re, Son of Re, Alexandros' its name, upon the shore of the Great-Green of the Hau-Nebu, Ra-ked [Rakotis] its earlier name.

The terms Great-Green and Hau-Nebu are very old ones, the former means 'sea', while the latter, 'those who are in their baskets/islands', by the Late Period had come to mean 'Greeks'. This short reference effectively proclaims both the establishment of Rakotis (Alexandria) as the royal residence of the Macedonian kings of Egypt and the direction that city would face – towards the Hellenistic world of the Mediterranean.

The Satrap Stela is one of a group of royal stelae produced during the Ptolemaic Period to establish and regulate donations of land and other economic resources to temples, sometimes with multilingual texts. The Rosetta Stone is the most famous of these stelae.

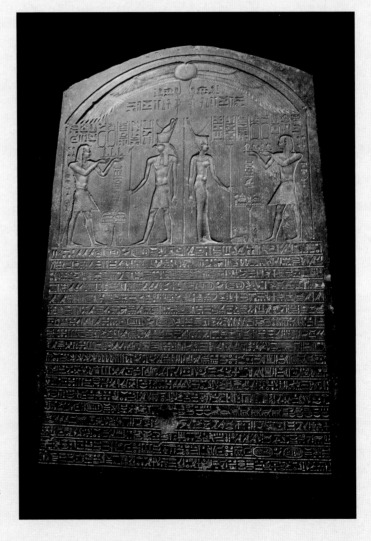

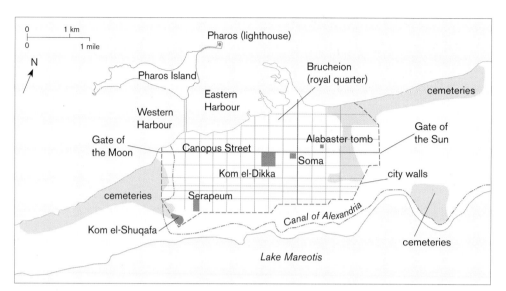

Plan of Alexandria showing some of the major features of the city in the Ptolemaic and Roman Periods.

letters of the Greek alphabet. The core of the city was two long roads, which crossed each other at right-angles, and from which other roads led off. These major thoroughfares were Canopus Street, which ran the entire length of the city from the Gate of the Moon in the west to the Gate of the Sun in the east. Running north-south was Soma Street, which stretched from the great Eastern Harbour to the harbour on Lake Mareotis to the south of the city. It was named after the

Soma, a building located where the two main streets crossed, and which housed the tombs of the ruling dynasty including that of Alexander himself. In the same area was the Museion, a centre of learning that was intended to establish Alexandria's credentials as the cultural capital of the Hellenistic world.

Other parts of the city are less easy to identify apart from a few archaeological survivals such as the Serapeum – the temple of the new

The location, or locations, of the tomb(s) of Alexander the Great at Alexandria are still much disputed. The 'Alabaster tomb' in the eastern part of the city has been proposed as one of the potential candidates.

Hellenistic-Egyptian god Serapis, which is in part of the city now marked by a triumphal column of the emperor Diocletian, erroneously referred to as 'Pompey's Pillar'.

The Royal Quarter

The Brucheion or royal quarter was located on the sea front of the eastern harbour; according to Strabo it occupied between a quarter and a third of the total area of the city. Changes in sea-levels, and the effects of the earthquakes the city later suffered, mean that a significant proportion of the Brucheion and its royal palaces lie under the waters of the Eastern Harbour, from where they are currently being recovered. Although it is difficult to reconstruct the royal quarter in any detail, it is clear that public buildings in the city were often a combination of traditionally Egyptian and contemporary Classical styles. Ancient Egyptian monuments such as obelisks

Little now remains of the Serapeum, perhaps the most important temple building in Alexandria, although the mixed Egyptian and Graeco-Roman character of the site is still attested through this Egyptian sphinx and Roman column.

The Pharos

If Alexander's tomb symbolized the origins of the city and its self-image as the heart of the Hellenistic world created by Alexander's conquests, the real emblem of the city was the Pharos, built by Sostratus of Cnidus. This great lighthouse stood on an artificial island at the end of a causeway a kilometre long, the Heptastadion, which divided the port's two harbours. Today the mediaeval Qait Bey fort sits on the spot from which it once rose over 100 metres (328 ft) in height.

An architectural and engineering marvel, and one of the seven wonders of the ancient world, the Pharos seems to have consisted of a tower of three storeys: a square pedestal surmounted by an octagonal block surmounted by a cylinder. The artificially magnified fire on top of the lighthouse could be seen as a beacon from a very great distance. As well as a practical navigation aid the Pharos made a powerful statement about the cultural ideals with which Alexandria and the Ptolemies identified – it, and they, looked out towards the Mediterranean rather than inwards towards the Delta and Valley of Nilotic Egypt.

The Pharos of Alexandria collapsed after a series of earthquakes. This smaller lighthouse, at Taposiris Magna along the coast to the west of Alexandria, perhaps gives an indication of its original appearance.

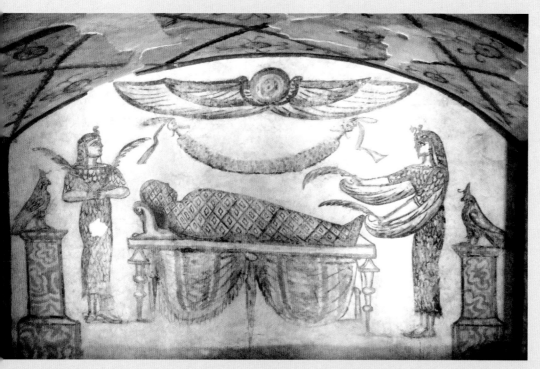

This wall-painting from a tomb in the Kom el-Shuqafa cemeteries at Alexandria is an excellent example of traditional Egyptian themes – in this case the body of the deceased protected by the goddesses Isis and Nephthys – depicted in Hellenistic style.

and statues were imported in large numbers from sites such as Heliopolis and Sais to embellish the new capital of Egypt.

Cemeteries and Suburbs

The most substantial parts of ancient Alexandria that can be seen today are its cemeteries. Located in the eastern and western suburbs, in the southern part of the main city, and on an expanded Pharos Island, these subterranean tombs are architecturally a local adaptation of Hellenistic tombs, but with decorative motifs and scenes drawn from Egyptian views of the afterlife. In line with much of what we know about Alexandria, the combination between Classical and Egyptian traditions is a dominating theme.

Alexandria's Decline

The decline of Alexandria was gradual. There had been relatively little in the way of major architectural innovation during the 1st and 2nd centuries AD, although most of the important landmarks of the Ptolemaic city – including the Serapeum, Pharos and Museion – were

maintained and occasionally renovated, as when the Serapeum burnt down in 181 and was replaced by a larger Roman version. Significant damage was done when the emperor Aurelian recaptured the city from Queen Zenobia of Palmyra in 272, and by the emperor Diocletian during his eight-month siege of 298. Civil unrest as a result of the friction between the emerging Christians and traditionalist pagans was another destabilizing factor, although the specific effect of these riots on Alexandria's pagan buildings is difficult to assess.

In addition, the impact on the city of the series of earthquakes in 365, 447, 535 and 792 was not a happy one. The first half of the 7th century AD was a dramatic period during which possession of Alexandria quickly changed hands, from its capture by the Sassanid Persians in 619, its recapture by the Byzantines in 629 and finally, after a 14-month siege, its conquest by Amr Ibn al-As in 641 as part of the Arab invasion of Egypt. The subsequent development of Alexandria as a mediaeval and modern city – second only to Cairo – has meant that there is relatively little to see of what was one of the great urban centres of the Graeco-Roman world.

The Faiyum in the Graeco-Roman Period

One region benefited more than any other from new Ptolemaic settlement – the Faiyum. Like their Middle Kingdom predecessors, the Ptolemies recognized the concentration of agricultural potential of the Faiyum – which they named the Arsinoite Nome after Queen Arsinoe (sister and second wife of Ptolemy II) – and exploited it through a project of draining Lake Moeris to create new agricultural land. The ancient regional capital of Shedet (on the site of what is now the modern regional capital of Medinet el-Faiyum) became known as Krokodilopolis (after its local god, the crocodile-headed Sobek) or Ptolemais Euergetis after 117 BC (the date it passed into their hands). Krokodilopolis was the only *polis* in the Arsinoite

nome, the other settlements each being termed a *kome* – village. Nevertheless, these villages could be substantial in size: Krokodilopolis was probably 288 hectares in area at its greatest extent, but the 'village' of Karanis – the next largest settlement in the Faiyum, was a not-inconsiderable 79 hectares.

Greeks and Egyptians in the Faiyum

Although Greek place names are commonly used in official, Greek documents, ancient toponyms continued to be used by the Egyptian population. German scholar Katja Mueller gives the example of 'The town of Sobek Ratakheny which is called the Hall of Ptolemy'. 'The town of Sobek' is a prefix often given to settlements in the Faiyum to stress their connection with the local god; Ratakheny is the traditional dynastic name, while 'Hall of Ptolemy' is the Greek name for the site, Ptolemais Hermiou. The local Egyptian population would have used the ancient, traditional name Ratakheny. Today we know this town as Illahun.

For new settlements, a regular, Hellenistic street-plan was the norm. The archaeological exploration of the site of Philadelphia (Kom el-Kharaba el-Kebir), established in the Faiyum by Ptolemy II, has revealed a settlement of probably 1,000 by 500 metres (3,280 by 1,640 ft), laid out on a very regular grid-plan of right-angled streets and *insulae* – housing blocks of 100 by 50 metres (328 by 164 ft), each of which contained up to 20 mudbrick houses with a footprint of 12 by 12 metres (39 by 39 ft). The settlement at Dionysias (Qasr Qarun) on the western edge of the Faiyum also had a strict orthogonal plan with square *insulae* of 50 by 50 metres (164 by 164 ft). However, other settlements had a more traditional Egyptian feel to their planning because the key factor was the dominant presence of a temple whose *dromos* (avenue) acted both as

a processional route and a main street, echoing the key principles of the planning of New Kingdom royal cities such as Thebes and Amarna.

Karanis

Karanis, although technically a village, was very large indeed: its archaeological remains cover an area of 1,050 by 750 metres (3,445 by 2,460 ft) and by the 2nd century AD its population was perhaps 4,000. At this time the influence of the temple-centred major settlement was still present in the provinces, and the two most striking architectural survivals are its two large temples: the stone-built southern temple was 15 by 22 metres (49 by 72 ft) and was located within a sacred enclosure of 75 by 60 metres (246 by 197 ft). The god worshipped here, as in several places in the Faiyum in the Graeco-Roman Period, was a form of Souchos, the Classicized name of the crocodile-god Sobek. At Karanis, Souchos was worshipped in the form of the paired deities Pnepheros and Petesouchos. As was typical of the Late and Graeco-Roman Periods, the worship of gods who had animal forms developed into reverence for sacred animals themselves and a necropolis of mummified crocodiles grew up at

The excavations by the University of Michigan at Karanis (here shown during their 1924–25 season) are one of the most important and large-scale excavations of a provincial settlement of the Graeco-Roman Period.

Karanis, impressive for a 'village', but nothing to rival the catacombs at Hermopolis Magna where ibises and baboons were mummified and interred to honour the local god Thoth.

The most important aspect of Karanis is that, a desert-edge town-mound, it was abandoned before the end of the Roman Period and not re-occupied later. Karanis has principally been excavated by a team from the University of Michigan. It is therefore the best example to have survived of a settlement site of Graeco-Roman Egypt; its two- or three-storey mudbrick houses, clustered together in complex localities, give a strong impression of what life must have been like in a 'real' town of this period. It provides a counterpoint to the site of **Oxyrhynchus** in Middle Egypt, which has provided a mass of documentary evidence for life in a provincial town, but relatively little in the way of coherent archaeological remains.

The inhabitants of Oxyrhynchus dumped their rubbish in the desert to the west of the town where it was well preserved. This rubbish included papyrus documents, most written in Greek, many of which were recovered in the period 1896 to 1907 by the British papyrologists Bernard Grenfell and Arthur Hunt. Some of these papyri were fragments of plays by Classical authors or early versions of the New Testament, but 90% were administrative documents or private correspondence. The ongoing project to translate this huge archive is gradually revealing the life of the town in the period from the 4th century BC to the 7th century AD.

Decline

The population evidence from the Faiyum suggests an overall population decline during the 2nd century AD. In the AD 160s, Egypt suffered from a very serious plague, which had the effect of depopulating much of the country. Where figures exist, or can be estimated, the decline was dramatic and long-lasting. In the 50 years between AD 150–200 the population of Karanis fell by 40 per cent and seems not to have recovered, since by the 4th century it stood at only 10 per cent of its 2nd-century level. Elsewhere in the Faiyum, other large villages suffered a catastrophic decline in population and some were completely abandoned.

The extensive, if rather bleak, remains of Karanis (Kom Aushim) constitute one of the largest archaeological sites in the Faiyum.

Middle Egypt in the Graeco-Roman Period

Almost facing each other across the Nile in Middle Egypt, the cities of Hermopolis Magna and Antinoöpolis were two of the most important urban centres of the Graeco-Roman Period in the Nile Valley. They also provide a fascinating comparison in the development of cities of this era, since the former had a long and illustrious history, and was able to retain much of that character well into the Roman Period, while the latter was, essentially, a creation of the early Roman Period.

A Favourite City – Antinoöpolis

The foundation of Antinoöpolis (modern Sheikh Abada) can be dated with a rare precision – 30 October AD 130. Although the presence of a temple inscribed by Ramesses II indicates

that there was an existing dynastic settlement at the site, the desire of the emperor Hadrian to found a city to commemorate his drowned favourite Antinous seems to have resulted in the establishment of a city – the only *polis* founded

Below The *tetrastyle* at Antinoopolis drawn in Napoleon's *Description de l'Égypte*. Since then, it has, unfortunately, been destroyed.

by the Romans, to add to Alexandria, Naukratis and Ptolemais Hermiou – on a much greater scale than whatever was there. It is interesting to note that this new city was founded on a, presumably, under-used piece of land on the east bank of the Nile, not far away from Amarna, where Akhenaten had had a similar idea.

Initially the city seems to have had a Hellenistic character; it was called 'Antinoöpolis of the New Hellenes/Greeks' and this would accord with Hadrian's well-known Hellenophilia. More practically, it formed the Nile Valley terminus for the Via Hadriana, which crossed the Eastern Desert from the Red Sea port of Berenike. The city benefited from being settled by army veterans under the emperor Antoninus Pius (AD 138–61) and from building works by another emperor, Severus Alexander (222–35).

The skeleton of the city was, unsurprisingly, its main thoroughfares, the north–south 1,162-metre (3,812-ft) long *cardo* and the east–west 1,014-metre (3,327-ft) long *decumanus major*, which were both provided with colonnades totalling over 1,000 stone columns; the *decumanus minor* was a second important east–west street. The intersections of these streets formed the major hubs of Antinoöpolis and each was marked by a *tetrastyle* – a monument comprising four large columns topped with statues.

The city was surrounded by a double enclosure wall on three sides. The fourth – the river side – was dominated by a triumphal arch at the western end of the *cardo*. Although the site has only been patchily excavated, the most obvious large structures to have been built at Antinoöpolis are its baths, its theatre and, outside the town, an extraordinary hippodrome 307-metres (1007-ft) long and 77-metres (253-ft) wide.

City of Hermes – Hermopolis Magna

Hermopolis Magna was very different from Antinoöpolis in that it had a long and distinguished history, which was reflected in its appearance in the Graeco-Roman Period. Known anciently as Khmunu 'Eight Town', it was mythologically connected to eight local creator

Opposite above The ruins of Antinoöpolis (Sheikh Abada) constitute a huge, and largely unexplored, archaeological site.

The large and impressive town-mound at Hermopolis Magna attests to its long period of significant occupation, from the remains of mudbrick settlements (background) to stone statues like these seated colossi of Ramesses II (in the foreground).

gods, the Ogdoad. In this way, the city could be said to be as ancient as it was possible to be, since the creation of the world itself took place here.

Not much remains of the city from before the New Kingdom apart from the limestone gateway to a Middle Kingdom temple, built by Amenemhat II. One other survival from this period is the name Khmunu, which finds an echo in the current name for the large village that covers the southern part of the ancient mound, el-Ashmunein. Up to the Late Period the city seems to have been a typical temple-town: a main temple complex orientated north–south, which was added to by Amenhotep III (his embellishments included eight colossal quartzite baboons), Horemheb and Ramesses II (who used *talatat*-blocks of the Amarna Period as the fill for a pylon (monumental entranceway) he erected).

Right Plan of Hermopolis Magna in the Graeco-Roman Period, showing both new buildings and those adapted from earlier periods.

Below The Portico (pronaos) of the temple built by Philip Arrhidaeus for the god Thoth at Hermopolis Magna, as illustrated in the *Description de l'Égypte*. Only the column bases of this structure now remain, as it was destroyed in 1826.

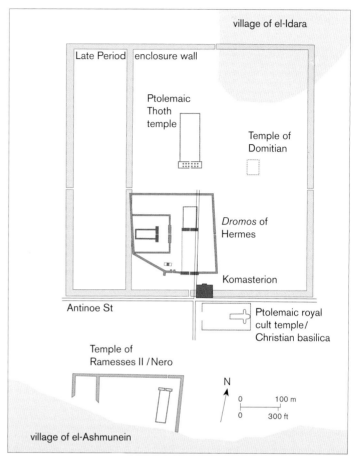

The temple was dedicated to the god Thoth, an association that continued into the Graeco-Roman Period, as Thoth became identified with the Greek god Hermes. Additions to the temple-complex took place under the 20th Dynasty, and during the Third Intermediate Period houses were built to the west of the temple area.

During the 30th Dynasty, a massive mudbrick enclosure wall surrounded an expanded temple area and effectively created a huge temple enclosure that dominated the northern part of the city, while most of the later residential area probably still lies under modern el-Ashmunein. This enclosure gave shape to the city, and later additions fitted within its existing structure. The temple of Thoth was extended at the very beginning of the Ptolemaic Period and the main processional route that ran to this new building, and south out of the temple enclosure, the *Dromos* of Hermes became the main north–south street of the city. The main east–west road,

Antinoe Street, crossed the *Dromos* at right angles immediately to the south of the temple enclosure; this became the heart of the Graeco-Roman city, marked by a tetrastyle and a series of Classical-style buildings. Also at this important crossroads was a temple to Ptolemy III and Berenike, later overbuilt by a Christian cathedral whose red granite columns are the most striking part of the site visible today. Within, and outside, the temple enclosure, small Egyptian-style temples continued to be built or added to by later rulers, including the emperors Nero and Domitian.

One of the largest and most important cities of the Graeco-Roman Period, Hermopolis Magna is an intriguing combination of the ancient and the modern.

The importance of Hermopolis Magna in the early Christian Period is attested by the impressive granite columns of a now largely destroyed major church.

PART V

Gazetteer of Cities and Towns of Ancient Egypt

Gazetteer of Cities and Towns of Ancient Egypt

So far we have looked at some of the most important and distinctive features of cities and urban life in ancient Egypt. In doing so, we have examined evidence from a range of sources including archaeological excavation, depictions on tomb walls, texts written by the Egyptians themselves and the speculations of modern scholars. This kaleidoscope of sources has not been consistent or even, but has been a product of the accidental survival of different types of evidence. We have been able to look at daily life in the New Kingdom at Deir el-Medina and the organization of a Middle Kingdom settlement at Kahun, but our understanding of where the inhabitants of the great ancient cities of Thebes or Memphis lived and worked is patchy to say the least.

This chequered pattern of good and poor levels of evidence is also very much apparent as we journey down the Nile from Elephantine (Yebu) to the Mediterranean, through the Nile Valley of Upper (southern) Egypt to the broad Delta of Lower (northern) Egypt, and to the adjacent areas of the Faiyum, the Western Desert Oases,

Nubia, Sinai and the Mediterranean Coast. We shall see cities, such as Amarna, whose detailed layout has been reconstructed through many years of patient research, abandoned towns such as Balat in the Dakhla Oasis whose remains have been preserved under centuries of drifting sand, and we shall look in vain for substantial traces of some of the major settlements of the Nile Valley and Delta whose presence is only known to us through the survival of their desert cemeteries or references in the works of ancient authors.

Although the task of providing a complete gazetteer of all the important cities and towns of ancient Egypt is bound to be one with substantial gaps (even if some are being and will continue to be plugged by the work of current and future archaeologists), this is a task that would have been both understandable to and approved of by the Egyptians themselves. They – or at least their scribes – were people who loved a good list, and the Gazetteer that follows here is very much in the spirit of a document we have already seen (pp. 35–37), the *Onomasticon of Amenemope.*

The Nile, and its fertile floodplain, as viewed from the tomb of Ankhtifi at Moalla in Upper Egypt. The cattle in the foreground are grazing on a temporary island in the middle of the river.

Previous pages
Reconstruction of the city of Memphis during the New Kingdom.

Elephantine and Aswan

The town of **Elephantine** (ancient Yebu) is unique. No site in Egypt is more thoroughly surrounded by water and yet it has archaeological remains, with a high level of preservation, that stretch back through the dynastic period to its predynastic settlement. The reason for the unique nature of Elephantine is its specific geographical location on a granite island that forms part of the band of hard stone making up the First Cataract of the Nile. That same landscape feature formed a natural southern border for ancient Egypt, and so for much of its history Elephantine was effectively a border town, and developed a number of important functions because of this location. Elephantine has been the subject of a long-term project of excavation and reconstruction by German and Swiss

archaeological institutes who have been working at the site since 1969.

The Development of Elephantine

Today Elephantine is an island that measures 1,500 m (4,920 ft) north to south and 500 m (1,640 ft) at its widest east–west point. It is a relatively small element of the large and still-expanding city of **Aswan** (Sunu); in ancient times this situation was reversed, with Elephantine the important settlement and Aswan a small off-shoot on the east bank of the Nile. The current island only became a single entity when the base-level of the Nile lowered during the First Intermediate Period; before this, there

Elephantine
/Aswan

Aerial view of Elephantine. The ancient settlement was concentrated on the southern part of the island.

were two islands, divided by marshland, which would flood during the inundation.

In the late Predynastic/Early Dynastic Periods, a town developed on Elephantine, surrounded by a defensive wall. As was the case throughout its history, space was at a premium and this early town seems to have been a tight cluster of buildings. By the late Old Kingdom, the region of the First Cataract, and Elephantine in particular, had become of even greater strategic interest to the Egyptian state, perhaps reflected in the well-organized public buildings and houses that appeared in the 5th to 6th Dynasties and continued through the Middle Kingdom. The town on Elephantine commanded a hinterland beyond the island: in addition to the subsidiary mainland settlement of Aswan, the elite cemetery of Elephantine was created at the Qubbet el-Hawa, a high ridge of cliffs on the west bank

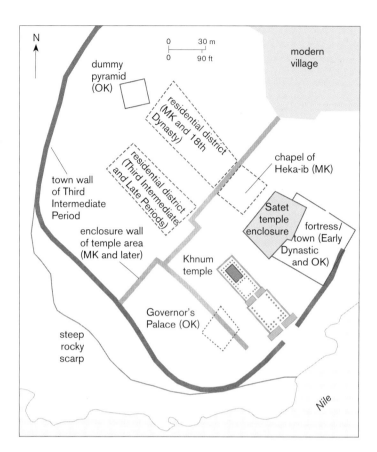

Right Plan of the town of Elephantine, showing some of the major buildings at different periods of the life of the settlement.

of the Nile a little to the north of the island. It is here that the officials and caravan-leaders of Elephantine inscribed their tombs with autobiographical texts describing their (and Elephantine's) role as the heart of trade with Nubia and central Africa beyond. To the south of Elephantine were an important series of granite quarries on both the east bank of the Nile (the 'Northern' and 'Southern' quarries) and islands in the Nile, especially Sehel, which has produced an astonishing series of graffiti, mainly the work of officials sent on stone-procuring missions to the region or en-route further south into Nubia.

Opposite below View looking northwest across an area of partially reconstructed Middle Kingdom administrative buildings.

Above The high degree of survival of the archaeological remains at Elephantine from the Early Dynastic to the Graeco-Roman Periods make it one of the most important towns from ancient Egypt whose development can be traced in some detail.

Left This substantial rock graffito on the island of Sehel commemorates an expedition to acquire obelisks by the high official Amenhotep, who may have lived during the reign of Hatshepsut.

Left The earliest substantial settlement remains at Elephantine are the Early Dynastic/ Old Kingdom fortress and town in the northeastern part of the town.

Temples at Elephantine

As with most large towns in dynastic Egypt, the temple of the local god(s) was at the very heart of Elephantine. The earliest deity to be associated with the town seems to have been the goddess Satet, whose first temple was a grotto within a cluster of granite boulders. This temple was expanded and developed in a way that retained its ancient core, but also saw important additions in the Middle Kingdom, New Kingdom and Ptolemaic Period. By the Middle Kingdom, Satet had acquired a male partner, Khnum, whose temple buildings are now the most striking at Elephantine, especially the monumental additions made in the Late and Graeco-Roman Periods. The third major deity at Elephantine was the goddess Anuket, daughter of Khnum and Satet, who was especially associated with the nearby island of Sehel. The most striking aspect of temple building on Elephantine is the extent to which its development can be traced over a long period of time.

Below Perhaps the most obvious indications of the importance of Elephantine in the Late and Graeco-Roman Periods are elements of temple-building on an enormous scale, such as this monolithic *naos*-shrine in the Khnum temple.

Jewish Mercenaries on Elephantine

One of the most remarkable discoveries made on Elephantine – not least as an example of the high level of preservation of delicate objects on this island – are a group of papyrus documents written in Aramaic, recovered during the early years of the 20th century. These documents refer to the existence of a community of Jewish mercenaries resident at Elephantine from *c.* 525 to *c.* 400 BC as part of the Persian occupation of Egypt. This community had built a temple to Yahweh, which had been destroyed in 410 BC as part of an ongoing conflict with the priesthood of Khnum. Nevertheless, this temple – whose location has not yet been discovered – was re-established after permission to do so had been granted from Jerusalem.

Southern Egypt

The stretch of the Nile between the major cities
of Elephantine and Thebes, comprising Upper
Egyptian Nomes 1–3, contained a number of
important settlements. Unfortunately, the level
of survival of these ancient towns has been rather
poor, with some partial exceptions.

Kom Ombo

The ancient city of Ombos has an especially
striking location – on a promontory overlooking
the Nile to the west and, to the east, an unusually
(for this part of southern Egypt) substantial
basin of well-watered agricultural land. The
natural advantages of the site made **Kom Ombo**
an obvious choice for settlement from as early
as the Upper Palaeolithic. Little work has taken
place on the surviving settlement mounds, on
this promontory, although they may date back
as early as the Old Kingdom, apart from the
clearance of the monument for which the site is
now famous, the Ptolemaic double-temple of the
gods Sobek and Haroeris.

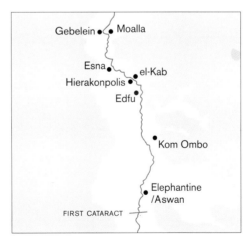

Edfu

This site is best known for its enormous temple
to the god Horus, built during the Ptolemaic
Period; it is the best-preserved temple in
Egypt. However, immediately to the west of the
enclosure of the Horus temple there still exists
a substantial town-mound, **Tell Edfu**. This was

Top Kom Ombo is
best known for its
impressive Graeco-
Roman temple, but it
also has substantial
settlement remains
(for example, the large
mound on the left of
this view), which have
hardly been explored.

excavated by a French/French–Polish team from 1921 to 1939 and has produced substantial evidence for a long occupation of the town (known as Behdet, then Djebat) from at least as early as the late Old Kingdom.

Unfortunately, it appears that the levelling of the ancient town-mound to create the space for the Ptolemaic temple ripped the heart out of the earliest settlement remains, and there are only a few traces of Old Kingdom walls to the west of the temple. However, an important cemetery in the southwest part of the surviving mound has preserved tombs of local officials dating from the Old and Middle Kingdoms. In addition, significant portions of walls from the First Intermediate Period town have also survived, indicating that the town probably doubled in size from *c.* 7 hectares (17 acres) to *c.* 13 hectares (32 acres) during the First Intermediate

Period, probably reflecting the status of Edfu as an important provincial centre at this time. Excavations conducted since 2005 by Nadine Moeller for the University of Chicago have emphasized this importance with the discovery of administrative buildings of the Middle Kingdom and a set of large grain silos from the Second Intermediate Period.

Above Edfu's settlement remains have been the subject of some detailed archaeological investigation, though, like Kom Ombo, it is best known for its Graeco-Roman temple.

Recent excavations at Edfu have determined the importance of the town during the Second Intermediate Period.

Hierakonpolis and el-Kab

Despite its role as perhaps the largest and most important of the first cities of Egypt, **Hierakonpolis** (Nekhen; see pp. 23–25) quickly became something of a provincial backwater after the Early Dynastic Period. On the opposite (eastern) side of the Nile, **el-Kab** (Nekheb), which replaced Hierakonpolis as the capital of the 1st nome in the New Kingdom, fared rather better. Long-standing fieldwork – a Belgian expedition has been working here since 1937 – and an impressive range of archaeological remains indicate a long occupation history. These remains include a large cemetery of the late Predynastic, an important series of rock-cut tombs from the New Kingdom and a series of temples in the Wadi Hillal, all in the desert immediately to the east of a huge rectangular mudbrick enclosure measuring 590 by 520 m (1,936 by 1,706 ft). This enclosure, probably the work of the 30th Dynasty, contains a series of temples from the New Kingdom and later, as well as unexcavated parts of the ancient city, suggested by the presence of tombs of the Old and Middle Kingdoms built close to the north and east walls of the enclosure.

Unexcavated Sites

All that is visible today of the town of **Esna** (Iunyt) is the inner portico at the entrance of its Graeco-Roman temple, visible at the bottom of a huge hole 9 m (30 ft) deep below the ground level of modern Esna. Beneath the present houses, ancient Esna presumably still awaits excavation. The towns served by the important cemeteries at **Moalla** and **Gebelein** are unknown archaeologically although their First Intermediate Period tombs suggest that they must have been important centres, especially in that period.

Although surrounded by one of the most extensive sets of town walls in Egypt, the interior of the town of el-Kab (Nekheb) shown here has not survived as well as its New Kingdom tombs and desert temples.

Thebes

A city with many names, **Thebes** was known to the ancient Egyptians as Waset or simply Niwt, 'The City'. The Greeks called it Thebai and its modern name Luxor comes from the Arabic al-Uqsur, 'The Castles'. Compared to Memphis, its period of prominence as an important urban centre was relatively limited. It owed its status to history repeating itself: Theban local rulers brought an end to both the First and Second Intermediate Periods and subsequently embellished their home town with monuments, impressively in the Middle Kingdom and spectacularly in the New Kingdom.

There is perhaps more for the modern visitor to see at Thebes than at any other archaeological site in the world, but the dazzling array of astonishing temples and tombs does not really give much of a sense of what the city of Thebes, as a living community, actually looked like. Although New Kingdom scribes referred to Thebes being called Niwt since it was 'the model for every city', it is difficult to know to what extent Thebes was a typical city of the New Kingdom or indeed of any other period, since so much of downtown Thebes in the 18th and 19th Dynasties was probably built around and

Opposite above The temple of Medinet Habu, looking south. This important West Bank temple was not simply the mortuary monument of Ramesses III, but also an important administrative centre in the late New Kingdom and the core of the town of Maiunehes (see pp. 40–41).

Thebes

Reconstruction of the East Bank at Thebes in the New Kingdom, looking from Luxor Temple (bottom) towards Karnak along the processional road of the Opet festival. The extent of the settlement around the temples and road is speculative.

Opposite below An overview of the main archaeological remains at Thebes illustrates the dominance of monumental temple-buildings in terms of surviving structures, with the location and extent of most of the domestic settlement a matter for conjecture.

between the major East Bank temple complexes
at Karnak and Luxor – then subsumed beneath
the modern town.

However, despite the impression given today
that the city of Thebes consisted almost entirely
of royal monuments and private tombs, there
are a number of important pieces of information
from the New Kingdom that have helped us
to understand key elements in Egyptian urban
design of the period. The four most significant
conclusions we can derive from these are:

1 The monumental 'skeleton' of a city is often
   the core of its built environment, and the
   'home' of its patron god. Karnak temple as
   the house of Amun-Re (and his divine family)
   and the paved road of the processional route
   to Luxor temple provided the spine of the
   East Bank city of Thebes. An extension of
   this monumental skeleton on the West Bank
   included the royal mortuary temples of which

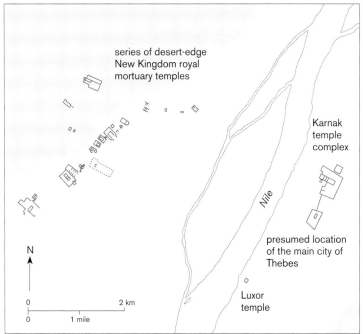

series of desert-edge
New Kingdom royal
mortuary temples

Karnak
temple
complex

Nile

presumed location
of the main city of
Thebes

Luxor
temple

N

0   2 km

0   1 mile

the best known are those of Hatshepsut at Deir el-Bahri, Amenhotep III at Kom el-Hetan, Ramesses II (the 'Ramesseum') and Ramesses III at Medinet Habu. Of course the royal burial site of the Valley of the Kings also formed an important part of the monumental aspect of Thebes, although not one that would have been accessible, or even visible, to the vast majority of the city's population.

2 Where space allowed, the different elements could spread out over a wide area, with agricultural land or even the Nile itself between those different elements. The distribution of existing clusters of buildings from Thebes, especially on the West Bank, makes this clear, especially as recorded in the house census centred on the town of Maiunehes (see pp. 40–41).

3 However, despite the city being widely spread, individual groups of houses and communities were often tightly packed together within an enclosing wall. The outstanding example of this is the workers' village at Deir el-Medina (see pp. 74–86).

4 The impetus for much of the building activity in major centres – 'royal cities' – came from the king. This is best illustrated in temple construction, but also in the sometimes extensive palace complexes they built. That at Malkata, built by Amenhotep III on the West Bank at Thebes (see pp. 47, 49) is one of the best examples of what is effectively a town within a city.

Thebes may not be the place where we can most clearly see what a great ancient Egyptian city looked like in totality – for that we must go to the briefly occupied Amarna – but it has provided us with a great deal of evidence to help us understand a number of major components that went to make up Egyptian cities and towns; this then enables us to see that, in its core features, Amarna does not seem to be unusual as a large urban centre of the New Kingdom – a very important factor given that we rely so much on its evidence to understand ancient Egyptian urban life (see pp. 155–63).

The Theban/Coptite Region

Apart from Thebes itself, most of the major towns and cities on the Qena Bend of the Nile share some common attributes. They are all urban centres that have a relatively long history, as attested by their temples, which have long periods of use and rebuilding on or near the same spot. This suggests a continuity of occupation of the town or city to go along with its temple. In the case of **Tod** (just to the south of Thebes), the temple was probably in existence during the Old Kingdom and continued until the Ptolemaic Period; at **Armant** (across the river from Tod) the temple spans the period from the 11th Dynasty to the Romans; and at **Medamud** (north of Thebes) from the Old Kingdom to the Ptolemaic Period. Nothing is known about the settlements that were attached to these temples. The importance of **Nagada** in the late Predynastic Period has already been noted (p. 23).

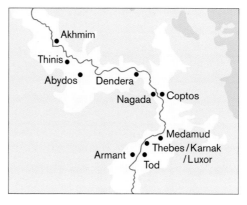

Coptos

Coptos had an even earlier history, as attested by Petrie's excavations of the Predynastic/Early Dynastic temple in 1893–94, and was clearly the most important town in this part of Egypt apart from Thebes, but once again it is only known archaeologically from its extensive temple complex, added to until well into the Roman Period, within the modern city of Qift.

Dendera

Best known today for its impressive Graeco-Roman temple, **Dendera** in fact also has, to the east of the enclosure wall of this temple, a substantial amount of its town-mound yet to be excavated. To the south of the temple enclosure, on the desert edge, is an important cemetery whose most significant excavated tombs are the substantial *mastaba*s built for local administrators in the late Old Kingdom and First Intermediate Period, an indication of the importance of Dendera as a semi-autonomous regional centre in southern Egypt at that time.

Abydos (and Thinis)

An unusual site, **Abydos** owed its importance to religious, or rather funerary, concerns. It was the site of the pre-eminent royal cemetery for the Early Dynastic Period and later (and relatedly) was associated with the Osiris cult, because it was seen as the place where the god was buried. It therefore developed an importance different from that of other 'towns', for it was distant from the Nile and had a population that was probably almost entirely geared to servicing the tombs and other funerary monuments, not unlike the situation we have seen in the Middle Kingdom town of Wah-Sut (see pp. 68–70) and the New Kingdom 'Ahmose Town'. The longest-lasting settlement at Abydos was relatively limited and dates from the Old Kingdom to the Second Intermediate Period. It developed close to the temple of Osiris at the Kom es-Sultan at Abydos. The nome capital for Abydos was at the now-lost town of **Thinis** which may be beneath the modern city of Girga.

Akhmim

Another particularly spectacular example of traces of an ancient city poking through a modern one is at **Akhmim**, capital of the 9th Upper Egyptian nome, where a very large town-mound is substantially covered by the

modern city, with the significant exception of the accidental discovery of a Ramesside temple whose major surviving element is a re-erected colossal statue of Meritamun, daughter of Ramesses II.

The modern city of Akhmim largely obscures the ancient city, whose importance in the New Kingdom is nevertheless obvious thanks to the presence of this colossal statue of Meritamun, daughter of Ramesses II.

Middle Egypt

Although **Hermopolis Magna** (see below, pp. 164–65) has one of the largest surviving expanses of settlement remains in the Nile Valley between Memphis and Thebes, and the city of Amarna (the next city to be discussed in this Gazetteer) is perhaps our best example from any period, there is plenty of evidence to suggest that the stretch of the Nile between Asyut and Memphis contained other substantial towns and cities. Some of these are best represented by their latest, Graeco-Roman, phase, such as Hermopolis, and **Oxyrhynchus**, a site famous for its important finds of papyri (see p. 135). A particularly interesting example here is **Antinoöpolis** (modern Sheikh Abada) on the east bank of the Nile, close to Hermopolis, where a major refounding of the city after the reign of Hadrian (see pp. 136–37) mostly conceals earlier phases of occupation, apart from a temple built by Ramesses II.

Missing Towns of Upper and Middle Egypt

A significant number of ancient towns and cities in the Nile Valley are known to us only through the survival of the cemeteries that once served them. This is especially the case for the important rock-cut tombs of Middle and Southern Egypt where the steep face of cliffs close to the Nile provided an ideal location for elite tombs, high and dry above the floodplain that both nurtures and eventually obliterates traces of the settlements in which once lived the occupants of those tombs. While some examples of both cemetery and town do survive (e.g. the Qubbet

el-Hawa cemetery and the town on Elephantine Island) these tend to be exceptional. Especially for the period from the late Old Kingdom to the end of the Middle Kingdom, the rock-cut cemeteries of nome leaders provide the best indication of the existence, and possible nearby location, of what was usually the most important town of the district, the nome capital.

Cemetery	Nome	Missing Nome Capital	Possible Location of Nome Capital
Qau	10	Tjebu/Djew-qa	Village of Qau el-Kebir (Graeco-Roman Antaeopolis)?
Deir Rifeh	11	Shashotep	Village of Shutb?
Deir el-Gebrawi	12	not known	not known
Asyut	13	Sawty	Traces of ancient buildings have been recovered in the city of Asyut itself
Meir	14	Kis	Village of Qusiya?
Beni Hasan	16	Menat-Khufu	Near the city of el-Minya?

Amarna – The Complete City?

The ancient city now known as **Amarna**, or Tell el-Amarna, is a curious paradox. It is a place where a huge amount is known about the layout of the city and its individual buildings, and it is possible to reconstruct in some detail how the city operated for its residents, from the king down to the humblest worker. It is the only ancient Egyptian city whose ground plan is known to any real degree of completeness, and it provides a varied range of sources of evidence to tell us about the city, its purpose and its contents. Yet it is also a site that can disappoint the visitor. Apart from the modest reconstructions of parts of the city by modern archaeologists, there is virtually nothing to be seen of the city of Amarna, especially its monumental centre. Indeed the best preserved parts of Amarna are very much on its periphery – the tombs and boundary stelae – yet these are the very structures that are some of the most useful in understanding what Amarna once looked like.

The Founding of the City

> Behold, it is Pharaoh, who found it – not being the property of a god, not being the property of a goddess, not being the property of a male ruler, not being the property of a female ruler, and not being the property of any people.
>
> from the boundary stelae at Amarna

The creation of the city of Amarna was the result of an individual royal initiative. This is not in itself unusual – many of the towns described in this book were created as part of a royal project, especially those built to service royal mortuary projects, such as the workers' town at Giza or the pyramid town at Kahun. Nor is the foundation of an entirely new city unknown in the context of ancient Egypt, although Amarna is the earliest known example of an entire city effectively being founded and built during the reign of a single king – it may be that the example of Amarna influenced the creation of Pr-Ramesses just a few decades later. The single most important reason for the foundation of Amarna, and the resultant deployment of royal resources, seems to have

been the desire of Amenhotep IV/Akhenaten to create a suitable arena for the worship of 'his' god, the solar deity Aten.

Presumably, attempts early in his reign to remodel parts of the pre-eminent royal 'religious' city – Thebes – were recognized as something of a failure within a monumental landscape that had, for the previous two centuries, been the subject of continual and intensive royal investment in buildings whose focus was the cult of the god Amun. It seems that a clean break was required

Amarna

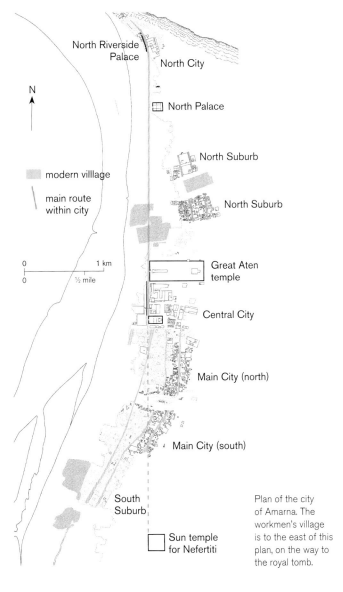

N

modern village

main route within city

0   1 km
0   ½ mile

North Riverside Palace

North City

North Palace

North Suburb

North Suburb

Great Aten temple

Central City

Main City (north)

Main City (south)

South Suburb

Sun temple for Nefertiti

Plan of the city of Amarna. The workmen's village is to the east of this plan, on the way to the royal tomb.

and a virgin spot was sought for a new city whose main inhabitants would be the Aten, the royal family, the court and a population that serviced the elite residents. The site chosen, Akhetaten, 'The Horizon of the Aten', was in Middle Egypt, roughly halfway between the two major urban centres of 18th-Dynasty Egypt, Memphis and Thebes, a naturally dramatic setting where the riverside cliffs swing away from the river to create a 'bay' 10 km (6 miles) long and 5 km (3 miles) at its widest point.

Boundary Stelae

Akhenaten was determined to prescribe the limits of Akhetaten. The physical integrity of the natural desert 'bay' at Amarna was emphasized by a series of monumental stelae, which marked the city limits. Sixteen of these stelae – carved into the face of the surrounding cliffs themselves – are known today. They were carved in the king's regnal years 5, 6 and 8 in two versions known as the 'Earlier Proclamation' and the 'Later Proclamation', right at the beginning of Akhenaten's activities at Amarna. Although the boundary stela itself was not a new concept – stelae are known marking the extent of Egypt's empire in the early 18th Dynasty, and the boundaries between different nomes during the Middle Kingdom – the idea of a ring of stelae marking the boundaries of an individual city is unique to Amarna. The stelae are useful in a number of ways.

First, they show us what Akhenaten intended to be the boundaries of the domain of the Aten at Akhetaten: the eastern stelae are carved into the desert cliffs only a few kilometres east of the central city, and use the same rock face as the elite tombs of Akhenaten's courtiers, but the western stelae are much more distant.

> Now, as for Akhetaten, starting from the southern stela of Akhetaten as far as the northern stela, measured between stela to stela on the eastern mountain of Akhetaten, it makes 6 *iteru*, 1¾ rods, 4 cubits.

> Similarly, starting from the southwestern stela of Akhetaten to the northwestern stela upon the western mountain of Akhetaten, it makes exactly 6 *iteru*, 1¾ rods, 4 cubits six *iteru* one and three-quarter rods and four cubits.

The best known of the stelae is that at the site of Tihna el-Gebel, one of the desert cemeteries of the city of el-Ashmunein (see pp. 138–39), indicating that this important ancient city of Middle Egypt and its agricultural hinterland were seen as part of a 'Greater Akhetaten', totalling 200 square km (77 sq. miles) in area.

> As to the interior of the four stelae, starting with eastern mountain of Akhetaten as far as the western mountain of Akhetaten, it is Akhetaten in its entirety. It belongs to my Father, the Aten … consisting of hills, flatlands, marshes, new lands, basin lands, fresh lands, fields, waters, towns, banks, people, herds, orchards and everything that the Aten, my father, has made and caused them to come into existence forever and ever.

Secondly, the stelae provide a commentary on the founding of the city itself. Their extensive texts, composed by Akhenaten, describe his desire to find a new site for his god, and his unwavering intention (he specifically states that he will not let anyone – even his wife Nefertiti – dissuade him from this purpose) to build a city there:

> Now, it is the Aten, my father, who advised me concerning it, namely Akhetaten. No official ever advised me concerning it, nor any of the people who are in the entire land ever advised me concerning it, to tell me a plan for making Akhetaten in this distant place. It was the Aten, my father, who advised me concerning it, so that it might be made for Him as Akhetaten.

It is a remarkable insight into Akhenaten's mindset – the relationship between king and god as the main driver in the deployment of the resources of the world's richest empire. It is ironic that Akhenaten had inherited that empire from his father Amenhotep III, a king who had done as much as any to embellish the Amun-focused landscape of Thebes.

Thirdly, and most usefully here, the Amarna boundary stelae provide an exceptional amount of detail in describing the buildings of Akhetaten itself. They can be seen as a statement of intent by Akhenaten for the creation of a new city, down to the detail of individual structures. Looking over the city itself, they are also an invitation to compare what Akhenaten says he will build

with what he actually built. It has to be said that his record in bringing this building schedule to completion is an impressive one. Selected extracts from the boundary stelae provide a sense of what were considered to be the core buildings of the new city:

I shall make the 'House of the Aten' for the Aten….

I shall make the 'Mansion of the Aten' for the Aten….

I shall make the 'Sunshade of the Great King's Wife [Nefertiti]' for the Aten….

I shall make the 'House of Rejoicing' for the Aten, my father, in the island of 'The Aten, Distinguished of Jubilees'….

I shall make the 'House of Rejoicing in Akhetaten' for the Aten, my father, in the island of 'The Aten, Distinguished of Jubilees'….

I shall make for myself the apartments of Pharaoh … and I shall make the apartments of the Great King's Wife in Akhetaten.

Let there be made for me a tomb in the eastern mountain….

Reconstruction drawing of Boundary Stela 'N', from the cliffs to the south of the city of Akhetaten (Amarna). Flanking the stela, and also cut from the desert cliffs, are statues of Akhenaten and Nefertiti with their eldest daughters, Meritaten and Meketaten.

Let the burial of the Great King's Wife Nefertiti
be made in it....

Let the burial of the King's Daughter,
Meritaten, be made in it....

Let a cemetery be made for the Mnevis Bull
in the eastern mountain of Akhetaten....

Let the tombs of the Greatest of Seers, of the
God's Fathers of the Aten and the ... of
the Aten be made in the eastern mountain
of Akhetaten....

Let the tombs of the priests(?) of the Aten
be made in the eastern mountain of
Akhetaten....

It is obvious that the 'prospectus' for the new
city carved on the boundary stelae is deeply
concerned with describing the provision that
will be made for the king, his immediate family,
the god Aten and those religious officials who
were to be involved with the cult of the Aten. It is
equally obvious that it utterly ignores the needs
of the vast majority of the population of Amarna,
people who would have been moved (possibly
unwillingly) from their homes to inhabit the
new city.

The City of the Aten

It is possible to identify most of the places
mentioned in the boundary stelae with actual
buildings at Amarna, with a good deal of
accuracy.

The 'House of the Aten' (*Per-Iten*) is the Great
Temple of the Aten, which dominated the north
part of the central city. The 'Mansion of the Aten'
(*Hwt-Iten*) is the smaller Aten temple (which has
been identified as Akhenaten's mortuary temple)
to the south of the King's House. The 'Sunshade'
(*Shwt-Ra*) of Nefertiti is not known, although
other sunshade temples for royal women are,
including the Maru-Aten (for Akhenaten's
secondary wife Kiya then his daughter Meritaten)
in the southern part of the city. The two
structures called 'House of Rejoicing' (*Per-Hay*)
are more difficult to identify, with possibilities
being parts of larger buildings such as the 'House
of the Aten' or perhaps the Great Palace itself.

The location of the 'apartments' (*Perytu*) of
Akhenaten and Nefertiti are also uncertain. They
might be the King's House and the harem area
in the Central City, but they might also refer to
the more generally accepted residences of the
King and Queen in the North Riverside Palace

Model of the *Per-Iten*,
'House of the Aten',
the main temple at
Akhetaten. The temple
building is based
on a series of pylon
gateways and open
courtyards, but the
most striking feature
are the vast rows of
small offering tables
outside the central
building.

and the North Palace. More likely, the reference
is deliberately vague, as Akhenaten's plans for his
own domestic arrangements in Year 5 were less
well formulated than those for the main religious
structures (including tombs) at the site.

The tomb of Akhenaten himself was completed
in a wadi to the east of the city, just as he says
in the boundary stelae, but no separate tomb
were completed (or at least none has yet been
discovered) for Nefertiti, Meritaten and the
Mnevis bull, although other tombs were planned
and begun in the area of the king's tomb. More
substantial are the tombs of the elite priesthood
at Amarna who, along with other high-ranking
members of Akhenaten's court, were given rock-
cut tombs high in the cliffs overlooking the city.
These tombs also have an important contribution
to make in our understanding of Akhetaten.

Tombs and the City

Superficially, the elite private tombs at
Amarna were not unlike similar tombs at
Thebes. However, their interior decoration
was significantly different. Private tombs of the
18th Dynasty at Thebes and in other regional
cemeteries had as their main decorative theme
the life-experience of the tombowner, particularly
emphasizing how his activities were so important
that they attracted the notice and favour of
the king. Similar tombs at Amarna demoted
the tombowner from main actor to spectator,
specifically a spectator of royal activity within
the physical context of Amarna itself. Wall
decoration in these tombs often consisted of
huge undivided scenes covering an entire wall,
and the major themes of this decoration were,
first, the relationship between the royal family
and the Aten, secondly the city of Akhetaten
itself and, last but certainly not least, the
tombowner himself.

Closeness to the king can be indicated here
by showing the tombowner as an observer or
a minor participant in royal activities such as
chariot-processions by Akhenaten, the royal
family being blessed by the life-giving rays of
the Aten or scenes of the arrival of foreigners to
bring tribute to Akhenaten. The very best that
the tombowner could hope for was to appear
as a tiny figure being rewarded by the king with
some piece of jewelry thrown down from the

'Window of Appearance'. Although this inability
to show himself as the dominant figure in his
tomb-paintings may have been unsatisfactory
for the tombowner, the fact that we have instead
many images of a wider urban context is very
helpful for our understanding of the appearance
of buildings at Amarna. If the boundary stelae
identify the most important structures at
Amarna, and archaeology has provided many of
their groundplans, illustrations within the elite
private tombs of Amarna give a good sense of
how these now-destroyed buildings appeared in
their heyday.

The ways in which the royal family related
to these core elements of Akhetaten – its
monumental heart – are central to these
depictions. They also include a further major
part of the city, the great royal road (the 'Sikket
es-Sultan'), which linked the main royal residence
of the North Riverside Palace to the Central City
and which served as the route of royal chariot
processions depicted on the walls of the Amarna
private tombs.

Depictions of the Great Temple of the Aten
are standard in these tombs, often in great detail.

This depiction of a
banquet comes from
the Amarna tomb of
Huy, steward of Queen
Tiye. On the right is
Tiye herself and on the
left her son Akhenaten,
Nefertiti and two of
their daughters. Huy
himself is the tiny
figure at Tiye's feet.

In the tomb of Meryre the whole of one wall is covered with a composite set of images that show the temple and the nearby King's House. Ancillary buildings include temple storerooms (and their contents), granaries, gardens, cattle in their stalls and boats on a quayside. A more detailed depiction of the harbour at Amarna is shown in the tomb of May. Perhaps the most informative rendition of the temple itself is that from the tomb of Panehesy where the individual pylon gateways, courtyards and offering-stands lead towards the central altar of the god Aten.

Although the formal agenda of these scenes is clear enough – they are a form of propaganda emphasizing the reliance that even the elite of Amarna had on the King and the Aten, manifest in the 'Horizon of the Aten' – some have an undeniable charm when the images of the city are populated by figures of its inhabitants. Perhaps the most appealing of these are the scenes of the royal harem in the tomb of Ay, where doorkeepers, servants and the women themselves are shown going about their daily business.

The Heart of the City

The buildings described in the boundary stelae and depicted in the private tombs comprise most of the elements of Akhetaten that were important to the king – the monumental heart of the Central City. This core area was organized for the convenience of the king and his god, down to such details as the bridge that crossed the royal road to allow the royal family to pass from the ceremonial venue of the Great Palace to the city apartments of the so-called King's House. Other, non-ceremonial buildings in the Central City included administrative departments, most famously the 'Office for the Correspondence of Pharaoh', which produced the 'Amarna Letters' – the filed correspondence from foreign rulers that allows us to reconstruct foreign affairs during the Amarna Period in some detail.

The Noble Villa

Houses at Amarna came in a variety of shapes and sizes. Some bear comparison with similar structures at other sites – the parallels between the workmen's villages at Deir el-Medina and at Amarna have already been discussed (pp. 86–87).

Aerial view looking westwards over the central part of the city of Akhetaten. The distinctive rectangular building in the centre left is the Small Aten Temple. The road running north–south near the cultivation is the course of the ancient royal road, and the remains of the Great Palace can be seen on the far side of the road near the trees.

Royal palaces are also found at other sites, although not in such quantity and variety at a single location as at Amarna. But the most important single contribution Amarna has made to our understanding of houses and how they were used in ancient Egypt is in its villas – the residences of the elite – which are not known from any other site. This is not to say that such residences did not exist elsewhere, because it is easy to imagine the outskirts of Memphis, Thebes or a whole range of other towns and cities having such magnificent dwellings, particularly as they are often shown on the walls of the tombs of their New Kingdom owners. Indeed we have already come across a description of such a luxurious elite villa as described in the Ramesside Papyrus Lansing (see p. 88).

But how does this vision compare to the reality of the Amarna villa? The first thing to note is that, among the Amarna villas excavated to date, there is no single blueprint for how such a structure should appear – personal choice and the dictates of expense and space give each one its own individual character. However, there are a number of elements that are common to these houses and these are listed below. They can be identified on the groundplans of two examples of Amarna villas, that belonging to General Ramose (P47.19) in the North Suburb, and that of the 'Overseer of Work' Hatiay (T34.1) in the North Suburb.

1 A short entrance stairway leading to two entrance rooms ('porter's lodge'), whose position and doorways make the person entering the house double back on themselves into…

2 A long, columned room, which might have been open on its exterior wall, allowing cool breezes to enter this (north-facing) loggia, making a pleasant shaded area. The central inner wall of this loggia has a doorway leading to…

3 The central living room. A square room, usually the largest in the house, provided with pillars, supported a roof that was probably higher than that of surrounding rooms in order to let light and air enter via clerestory windows. These rooms were often provided with limestone stands for waterjars

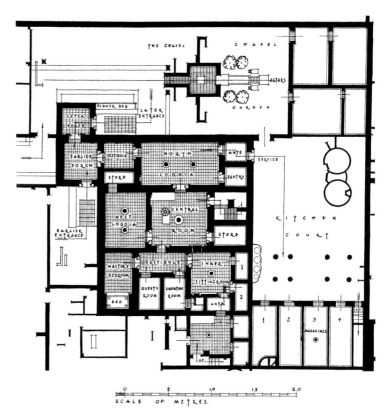

– possibly indicating washing associated with entertaining guests for dinner. The necessity of providing a water-resistant area for the splashing of water in a house primarily made of unfired mudbrick is obvious. Several rooms opened off this central room, including…

4 Relatively large living-room-like spaces whose purpose is much debated. They have been identified as an office for the householder or as a place that was specifically reserved for female members of the household. It is more likely that no single purpose was invariably assigned to such rooms, but that they were available space that could be used flexibly based on the individual demands of individual households.

5 At least one (master?) bedroom, identifiable by its private, inner location within the house, and also by its distinctive raised bed platform.

6 A bathroom, identifiable by its specific facilities, including a toilet stall and a limestone shower tray.

7 Smaller rooms, probably too small for human activity, but useful as storage areas within the main house.

Plan of the villa belonging to the Overseer of Works Hatiay. The plan is that of the original excavators, as is the identification of the function of individual rooms.

8 Stairs leading to the roof. The use of roof space is difficult to assess, given the poor state of preservation of most of these Amarna houses.

The grounds of these villas were filled with a variety of facilities. The largest villas possessed a shrine, probably for the worship of the royal family, in its own grounds, and sometimes with a separate entrance from that of the main villa. Another unsurprising element within the grounds was a garden, but one capable of growing fruit and vegetables as well as flowers. Water supply was a crucial issue, and self-sufficiency via a well was a major asset (see pp. 105–7). Further aspects of food production and storage were served by a series of domed granaries, averaging 2.5 metres (just over 8 ft) in diameter, sometimes replaced for more substantial quantities of grain by long, vaulted chambers similar to those found in the storage areas of temples of the same period. Animal sheds can be identified by their mangers and stone tethering posts, while a kitchen area was dominated by clay ovens for the baking of bread – the main staple.

The Villa in Pictures

Although we have been referring to this house type as the 'Amarna Villa', it is likely to have been a relatively common form of elite house throughout the New Kingdom. At Thebes especially there are illustrations of large houses within New Kingdom tombs and although the conventions of Egyptian art make these illustrations difficult to interpret, it is likely that they represent Amarna-style houses. The simplest of these illustrations include the house of the well-known early 18th-Dynasty architect Ineni. The image of his house from his tomb shows, in elevation, a house set within walled grounds, whose garden includes trees. Although the perimeter wall bars our view of the lower part of the house, the visible upper parts show either the high windows of a tall, single-storey residence or, perhaps more likely, the upper floor of a two-storey house.

Illustrations of large houses also appear on Amarna Period *talatat*-blocks recovered at Karnak. These blocks have been used by French Egyptologist Claude Traunecker to reconstruct the houses they depict, presumably built at Thebes early in the Amarna Period. Traunecker's reconstructions are remarkably similar to the groundplans of the Villas at Amarna, further suggesting that this was a well-known and well-used house type in New Kingdom Egypt.

More complicated is the depiction of the house of Djehutynefer from his tomb at Thebes. Although this illustration appears to be a cut-away elevation of a tall, multi-storey house, it is more likely to be the result of the creation of a composite drawing where the interior of each room is faithfully rendered, but with no attempt to give a realistic overview of the whole house. Most attempts to reconstruct the house based on a (to us) more faithful depiction of the proper relationship of individual parts of the house have produced something very Amarna Villa-like, except that the activities of each room (from the weaving sheds to the living room, via servants moving around the house) are populated with images of people going about their daily tasks.

The Suburbs

Most of the elite villas were located within two residential areas, usually referred to as the North and South 'Suburbs', although they are located much closer to the central city than the term suburbs usually implies. Together, these two areas housed up to 90 per cent of the total population of Amarna (which has been estimated to have been anything from 20,000–50,000).

This pig-pen (left) and mixing trough (right) are evidence of the reality of everyday life in the Amarna Workmen's Village.

The South Suburb was the earliest major residential area within Amarna and came to cover over 1.5 sq. km (⅔ sq. mile) and contain well in excess of 2,000 individual houses. It was not physically separate from the Central City, but merged into it. This area included workshops as well as houses, most famously that of the chief sculptor Thutmose, which was found to contain the famous bust of Nefertiti when it was excavated by the German archaeologist Ludwig Borchardt. The most notable residents here – usually identified by inscriptions on the stone doorframes of the largely mudbrick houses – include High Priests Pawah and Panehesy (whose tomb is one of those that has been excavated in the necropolis – see above), Vizier Nakht and General Ramose.

The houses in the South Suburb display what British archaeologist Ian Shaw has referred to as 'an intricate patchwork of production and consumption, involving individual families and neighbourhoods specialising in particular forms of manufacture.' However, as we have seen, the redistribution of the main food staple, grain, was carried out from large houses to small ones.

Unlike the South Suburb, the North Suburb was clearly detached from the Central City, and has the appearance of a coherent residential area. It was founded later than the South Suburb, and is significantly smaller; although it has suffered from later natural and human damage, it is likely that it contained about 600 houses. The only one of these houses that can be assigned to an important official is that belonging to the 'Overseer of Work' Hatiay. A number of scholars who have excavated at, or worked on material from, the North Suburb – including Henri Frankfort, John Pendlebury and Ian Shaw – have suggested that this district can be divided into a series of 'Quarters', each with its own distinct character. This character was originally suggested by architecturally identifiable 'clusters' of houses, but was later refined by an examination of the artifacts they contained. Examples of this characterization include the high incidence of bronze tools in the northern quarter of the North Suburb (including the house of the Overseer of Works Hatiay), leading to the suggestion that this neighbourhood specialized in woodworking. In contrast, the western side of the North Suburb produced a high number of hooks and other fish-related objects – perhaps this was a district of fishermen.

A further 'suburb' can be identified at the northern part of the Amarna bay, where the royal road leads to a cluster of structures that seem to constitute a 'royal suburb'. These buildings include the North Palace, the North Riverside Palace, the North City and the North Administrative Building. Together these make up a sort of extended royal compound that housed the royal family and those court officials who were especially close to the family.

This aerial photograph of part of the North Suburb of Amarna was taken in 1935, when some of the detail of the houses excavated by the Egypt Exploration Society between 1926 and 30 was still visible. It gives a good sense of the extent and density of housing in this part of the ancient city.

The End of Amarna

One of the many remarkable features of Amarna is the briefness of its occupation. With the death of Akhenaten in his Year 17 the 'Amarna Experiment' came to an end and the short reigns of his successors Smenkhkare and Tutankhaten/amun saw a shift back to both traditional forms of official religious orientation and more traditional sites of royal activity, especially Thebes and Memphis. The only part of Amarna that seems to have been occupied in the following Ramesside Period was the River Temple – part of a much larger building at the southern end of the site, which appears to have been the base for the workers involved in demolishing the stone buildings at Amarna so that the limestone blocks could be used elsewhere.

Other Middle Egyptian Cities

Although it is tempting to think of Amarna as being the outstanding example of an ancient city in Middle Egypt it was, of course, a very short-lived phenomenon compared with other major settlement sites in the region (see map p. 154) that had existed long before, and continued to exist long after, Amarna had been built, occupied and abandoned. Of these, the largest and most important was the city known in the Graeco-Roman Period as **Hermopolis Magna** (see pp. 137–39) and in the dynastic period as Wenu or, from the Middle Kingdom, Khmunu, perhaps referring to two separate but adjacent settlements that merged into one as they grew. Exactly when the city was first settled is not easy to say, since most of the pre-New Kingdom occupation levels are now well below ground water.

The site is impressive not only because of the size of its surviving town-mound (1.5 km, or 1 mile, from north to south; 1 km, or ⅔ mile, from east to west), but also because of the chronological spread of those remains, from a cemetery of the First Intermediate Period to remains of the late Roman Period. The town-mound has been sporadically excavated, both unofficially and officially, but the two most extensive sets of archaeological excavations were led by German Egyptologist Günther Roeder for Hildesheim Museum, between 1929 and 1939, and British Egyptologist Jeffrey Spencer for the British Museum, from 1980 to 1990.

The remains of the ancient city are almost 5 km (3 miles) from the Nile, in the middle of a wide tract of agricultural land, and connected to the Nile by canals. During the Amarna Period this rich fertile area (and Hermopolis itself) was included within the wider environs of the city of Akhetaten, as demonstrated by the presence of Amarna boundary stelae in the desert cliffs to the west of Hermopolis. By the Third Intermediate Period, the city was dominated by its sacred enclosure (bounded by a massive mudbrick wall), which contained a series of temples. The most important of these was the temple of Thoth himself, which was adapted and added to from at least as early as the Middle Kingdom (a stone gateway of Amenemhat II still survives) until the Ptolemaic Period, with especially

Above and opposite below The limestone gateway erected by Amenemhat II (above), is one of the few parts of the Middle Kingdom temple complex of the god Thoth to have survived the later remodellings of the sacred area at Hermopolis Magna, while the temple built by Seti II (opposite) made extensive use of *talatat* blocks of the Amarna Period for the construction of its pylon.

Opposite above Plan of Hermopolis Magna, showing known major structures erected up to the end of the New Kingdom.

important work done during the New Kingdom. During the Ramesside Period these additions were facilitated by using the *talatat*-blocks that became available through the demolition of the nearby Amarna temples.

Cemeteries at Hermopolis Magna

The earliest burial grounds that served the city were on the town-mound itself, as suggested by the First Intermediate Period cemetery excavated by the British Museum team. For the elite of Hermopolis and its nome, large rock-cut tombs were created in the distant east bank sites of Sheikh Said and el-Bersha, in the period from the Old to Middle Kingdoms. In the New Kingdom, the preferred burial ground switched to the closer western desert-edge site of Tuna el-Gebel; the best-known tombs from this cemetery are those belonging to the local elite of the Late Period, with their impressive superstructures built to mimic houses or temples. Other 'residents' of Hermopolis to be buried at Tihna el-Gebel are the thousands of examples of mummified baboons and ibises, sacred to Thoth, interred in vast underground catacombs.

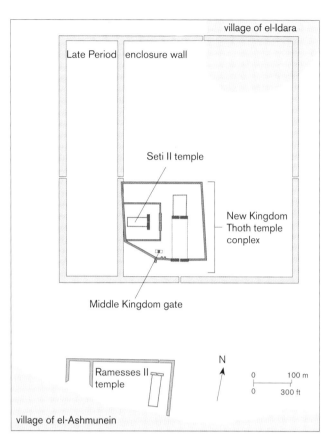

village of el-Idara

Late Period enclosure wall

Seti II temple

New Kingdom Thoth temple conplex

Middle Kingdom gate

Ramesses II temple

N

0   100 m
0   300 ft

village of el-Ashmunein

Petosiris Builds Temples for Thoth

One of the best-known examples of the way in which local leaders could initiate building work in their cities comes from the Tihna el-Gebel temple-tomb of Petosiris, High Priest of Thoth. Petosiris lived at the end of the Persian 31st Dynasty and the autobiography from his tomb outlines some of the major urban building projects he initiated, especially temples inside the sacred enclosure of the city, presumably beyond the control and/or interest of the Persian rulers of Egypt:

I stretched the cord and released the line to found the temple of Ra in the park....

I built the house of the goddesses inside the house of Khenu....

I built the house of Nehmetaway and the house of Hathor....

I made an enclosure wall around the park to prevent it being trampled by the rabble.... I made a solid work of the wall of the temple of Khenu.

Petosiris showed particular concern for the temple of Heket, which had suffered from regular flooding:

The water had carried it off every year until its foundation plan was no longer visible. It was only known by name as the 'House of Heket' since there was no brick or stone there.... I summoned the temple scribe of this goddess and gave him silver beyond counting to make a monument there from that day. I built a great rampart around it so that the water could not carry it off.

The superstructure of the tomb of the high priest Petosiris at the desert cemetery of Tihna el-Gebel is an early example of an architectural form, the columned *pronaos*, that would soon become standard in temples of the Ptolemaic Period.

Zawiyet el-Maitin

Ten km (6 miles) to the south of el-Minya is the site of **Zawiyet el-Maitin** (sometimes called Zawiyet el-Sultan). It clearly had some significance as early as the Old Kingdom because it contains one of the small 'dummy' pyramids attributed to king Sneferu of the 4th Dynasty. The site has not been systematically investigated, but a survey carried out from 1999 to 2001 by Nadine Moeller indicated that this is potentially an important multi-period town site.

Tihna el-Gebel

The town of Akoris (modern **Tihna el-Gebel**) lies 10 km (6 miles) to the north of el-Minya on the east bank of the Nile. Although it contains tombs of the Middle Kingdom, its substantial settlement remains date from the Third Intermediate Period and, especially, the Graeco-Roman Period.

el-Hibeh

In the Third Intermediate Period, the northern extent of Theban control, at least for some time, seems to have been marked by the site of **el-Hibeh**, 35 km (22 miles) south of the modern city of Beni Suef, which has been excavated since 2001 by Carol Redmount for UC Berkeley. The site was effectively a fortified settlement that took advantage of a strategic location, although its military function was supplemented by other structures including a temple of Shoshenq I in the 22nd Dynasty.

Herakleopolis Magna

Close to the entrance to the Faiyum and on the Bahr Yussef waterway, **Herakleopolis Magna** occupied an important strategic position and, as such, it became one of the largest and most significant cities in the stretch of Middle Egypt between Memphis and Hermopolis Magna. Its ancient name was (Hwt-)Nen-Neswt and its greatest time of political prominence came in the First Intermediate Period when it provided the origin, and perhaps base, of the 'kings' of the 9th and 10th Dynasties.

Although the site is mainly represented by a very large (*c.* 700 m (2,297 ft) north to south by *c.* 800 m (2,625 ft) east to west) ruin-field next to the modern village of Ihnasya el-Medina, neither its full extent (which presumably included Kom el-Aqarib, a nearby mound with a Ramesside

temple) nor basic ground plan are well understood owing to it never having been the subject of large-scale and systematic excavation. The most substantial fieldwork carried out there was by Swiss Egyptologist Éduoard Naville in 1891–92 and a Spanish team sporadically from the 1960s. The cemetery of Herakleopolis Magna was probably the nearby desert site of Sedment el-Gebel. The most striking remnants of the ancient city to be seen on the *tell* are an impressive granite gateway, probably dating to the Ptolemaic Period, and the remains of the Ramesside temple to the local ram deity Herishef, excavated by Petrie in 1904.

Itj-Tawy

The location of the Middle Kingdom administrative capital of **Itj-Tawy** (more fully Amenemhat-Itj-Tawy, 'Amenemhat seizes the Two Lands') is a mystery. It is likely, on circumstantial evidence, that it is to be found somewhere in the cultivated fields to the east of the pyramids of Amenemhat I and Senwosret I at Lisht. Since the hieroglyphic determinative sign for Itj-Tawy is a fortified enclosure rather than a town, it appears that the site was not very large in size and probably only consisted of a relatively small number of administrative staff, who worked for the royal court at this strategic location close to the traditional boundary of a newly unified Upper and Lower Egypt.

Although its temples have been much denuded of their stone – not least by early excavators at the site – the enormous blocks that remain (here from the temple of Ramesses II) clearly indicate the continuing importance of Herakleopolis Magna in the New Kingdom and later.

The Faiyum

The Faiyum basin was of great interest to the ancient Egyptians as a locality distinctly different from the Delta or Valley. It was also, by virtue of being connected to the valley by the Bahr Yussef waterway, also rather different from the oases of the Western Desert. Its most obvious geographical feature was the lake that dominated it to the north. Known today as the Birket Qarun, in the Classical Period it was called Lake Moeris and during the dynastic period She-Resy ('Southern Lake') and Mer-Wer ('Great Lake'). The local god, Sobek, appears in the Pyramid Texts as 'Sobek of Shedet', the patron deity of the principal town of the Faiyum.

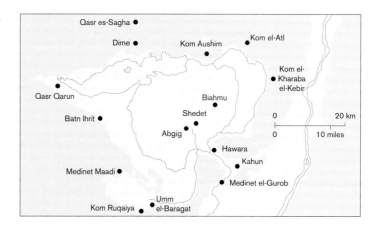

Shedet

Occupying a strategic position in the southern part of the Faiyum, **Shedet** has been the capital of the region since the Old Kingdom, although its name changed to Krokodilopolis in the Graeco-Roman Period and today it is known as Medinet el-Faiyum ('Faiyum City'). Unfortunately this longevity has not resulted in a significant body of surviving buildings, indeed the rapid growth of the city in the past century has put increasing pressure on the scant ancient remains. The most important concentration of the early settlement evidence is centred in an area of the modern city known as Kiman Fares; excavated structures have included at least one Middle Kingdom temple, but there is little for the visitor to see today.

Other Faiyum Sites

An important aspect of the history of the Faiyum was its role as the subject of a major project of royal land reclamation during the Middle Kingdom, especially the irrigation works represented by the Gadallah dam built

The Faiyum witnessed an increase in importance and royal interest during the Middle Kingdom, although much of the resultant work is now lost owing to later building and changes in the landscape. At the site of Biahmu, shown here, a pair of stone statue-bases once supported two colossal statues, which may have looked over the edge of the lake.

by Amenemhat II. Impressive traces of royal monumental activity that came on the back of this initiative, and presumably represent the expanded settlement of the Faiyum, can be seen in enigmatic structures such as the **Abgig** obelisk of Senwosret I (now re-erected on a roundabout in Medinet el-Faiyum) and the pair of colossal statues of Amenemhat III at **Biahmu**, which once perhaps overlooked a now-lost lake.

The location of the Middle Kingdom royal pyramids of Senwosret II at **Kahun** and Amenemhat III at **Hawara** – both at the mouth of the Faiyum – are also relevant here. However, our understanding of the specific nature of Middle Kingdom (and later) activities in the Faiyum has been significantly hampered by the extent to which the region was also intensively exploited during the Ptolemaic Period (see pp. 133–35), obscuring much earlier activity. The process is perhaps best exemplified at the site of **Medinet Maadi** in the southwestern Faiyum, where a small temple built for Sobek and Renenutet by Amenemhat III and IV in the Middle Kingdom has been absorbed within a much larger Ptolemaic structure; how much

of the vast Graeco-Roman town-mound around the temple conceals earlier settlement remains is unknown.

The substantial remains of significant towns of the Graeco-Roman Period are known from a number of locations in the Faiyum (see pp. 133–35 above). These are visible at **Kom Aushim** (Karanis), **Kom el-Atl** (Bacchias), **Dime** (Soknopaiou Nesos), **Umm el-Baragat** (Tebtunis), **Qasr Qarun** (Dionysias), **Batn Ihrit** (Theadelphia) and **Kom el-Kharaba el-Kebir** (Philadelphia).

Other marginal areas of the Faiyum that did not receive much attention in the Graeco-Roman Period, and thus have preserved their earlier settlement sites, are best represented by towns attached to royal projects, such as the Middle Kingdom pyramid town of **Kahun** and the quarrymen's town at **Qasr es-Sagha** (see pp. 70–71) and the New Kingdom Harem Palace at **Medinet el-Gurob** (see p. 48), while the Middle Kingdom rock-cut tombs at **Kom Ruqaiya** on the very southern edge of the Faiyum suggest that a town of that date might be found beneath the nearby settlement debris.

One of the few parts of the major town of Medinet Maadi to have been excavated is the small Middle Kingdom temple with its extensive Ptolemaic additions.

Memphis – The Shifting City

The toponym '**Memphis**' is a relatively recent one, used by Classical authors and deriving from the name of the pyramid complex of Pepi I at nearby Saqqara – Men-Nefer. In the dynastic period, Memphis was primarily referred to as Inbu-Hedj, 'White Walls'. The name of the central temple complex belonging to the god Ptah, Hwt-Ka-Ptah, was also used for the city as a whole and, when transliterated as Aigyptos by the Greeks, for the entire country.

Memphis was an important city for the whole dynastic period and well into the Ptolemaic Period – over 3,000 years – making it the longest-lasting major metropolis in the history of the world. Naturally, over such a long period, its fortunes rose and fell – in some periods, such as the Old Kingdom, it was effectively the only real city in Egypt and had a dominant role as the hub of economic and administrative life of the whole country. At other times (for instance, the Second Intermediate Period) it was marginalized.

But, as far as we can tell, it was always occupied; if its fortunes dipped they always revived, and it was probably always the largest population centre in Egypt, even when Thebes, Pr-Ramesses and Amarna were at their height.

However, there are two very significant problems in understanding the nature of Memphis over this long period. The first is in knowing where Memphis was at any given time. Apart from the late 18th Dynasty and the Ramesside Period, it is very difficult to give with any degree of certainty Memphis's location. This is because it moved, or rather parts of Memphis were abandoned and new areas created, to take account of the eastwards movement of the Nile during the dynastic period. The second problem, which is connected to the first, is that, for any given period of history, our knowledge of the extent and nature of contemporary Memphis ranges from the partial at best to unknown at worst. Unfortunately, for most of its history, Memphis is unknown.

Above A huge amount of Memphis is lost, but the area to the southwest of the Ptah temple enclosure, around Kom el-Rabi'a, still contains a number of important structures, including this 'oratory' shrine of Seti I.

Opposite A speculative plan of the major Memphite temples of the New Kingdom, produced by Ken Kitchen. It is based mainly on written sources, which provide important evidence for the location and relationship of buildings at Memphis.

The Founding of the City

The unification of Egypt and the foundation of Memphis seem to be almost contemporary events. More specifically, one seems to have been the natural consequence of the other, since a newly unified Egypt – especially if it included significant portions of the Nile Delta – would require an administrative centre that was more conveniently situated than the established Upper Egyptian power-bases of the victorious southerners at places like Hierakonpolis.

Diodorus Siculus notes that 'Uchoreus founded Memphis, the most famous city of Egypt. He chose the most favourable spot in the whole land….' His identification of the city's founder may be erroneous, but his recognition of the outstanding strategic location of Memphis (which acquired the epithet 'Balance of the Land') as a natural national capital is not. Herodotus states that 'priests informed me that it was Min, the first king of Egypt, who built the dam which created Memphis', while Manetho refers to 'Athothis, son of Menes' building a palace at Memphis. The relationship between unification and urbanization is a complex one, but the establishment of Memphis as the capital of a newly unified Egypt seems to have effectively brought to an end the urban multiplicity of important regional centres in Upper Egypt (such as Hierakonpolis and Nagada), and, we assume, Lower Egypt.

Although the specific location of Memphis as a royal centre may indeed have been a virgin site, the general area had already been recognized as offering a good number of natural advantages in terms of both agricultural potential and trading/mineral exploitation links into the eastern desert and beyond. On the east bank of the Nile the sites of Maadi at the mouth of the Wadi Digla (which may have been a major eastern trade route to Sinai, the Levant and beyond) and Helwan/Omari at the mouth of the Wadi Hof were already significant centres in the Late Predynastic Period. Indeed the enormous Early Dynastic cemetery at Helwan suggests that there may well have been an 'east bank' Memphis at this time.

Drill corings taken in the floodplain below North Saqqara/Abusir by a team led by British archaeologist David Jeffreys have revealed concentrations of Early Dynastic material close to the foot of the escarpment. It is likely that the Memphis of the 1st and 2nd Dynasties was located here, although its nature and extent are, as yet, unclear. During this time, it appears that Memphis functioned as the administrative and economic hub of the Egyptian state. Evidence for this comes from the titles of the high state officials who were buried in massive *mastaba* tombs on the desert edge at North Saqqara, although for kings of the Early Dynastic Period, burial in the ancestral necropolis at Abydos remained the traditional norm. Manetho refers to dynasties from the 3rd onwards as being 'of Memphis', reflecting the shift of royal cemetery to Memphis during the Old Kingdom proper (3rd–6th Dynasties). Remarkably, the only significant physical evidence for the existence of Memphis as the dominant metropolis of the Old Kingdom and administrative/economic hub for the entire state, is in the form of the royal cemeteries of the Old Kingdom, running along the edge of the desert to the west of Memphis from Abu Roash

Memphis

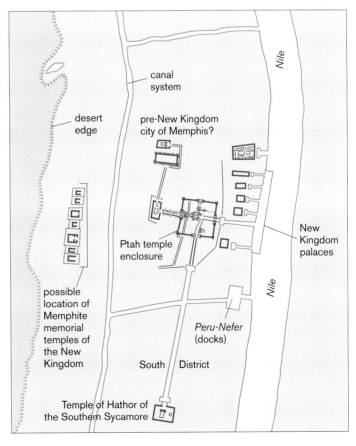

171

in the north to Dahshur in the south. Exactly which part of the Nile floodplain overlooked by these pyramids was the specific location of Old Kingdom Memphis is a problem yet to be solved.

The Archaeology of Memphis

The visible archaeological remains of Memphis today occupy an area roughly 4 km (*c.* 2½ miles) from north to south and 1.5 km (*c.* 1 mile) east to west. Most of these remains consist of fragments of elevated town-mound in and around a group of modern villages, especially Badrashein, Mit Rahina and Azziziya. The site consists of a series of mounds, identified by the descriptor *kom* (see p. 36). Although these appear as individual mounds, they were probably less distinct in the not-too-distant past, with the areas between and around them artificially 'enhanced' since the 19th century by human activities such as the digging out of *sebbakh*, brick-earth and saltpetre.

Individual Mounds in the Memphite Ruin-Field

The most prominent of the mounds in the ruin-field of Memphis, and the most significant archaeological remains they have produced, are as follows (see also plan, p. 174):

Kom el-Qal'a 19th Dynasty and later, including a palace and temple of Merenptah, a temple to Ptah and Sekhmet built by Ramesses II and a granite colossus of Ramesses II, which was moved to Cairo in 1956.

Kom el-Rabi'a monuments of the New Kingdom and later, including the 'oratory' of Seti I, small temples to Ptah and to Hathor of the Southern Sycamore built by Ramesses II, a limestone colossus of Ramesses II and tombs of the 21st and 22nd Dynasties.

Kom el-Fakhry a cemetery of the First Intermediate Period/early Middle Kingdom.

Mit Rahina rising 13 m (43 ft) above the surrounding fields, this mound is largely covered by the modern village of Mit Rahina, which means that no extensive excavation has been possible here, although fragments dated as early as the Middle Kingdom (a lintel inscribed by Amenemhat III) have been recovered; it is more than likely that parts of pre-New Kingdom stone monuments were reused in different parts of the city.

The '*Birka*' the name is the Arabic for 'lake', a designation that reflects the appearance of this large sunken depression, which is the location of the temple enclosure of the great New Kingdom Ptah Temple (see below).

The colossal statues of Ramesses II, some of which are still to be found at Memphis, are one of the the most obvious indicators of royal patronage of the temple of Ptah during the Ramesside Period.

Kom Tuman rising 20 metres (66 feet) above the surrounding plain, this is the highest part of the site, consisting of the foundations of a (probably fortified) palatial building of the Late Period, which, because of the fragments of colossal inscribed column fragments found there, has been termed 'The Palace of Apries'.

Memphis in the Middle Kingdom

On the west side of the Kom el-Rabi'a mound are the remains of a settlement site that was in almost continuous occupation from the Middle Kingdom to the Late Period, apart from the Second Intermediate Period. David Jeffreys, who has led attempts to detect and understand early Memphis, believes that this evidence suggests that the now-invisible pre-New Kingdom city of Memphis is to be found to the west of the current ruin-field, underneath the fields of the raised flood plain. This is supported by the presence of the Middle Kingdom burials at Kom el-Fakhry, which is also on the western side of the main ruin-field. It is also likely that the New Kingdom

building projects at Kom el-Qal'a and at the Birka were founded on virgin ground, reclaimed from the eastwards movement of the Nile (see plan p. 174).

Perunefer – the 'Bon Voyage'

From the reign of Thutmose III onwards, the name 'Perunefer' (which means 'a good going', or 'Bon Voyage') appears, referring to a major naval base whose main role seems to have been the servicing of the Egyptian fleet (instrumental in the conquest of Egypt's New Kingdom empire in the Levant). Although it is not universally agreed, many scholars believe that Perunefer was the port of Memphis during the 18th Dynasty, not least because much of the evidence for Perunefer comes from the titles of its officials and workers found in tombs in the Saqqara necropolis.

As well as an important military base, Memphis was an important international trading centre during the New Kingdom, with ships from the Eastern Mediterranean able to access this inland city by travelling along the major Pelusiac branch of the Nile. It is clear that New Kingdom

Recent fieldwork at Memphis includes the work of David Jeffreys for the Egypt Exploration Society, including this excavation of silos and buildings of the late Middle Kingdom/ Second Intermediate Period.

Memphis, with its influx of foreign goods, foreign religious cults and foreigners themselves, was an outstandingly cosmopolitan metropolis, what today we might call a 'world city'.

The name Perunefer disappears from our records at the end of the 18th Dynasty. This may be because the harbour became unusable owing to silting and movements of the Nile; it is probably no coincidence that the early 19th Dynasty saw the development of new building works on virgin land created by the eastward shift of the river. However, this is difficult to prove as, archaeologically, Perunefer remains undiscovered.

Memphis in the Ramesside Period I: The Ptah Enclosure

Today the most substantial visible remains of the city of Memphis are parts of buildings connected with the great New Kingdom sacred enclosure containing the temple of the god Ptah. Remarkably, the main temple itself, which must have rivalled Karnak at its height, is now lost under a forest of date-palms. However, the lower courses of a western extension to the temple –

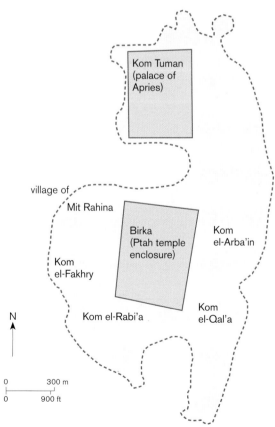

a columned hall with massive pylon gateway – which was probably built to celebrate one of the jubilees of Ramesses II – are still visible. The temple complex of Ptah was an important structure, indeed even more so than in most New Kingdom metropolitan centres, the high walls of the sacred precincts at Memphis seem to have been a real nucleus of the city. This gave rise to the development of a form of crenellated shrine that represented the outer walls of the Ptah Enclosure, sometimes decorated with ears to represent the fact that Ptah was receptive to the prayers of his worshippers.

Examples of this type of minor monument include variants that contained statues of the god Ptah (sometimes with his consort Sekhmet) or stone water-tanks. These objects were intended to symbolize the city of Memphis as home of Ptah, the Hwt-Ka-Ptah, in microcosm. Most remarkably it is used in the 'oratory' shrine of Seti I – perhaps built to celebrate the initiation of the major building works of the 19th Dynasty – which contained a statue of Ptah and two female deities, both of whom are shown nursing Seti I

as an infant. The two goddesses are Mennefer and Tjesmet – one a personification of Memphis and the other a personification of the temple wall – while in front of the chapel was a cult-model of the Memphite tower, the _tsmt_ (tjesmet) itself.

Memphis in the Ramesside Period II: The South District

Although it is difficult today to imagine Memphis as a 'real' city with areas of housing and industry around its monumental core, there is one intriguing set of documents that paint a picture of early Ramesside Memphis as having a somewhat similar character to Amarna, with its suburbs, large villas and adjacent modest houses. These texts are a series of administrative documents, written on papyrus, of unknown provenance. They date to the first three years of the reign of Seti I and document a census made of large timbers in a variety of locations in the 'South District' of Memphis (the Egyptian word translated as 'District' is _iwyt_), and also the later requisitioning of timber for state purposes. The

Opposite above
Although it is now in very poor condition, the surviving column capitals of this building at Kom el-Rabi'a identify it as a small temple dedicated to the goddess Hathor.

Opposite below
Plan of New Kingdom Memphis, showing the extent of the Ptah temple enclosure and the modern names for different parts of the ancient remains.

Below The Ramesside 'Small Ptah Temple', close to both the Hathor temple and the 'oratory' shrine of Seti I, demonstrates one of the most potent threats to stone buildings (especially of porous limestone): a high level of groundwater.

location of the 'South District' is not known with any precision, but it is likely to be somewhere in the area to the south of Kom el-Rabi'a/Kom Qal'a.

The documents refer to a dozen officials who have the title *wartu*, which we might translate as 'District Officer' – individuals who were responsible for at least some official functions in the South District. The nature of the timber census and requisitioning suggests that the District Officers were government officials with responsibility for the administration of this part of Memphis. One of the District Officers, Meryre (who is referred to as an ex-Chief Porter) is responsible for a royal granary in his district. The South District was divided into a series of smaller units, each of which was the responsibility of a named District Officer, but these sub-districts were not given independent topographical designations, but simply named after their District Officer, so any given sub-district would be called 'The South District of the District Officer X'.

The majority of the timber noted in the papyri consists of large parts of boats – masts, ribs, support-beams and planks, made of coniferous wood, averaging 4 to 5m (13 to 16 ft) in length, although one of the masts is over 17 m (56 ft) in height. It is not explained why so many houses in the South District of Memphis have bits of ships lying around in their back yards. The documents only concern themselves with locations within the South District that received deliveries of timber – 70 houses, 6 chapels and a group of royal institutions – so they only deal with a small sample of every building and institution in the South District, but they do provide some insights into the nature of this non-monumental part of Memphis.

It is difficult to use these documents to get a sense of the range of residents in the South District. As the only individuals mentioned are ones who have the status or wealth to be in possession of large and expensive pieces of timber, we would not expect to see a representative cross-section of the community mentioned in the papyri. The highest-ranking individual mentioned is the 'City-Governor and Vizier, Nebamun' (who lives in an 'abode' rather than a 'house') and the lowest perhaps the 'Citeness Huy' – though this latter mention is nonetheless notable as a reminder that, in New Kingdom Egypt, women could be in possession of both real estate and movable items of economic value.

The basis on which these people lived in these houses is unknown (was it private property or did it go with their job, especially likely for military officers?). However, it is striking how many of the individuals mentioned are military officers (standard-bearers, chariot-officers) alongside a variety of middle-ranking officials (e.g. chief builders, bureaucrats of royal estates, royal granary officials, gardeners, stablemasters, royal heralds, dock agents). Individual bits of detail provide us with a sense of a vibrant and complex district, which incorporated the presence of foreign cults (the district of the District Officer Ramose contained 'The Chapel of Qasarti in Qasarti Street', the word for 'street' being *ḫ3r*, pronounced *khar*) and the intriguing possibility of private ownership of riverside storage and trading facilities (one of the most interesting areas mentioned is the 'Wharf of the Charioteer Herynefer').

One of the best-documented districts is that overseen by Anhurmose, which contained a chapel for Amun-Re and one for Ptah, as well as houses occupied by:
– the Army-Scribe, Piay
– the Merchant Huti, son of Qatna (who is in the house of the deceased Fortress-Scribe, Mery)
– the Merchant of the Estate of Menmaatre, Menty
– the Troop-Commander of the Army, Re
– the Attendant(?), Toemhab
– the Troop-Commander of the Army, Waa
– the Chief Craftsman of the Estate of Menpehtyre, Hat
– the Chief of the Medjay, Amenwahsu
– the Troop-Commander of Kush, Khay
– the Transport-Ship Crewman of the Estate of Seti I, Aia, son of Inena
– the Standard-Bearer of the Ship 'Khaemope', Paser
– the Priest of the Temple of Maat, Merymaat
– the Deputy of the Settlement, Ramose.

An analysis of this data has been carried out by British Egyptologist Kenneth Kitchen; he has produced a (speculative) reconstruction map showing the divisions of the South District.

Memphis in the Graeco-Roman Period

Even after the foundation of Alexandria and its rapid rise to prominence as the dominant city of Egypt in the Graeco-Roman Period, Memphis retained some of its importance. Part of this was due to its continuing importance as an economic and population centre, but also as a city that embodied traditional notions of Egyptian culture – for instance, Ptolemaic kings were crowned there. It appears that enough of the Graeco-Roman city of Memphis city remained occupied, or at least visible, in order for it to be described by Classical authors including Herodotus, Strabo and Diodorus Siculus.

However, the importance of Memphis as a national administrative centre during the Ptolemaic Period lessened under the Romans. More decisive in its decline was the foundation of the garrison-town of Fustat on the east bank of the Nile after the Muslim invasion. The northern expansion of this town to create the city of al-Qahira (Cairo) brought into being one of the great cultural and political centres of the Middle Ages. It is still the capital city today, but its development has been disastrous for Memphis, which was soon abandoned and lost beneath the series of villages that grew upon its ruins.

Heliopolis – City of the Sun

All that is to be seen now of the *in situ* remains of the ancient city of Iunu, **Heliopolis** (also known today as Tell Hisn), is a single shaft of granite, an obelisk erected in the Middle Kingdom by Senwosret I to embellish what was one of the largest and most important religious structures of ancient Egypt, the solar temple of Re-Atum. Part of the reason is the location of Heliopolis, now absorbed within the expanding city of Cairo itself, and part is the lack of systematic archaeological fieldwork when more of the site remained to be excavated.

The work that has been done, both to recover fragments of temple buildings and the statuary placed within them and to study texts that mention the city, has largely been concerned with trying to understand the layout of the temple enclosure – which seems to have been the largest in Egypt, larger even than Karnak – at different periods. This is especially the case for the Old Kingdom, when Heliopolis was clearly Egypt's predominant religious institution, but exactly what that means in terms of the functions of a city beyond this religious role (how many people lived there, and where?) remains a mystery, owing to the lack of surviving evidence, apart from that of some cemeteries from the Old Kingdom to the Late Period in the area to the east of the temple.

Heliopolis

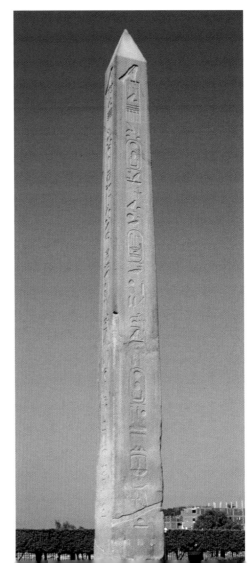

The still-standing obelisk of Senwosret I is a remarkable Middle Kingdom survival at Heliopolis, one of ancient Egypt's largest temples of which astonishingly little now remains.

The Memphite Region

Although Memphis was probably the most
populous city in Egypt throughout the dynastic
period, and Heliopolis a significant religious
centre for a similar period, these were far from
being the only towns or cities in the Memphite
region, especially during the Old Kingdom. To
us it appears that royal pyramid building was
the central activity of the state, especially during
the 4th Dynasty when the building activities
of Sneferu, Khufu and Khafre required huge
resources to build their monumental tombs. A
large proportion of those resources was human
labour, and so the housing of a relatively small
number of specialist craftsmen and a much larger
pool of unskilled manual labourers was one of
the great logistical feats in pyramid building.

Archaeologists have identified 'pyramid
towns' associated with a number of Old and
Middle Kingdom pyramids. The best known of
these is **Kahun** (see pp. 64–68), associated with
the pyramid of Senwosret II, which housed a
permanent community whose major function
was to ensure the continued operation of cult
ceremonies at the pyramid. Towns that housed
similar communities are known from other

pyramid sites such as **Dahshur**, or the priestly
community that came to occupy the valley
temple of the pyramid of Menkaure at **Giza**.
These 'priest's towns' are rather different from
the short-term accommodation required for
the workers who toiled on the construction of
the pyramid complex itself. Workers would be
conscripted as corvée labourers – people who
paid tax obligations through manual labour
– brought to the pyramid site from all over
Egypt to work for a given period of time on
this national project. These people needed to
be both housed and fed by the state.

Below Reconstruction
plan, based on Mark
Lehner's excavations
of the Giza Pyramid
Town, showing the
different areas of the
site excavated to date,
and the relationship
of the town to the
pyramids of Khafre
(left) and Khufu (right).

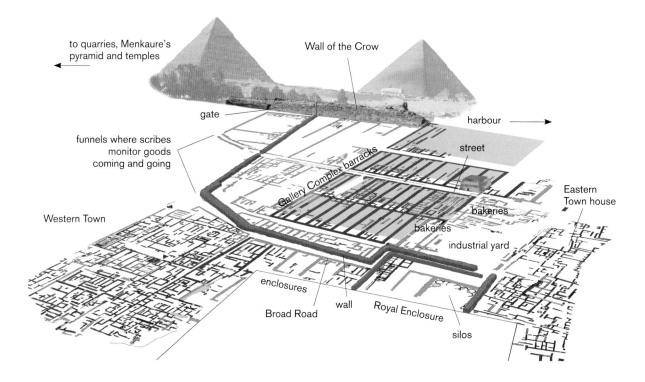

The Giza Pyramid Town

The best known, and apparently by far the most substantial, of these towns for pyramid workers is at **Giza**, just off the plateau itself, *c.* 400 metres (*c.* 1,300 feet) east of the valley temple of Menkaure. The town was separated from the monumental area of the pyramid complexes of Khufu, Khafre and Menkaure by a massive wall (200 metres long by 10 metres thick and 10 metres in height; 656 by 33 by 33 feet), known popularly today as the 'Wall of the Crow' (Heit el-Ghurab). The site has been excavated by American Egyptologist Mark Lehner since 1988, and the work of his multi-disciplinary team has produced many important insights into the logistics of housing a large pyramid-building workforce.

The northern district of the town was dominated by a series of long, narrow mudbrick galleries, organized into four 'sets', separated by streets, together covering an area of 150 by 75 metres (492 by 246 feet). Each 'set' contained eight galleries, which were usually 34.5 metres long by 4.7 metres wide (113 by 15½ feet). The centre of each gallery had a raised central 'bench'

into which were set column-bases for roof-supporting columns, while along both sides of this 'bench' were sleeping platforms, making these galleries substantial dormitories, which could house somewhere between 40 and 80 men, depending on whether the galleries contained a second storey, which may be suggested by the thickness of their walls. The total population of this huge dormitory block might therefore have been between 1,500 and 3,200 temporary labourers. Evidence suggests that baking took place in and around these dormitory blocks and, more surprisingly, the consumption of significant quantities of meat from sheep or goats and cattle.

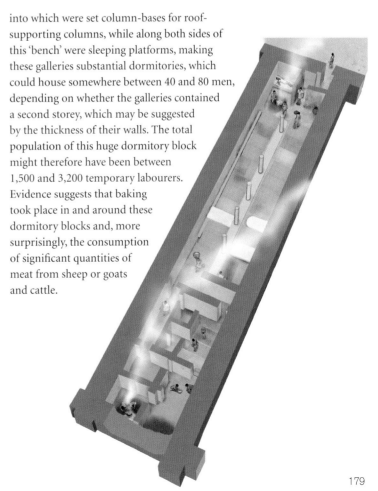

The town included a structure that the excavators have called the Royal Administrative Building, mainly on the basis of large numbers of mud sealings stamped with the names of Khafre and Menkaure. Since this structure contained a series of large grain silos it seems likely that this was a central depot for the distribution of food staples to the workmen. It has also been suggested that this building represents part of a significant royal administrative centre for Egypt as a whole during the 4th Dynasty, and that the dormitories contained not labourers, but a royal guards' regiment. The town, as excavated to date, also contained two other major areas. The 'Eastern Town' was largely made up of small residential units, which may have housed a permanent population of modest means, rather different from the temporary workers housed in the dormitories of the gallery area. The 'Western Town' contained some larger houses, which may have been occupied by higher-ranking individuals and their families, somewhat like the 'urban estates' at Kahun.

The Giza Pyramid Town seems to have been abandoned after the reign of Menkaure because the major focus for royal pyramid construction moved away from Giza to other sites, especially Abusir and Saqqara in the 5th and 6th Dynasties.

Above and left
One of the exciting aspects of the work at the Giza Pyramid Town has been the discovery of archaeological material relating to storage and food production, even though the function of some of these is still obscure, such as the 'Pedestal Building' (above) in the northern part of the Western Town. A distinctive, cone-shaped loaf, known by the Egyptians as 'bedja', was an important staple of the workers' diet, produced using large thick-walled moulds (left) in specialized bakeries.

The Delta

It is in the Nile Delta that the contrast between what we know of great ancient cities and the meagreness of the surviving remains is the most striking. Although the Delta contains some of the richest and most fertile land of ancient (and modern) Egypt, the very flatness of its green landscape gives a clue as to why its dynastic settlements have rarely survived: the vulnerability of low-lying land to the annual inundation of the Nile and the pressure on ancient sites by the demands of an increasingly large modern population mean that the ancient sites of the Nile Delta suffer the same pressures as the rest of Egypt, but to an even more significant degree. More positively, cities in the Delta are better documented by our classical sources, especially Herodotus (who claims to have visited Sais, Bubastis, Buto, Papremis and Pelusium), but this is small compensation for the severely degraded state of almost all major settlements in the Delta.

Of the dozen modern cities in Egypt that have an estimated population in excess of 300,000, the largest by far is Greater Cairo (*c.* 12 million) followed by Alexandria (4.25 million). Of the rest, three (Ismailiya, Port Said and Suez) have grown in association with the Suez Canal, two (Luxor and Asyut) are in Upper Egypt and one (Faiyum City) is in the Faiyum. The remaining four are in the Nile Delta – Mansura (*c.* 470,000), Mahalla al-Kubra (*c.* 450,000), Tanta (*c.* 430,000) and Zagazig (*c.* 320,000). The relative anonymity of these impressively large Delta cities even to Western visitors who claim to know Egypt well, is probably paralleled by the potential importance of little-known ancient cities in the Delta when compared with their monument-rich contemporaries in the south of Egypt.

The settlement of the Nile Delta has its own specific peculiarities that make it distinctly dissimilar from the Nile Valley. The most immediate difference is that, unlike in the Valley, the way sites relate to each other is more complex, in contrast with the largely linear distribution of sites in the Valley where they are either east or west of the river. The reason for this is that some 25–40 km (15–25 miles) north of Memphis, the Nile split into three major branches (Rosetta,

Damietta and Pelusiac), which along with a fourth that came off the Rosetta branch (named Canopic) and countless subsidiary waterways, formed the Delta. Like the river all the way up the Nile Valley of Upper Egypt, the Delta branches continually gradually moved and shifted in their courses. As a result, the distribution of nome boundaries is more complex and more fluid.

The significant distance from the desert for many Delta sites has important repercussions – unlike in the Valley, the desert edge is not the most obvious and convenient choice for burials, nor a convenient source of building stone. The location of cemeteries and the extent of reuse of stone therefore differ somewhat in the Delta and the Valley. In addition, the Delta saw the intensive use of *gezira*s (sometimes called 'turtlebacks') – naturally deposited sand islands found in parts of the Nile Delta – as prized locations for both cemeteries and settlement, since they often stood well above the waters of the inundation even at the height of the flood.

Nonetheless, despite the less-clear pattern of settlement in the Delta compared with the Valley, the major Nile branches dictated the

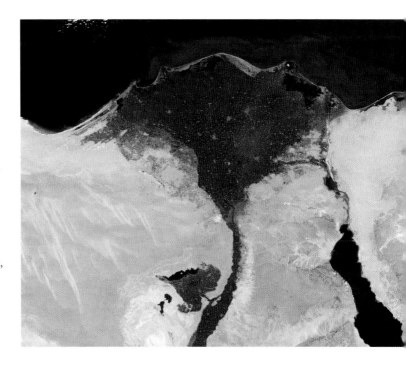

Satellite view of the Nile Delta, the Faiyum, and the northern part of the Nile Valley around Memphis and Herakleopolis Magna. The darker 'blobs' within the Delta are major modern cities.

key relationships between sites. The location of settlements in the Delta is closely linked to the position of the Nile branches, but the continuous movement of these branches over the millennia of major human settlement in the Delta creates a complicated picture of settlement distribution, which is difficult to unpick. The problem of a Nile that 'wanders' across its flood plain in the Valley (e.g. at Memphis) is much greater in the Delta where there are both multiple branches rather than a single stream, and no natural limits (apart from at its eastern and western borders) on a par with the constraining cliffs of southern Egypt.

It is clear from both ancient written accounts and modern archaeological work, which has attempted to locate ancient Nile streams through deep-core borings, that the location and even the number of Nile branches varied considerably over the period from the Predynastic to the present day. In addition, attempts to control all minor, and some major, Nile branches by turning them into canals (e.g. the ancient Pelusiac branch, which is now the el-Ibrahimiya Canal) has created a situation in which, from about

Pliny the Elder Describes the Branches of the Nile in the Delta

There are also, in the latter part of the course of the Nile, many towns of considerable celebrity, and more especially those which have given their names to the mouths of the river – I do not mean, all the mouths, for there are no less than twelve of them, as well as four others, which the people call the False Mouths. I allude to the seven more famous ones, the Canopic Mouth, next to Alexandria, those of Bolbitine, Sebennys, Phatnis, Mendes, Tanis and, last of all, Pelusium. Besides the above there are the towns of Butos, Pharbæthos, Leontopolis, Athribis, the town of Isis, Busiris, Cynopolis, Aphrodites, Sais and Naucratis, from which last some writers call that the Naucratic Mouth, which is by others called the Heracleotic, and mention it instead of the Canopic Mouth, which is the one next to it.

Pliny the Elder, *Natural History* 5.11

AD 900 onwards, there have been only two major 'natural' Nile branches in the Delta: they enter the Mediterranean at the modern cities of Rashid (this is the Rosetta branch) and Dumyat (this is the Damietta).

Cities of the Canopic Branch

The greatest city connected to the most western branch of the Nile in the Delta, the Canopic, was, of course, Alexandria (see pp. 127–33). However, even before the arrival of Alexander the Great, this waterway (which split off and travelled northwest from the Rosetta branch about half way along its course) was important as a major interface between cultivation and desert, or what was Egypt and what was not, during the dynastic period and before. As with elsewhere in the Delta, many ancient settlements have disappeared or are difficult to locate beneath agricultural or urban spread, such as the modern city of Damanhur whose current name suggests its ancient equivalent (Demi-n-Hor – 'Town of Horus').

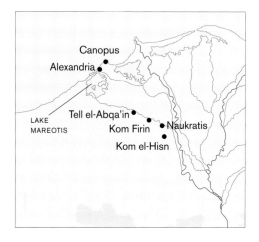

Kom el-Hisn

The ancient city of Imau has a sequence of occupation unequalled in the dynastic period

apart from by Sais. It has been the subject of fieldwork by several explorers, including Francis Ll. Griffith between 1885 and 1887, Mustafa el-Amir, Shafik Farid and Abdel Hamada in 1943–49, Robert Wenke in 1983–89 and

Cattle in the Delta

Excavations carried out at Kom el-Hisn by Robert Wenke for the University of Washington in the 1980s produced a wealth of faunal and botanical remains in settlement levels of domestic activity that have been dated to the late Old Kingdom. Much of this evidence – the bones of fish, fowl, sheep, goats and pigs – suggests a diet whose main protein component came from a mixture of hunting and domestication.

However, one additional intriguing discovery was that of substantial amounts of cattle dung, but very few cattle bones. This has led to the suggestion that Kom el-Hisn had a specialized function in the later part of the Old Kingdom, that of producing cattle that were transported to other parts of Egypt – perhaps Memphis – for consumption.

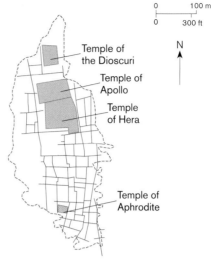

This plan of Naukratis, based on Petrie's excavations at the site, shows the two aspects of the town, with the traditional Egyptian temple enclosure to the south and the settlement containing several Greek temples to the north.

Christopher Kirby in the 1990s. Today the site is a low but extensive mound whose most distinctive feature is the rectangular temple enclosure. This temple, dedicated to the patron goddess of Imau, Sekhmet-Hathor, benefited from royal patronage, including a series of statues of Ramesses II and one of Amenemhat III.

The latter statue suggests Middle Kingdom activity at the site, which has been confirmed by the significant amounts of pottery of that date recovered by Kirby's survey. Unusually for the Delta, Kom el-Hisn has preserved a large cemetery dating from the First Intermediate Period to the New Kingdom, including a large decorated tomb for the 'Priest of Hathor, Overseer of Priests and Overseer of the Harim' Khesuwer.

Naukratis

One of the most strikingly individual towns founded on the ancient course of the Canopic branch was **Naukratis**, now represented by settlement mounds that have been heavily denuded by *sebbakh*-diggers, around the modern villages of Kom Ge'if, el-Nibeira and el-Nikrash. The name of the site derives from the Egyptian Niwt Keredj, the 'Town of the Carians', which indicates its role as a town with a distinct and

deliberately Greek character. The location of Naukratis made it an obvious port-town, with riverine links between Memphis and the sea, yet in reasonably close proximity to Sais (which was northeast from Naukratis on the nearby Rosetta branch). This strategic position was presumably the reason that it was chosen in the 7th century BC to be the home of a major Greek military and trading colony, as noted by Herodotus (see box overleaf).

Naukratis was first explored between 1884 and 1903 by Flinders Petrie, followed by Ernest Gardner and then David Hogarth. From 1977 to 1983 it was the focus of the 'Naukratis Project' led by William Coulson and Albert Leonard. The excavations at the site have largely confirmed Naukratis' role as an emporium that looked to the Greek world. In the northern part of the site, Petrie and his successors excavated the fragmentary remains of five Greek temples (to Apollo, Hera, Aphrodite and the Dioscuri, and the 'Hellenion'), as well as zones for manufacturing objects including scarabs, pottery, faience and – perhaps most interestingly – iron weapons, which were unknown in the rest of Egypt at this time.

The southern part of the town was dominated by the 'Great Temenos', a rectangular mudbrick enclosure 260 by 226 m (853 by 741 ft) that was either built or restored by Ptolemy II. In the northern part of the Temenos was an Egyptian temple to Amun, while the southern part of the Temenos was dominated by an enormous mudbrick platform, each side 55 m (180 ft) long; the function of this platform remains a matter of controversy.

Kom Firin

The principal excavations at this important site, whose ancient name is not known, were directed by Neal Spencer for the British Museum in 2002–10. *Sebbakh*-digging at **Kom Firin** has resulted in the creation of the most distinctive feature of the site: a series of artificial 'pedestals', some over 10 m (33 ft) tall, especially in the southeast corner of the site. The eastern part of the current *kom* is the one that is easiest to understand, based on Spencer's work. It consisted of a large (225 by 199 m, 739 by 653 ft) rectangular enclosure within which was a Ramesside temple. The massive size of the enclosure was probably deliberate, since, like Tell el-Abqa'in (see below),

The Establishment of Naukratis as an International Port

Amasis favoured the Greeks and granted them a number of privileges, of which the chief was the gift of Naukratis as a commercial headquarters for any who wished to settle in the country....

In the old days Naukratis was the only trading port in Egypt, and anyone who brought a ship into the other mouths of the Nile was bound to state on oath that he did so of necessity and then proceed to the Canopic mouth; should contrary winds prevent him from doing so, he had to carry his freight to Naukratis in barges all round the Delta, which shows the exclusive privilege the port enjoyed.

Herodotus II, 178–79

Kom Firin was established as a fortress-town to defend Egypt's western border from Libyan incursions during the late New Kingdom.

In the Late Period, the town, which had been based on the old Ramesside enclosure, seems to have been remodelled, with a new enclosure wall surrounding an area four times larger than that of the New Kingdom.

The cemetery of Kom Firin appears to have been located at the nearby site of Silvagou from the Middle Kingdom onwards, although no settlement remains as early as this have yet been found at Kom Firin itself.

The oddly shaped mudbrick 'pinnacles' at Kom Firin are the result of the long-term actions of the weather and *sebbakh*-diggers on the enclosure wall and major buildings at the site.

Tell el-Abqa'in

Tell el-Abqa'in consists of two substantial, adjacent mounds separated by a modern road, the smaller of these mounds being covered by a cemetery serving local villages. The larger mound was first examined by Georges Daressy in 1903. In 1941 it was excavated by Labib Habachi and since 1996 by Susanna Thomas for the University of Liverpool. Work carried out to date suggests that Tell el-Abqa'in was an important fortified settlement on the western fringes of the Delta.

As with Kom Firin, there is no evidence to suggest that the site existed before the reign of Ramesses II, although that king is very well attested at Tell el-Abqa'in through a variety of inscribed architectural elements and, most notably, a group of at least four wells in the southeast corner of the site, within a massive mudbrick enclosure wall. The western wall of that enclosure has largely been removed by *sebbakh*-diggers, creating an enormous trench whose eastern face suggests a complex internal stratigraphy for the site.

Cities of the Rosetta Branch

Most of the sites along the Rosetta Branch have not survived as well in the archaeological record as the desert-edge or near desert-edge sites of the Canopic branch to the west, or the Pelusiac branch to the east. Important ancient cities such as **Xois** (modern Sakha) have all but disappeared owing to a combination of natural erosion and human action, although there are some exceptions such as the remarkable mound of **Tell Mutubis** (ancient name unknown), which appears to be the remains of a significant settlement of the Late and Graeco-Roman Periods.

To the east of the Rosetta branch there are also the substantial remains of **Buto** (known in ancient times as Per-Wadjet (House of the Goddess Wadjet), modern Tell Fara'in). The visible remains of this long-lived city comprise three major mounds, one of which mainly consists of the temple enclosure. Archaeological work at the site between 1965 and 1967 by Veronica Seton-Williams and Dorothy Charlesworth for the Egypt Exploration Society concentrated on the Late Period and Graeco-Roman remains, while the work of the German Archaeological Institute led by Thomas von der Way has, since 1983, focused on developing an understanding of the Predynastic and Early Dynastic settlement.

However, the southern part of the Rosetta Branch does run close to the current desert edge, allowing some level of survival to sites such as **Merimde** (see p. 25 above) and **Kom Abu Billou**,

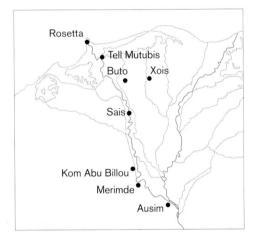

the Classical town of Terenuthis, whose Ptolemaic temple enclosure is in too poor a condition to encourage archaeological exploration, in contrast with its long-lived cemetery, which has produced burials as early as the 6th Dynasty and as late as the early Christian Period. Further south still, the town of **Ausim** (Egyptian Khem, Classical Letopolis), capital of the 2nd Nome of Lower Egypt, is known from textual sources to have existed as early as the Old Kingdom, but is an archaeological void, apart from a few architectural elements from the Late Period.

Sais

The ancient city of Sa, which was called **Sais** by Classical authors, has its name preserved in the modern toponym Sa el-Hagar ('Sa of the Stone').

It was capital of the 5th Lower Egyptian Nome, but is best known as being the royal capital of the 26th Dynasty (Saite) kings of a reunified Egypt, when it benefited from large-scale royal patronage, especially in the temple precinct of its patron goddess, Neith.

Description of the Site

Partly because of the remarkably poor state of preservation of its remains, relatively little systematic archaeological work has been carried out at Sais, with the exception of the programme of fieldwork under Penny Wilson since 1997.

Today the site falls into two distinct areas. To the south, fringed by the modern village of Sa el-Hagar, is a large depression, *c.* 400 by 400 m (1,312 by 1,312 ft), often referred to as the 'Great Pit'. This was created by a combination of *sebbakh*-digging, and digging for antiquities, and is now usually filled with water. To the north are the remains of a huge rectangular enclosure, 800 by 700 m (2,625 by 2,297 ft), whose massive mudbrick walls were visible to 19th-century visitors including Jean-François Champollion (who regarded it as the precincts of the Neith temple), Karl Richard Lepsius'

Prussian expedition and, in 1898, Antiquities Inspector Georges Foucart who did much to record the then current condition of many Delta sites. During the early 20th century, the intensive activities of *sebbakh*-diggers effectively removed these walls, although they can still be traced by following a track that runs on top of their ground-level courses on three of the four sides of the enclosure. Wilson believes that, during the Late Period, these two areas formed two distinct, massive rectangular enclosures, linked by a *dromos* or processional way (see plan opposite).

Sais before the Late Period

The association between the goddess Neith and Sais is an ancient one (a wooden label from the tomb of the 1st Dynasty king Aha shows the monarch visiting the Lower Egyptian towns or, rather, Neith's temples at Buto and Sais). Sais is depicted as a simple enclosure containing the totem of the goddess. The appearance of 'Neith' as part of the names of several royal women of the 1st Dynasty have led scholars to speculate that this was an aspect of dynastic marriage between the new rulers of a now-unified Egypt whose origins were at Hierakonpolis in Upper

Above Recent excavations at Sais have begun to explore the possibilities of urban archaeology at this superficially unpromising site.

Opposite Plan of Sais (above), showing the main visible areas of the site and a tentative reconstruction of how they might have been connected during the 26th Dynasty, and (below) a view of the 'Great Pit' surrounded by scattered fragments of ancient masonry.

Egypt (whose patron deity was Horus) and
female members of the most important of the
Predynastic Delta cities, Sais. It is certainly the
case that – along with Buto – Sais was regarded
by Egyptians of later periods as one of the most
ancient cities of Egypt.

Despite this reference to Sais as an important
cult centre at the very beginning of Egyptian
dynastic history, the archaeological evidence
for Sais during the following two millennia is
astonishingly meagre, although deep-coring by
Penny Wilson's team has produced evidence of
occupation during the Maadi/Omari Neolithic
phase and a relatively extensive Ramesside
settlement.

Sais in the Late Period

The emergence of Sais as a politically important
centre of the late Third Intermediate Period, as
the base of the short-lived 24th Dynasty and then
the Egypt-unifying 26th Dynasty, gave Sais a
hitherto unprecedented importance as a city that
was de facto capital of Egypt. Naturally enough,
a major royal city needed to have a major
monumental core. The form and extent of the
New Kingdom temple of Neith (for there surely
must have been one) is completely unknown:
it must have been entirely subsumed within or,
more likely, replaced by the building activities of
26th Dynasty kings, perhaps especially Amasis.

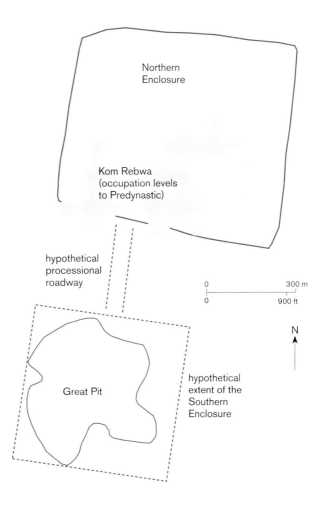

Wadjhorresnet Describes Sais in c. 520 BC

One of the most famous of the relocated monuments from Sais is a private statue of the Chief Physician, Wadjhorresnet. It is now in the Vatican Museums, probably having come from the collection of Egyptian monuments assembled by the emperor Hadrian at his villa in Tivoli. Wadjhorresnet describes his activities as a major Egyptian official serving Cambyses, Persian conqueror of Egypt and first king of the 27th Dynasty. Despite this foreign rule, Wadjhorresnet is keen to emphasize the way he used his influence with Cambyses for the benefit of Egypt in general and the city of Sais in particular, as the following extracts from the autobiographical inscription on his statue demonstrate:

An offering that the king gives to Osiris-Hemag ... for the ka of the one honoured by the gods of Sais, Chief Physician, Wadjhorresnet....

The Great Chief of all foreign lands Cambyses came to Egypt.... His Majesty assigned to me the office of Chief Physician. He made me live at his side as companion and administrator of the palace ....

I let His Majesty know the greatness of Sais, that it is the seat of Neith-the-Great ... and the greatness of the temple of Neith ... and the nature of the greatness of the castles of Neith and of all the gods and goddesses who are there; and the nature of the greatness of the Palace, that it is the seat of the Sovereign, the Lord of Heaven; and the nature of the greatness of the Res-Neith and Meh-Neith sanctuaries; and of the House of Re and the House of Atum....

I made a petition to ... Cambyses about all the foreigners who dwelled in the temple of Neith, in order to have them expelled from it, so as to let the temple of Neith be in all its splendour, as it had been before. His Majesty commanded to expel the foreigners who dwelled in the temple of Neith, to demolish all their houses and all their unclean things that were in this temple....

Cambyses came to Sais. His Majesty went in person to the temple of Neith ... he made a great offering of every good thing to Neith-the-Great.... His Majesty did this because I had let His Majesty know the greatness of Her Majesty Neith, that she is the mother of Re himself.

The statue of Wadjhorresnet, bearing a votive figure of the god Osiris in a shrine. His long robe is covered in the hieroglyphic texts describing his activities. The head is a reconstruction.

With the subsequent disappearance of these monuments, attempts to reconstruct the layout of Late Period Sais – including the identification of the forms and relationships of its principal buildings – have had to be based on references to those buildings in texts that come from the site. Remarkably, none of these texts has been recovered from Sais itself, but from relocated and reused monuments that were once set up at Sais. The evidence from these suggests that an enormous temple enclosure was created for the temple of Neith (note that the Late Period kings did not feel the need to copy their Third Intermediate Period predecessors at Tanis and other sites in the Nile Delta by creating a 'Thebes of the North' based around a temple complex for Amun), but this complex nevertheless also contained temples and shrines for other deities, most notably a local form of Osiris (Osiris-Hemag), who seems to have been provided with a tomb. There were also royal tombs for kings of the 26th Dynasty, a tradition following the precedent of burial within a temple precinct in the Nile Delta that had been started at Tanis and Leontopolis, and would be continued at Mendes.

The Dispersal of Sais

Once Sais was abandoned as a royal capital, its statues, obelisks and the very fabric of the monumental stone buildings themselves effectively became available for more active building projects, which required suitable monumental embellishment. Just as a significant portion of the Ramesside monuments of Pr-Ramesses had flowed downstream along the Pelusiac branch of the Nile to come to rest in Tanis during the Third Intermediate Period (see box p. 209), so the choicest antiquities of Late Period Sais could easily be transported down the Damietta/Canopic branches of the Nile to add to the necessary pharaonic ambience of Alexandria. In fact, largely unlike Tanis, Alexandria was not a final destination for many of these transplanted and rejuvenated antiquities: instead many went much further afield, becoming part of the collection of Roman emperors who used Egyptian artifacts to decorate both Rome and Constantinople, and indeed their own private collections. The most famous was that of the Egyptophile emperor Hadrian, whose extensive gardens at his villa in Tivoli were embellished with imported Egyptian artifacts, probably including the important statue of Wadjhorresnet from Sais (see box opposite). Statuary from Sais has turned up, or is now contained, in collections ancient and modern from locations as disparate as the islands of Delos and Cuba.

Although little remains to be seen of the once-magnificent temple buildings at Sais, stone fragments of its monumental past – shrines, sarcophagi, pieces of colossal statues – still litter its surface.

Herodotus Describes Sais in c. 450 BC

… in the temple of Athene [i.e. Neith], very near to the sanctuary, on the left of the entrance. The people of Sais buried within the temple precinct all kings who were natives of their province. The tomb of Amasis is further from the sanctuary than the tomb of Apries and his ancestors, yet it is also within the temple court; it is a great colonnade of stone, richly adorned, the pillars whereof are wrought in the form of palm trees. In this colonnade are two portals, and the place where the coffin lies is within their doors.

There is also at Sais the burial-place of him whose name I deem it forbidden to utter in speaking of such a matter [presumably the tomb of Osiris-Hemag]; it is in the temple of Athene, behind and close to the whole length of the wall of the shrine. Moreover, great stone obelisks stand in the precinct, and there is a lake hard by, adorned with a stone margin and well worked on all sides, circular in shape.

Amasis made a marvellous outer court for Athene at Sais, surpassing in height and grandeur, and in the size and splendour of the stones, all who had erected such buildings; moreover he set up huge images and vast man-headed sphinxes, and brought enormous blocks of stone for the building. Some of these he brought from the stone quarries of Memphis; those of greatest size came from the city of Elephantine, distant twenty days' journey by river from Sais. But let me now tell you of what I hold the most marvellous of all his works. He brought from Elephantine a shrine made of one block of stone; three years it was in the bringing, and two thousand men were charged with the carriage of it, pilots all of them. This chamber measures in outer length 21 cubits, in breadth 14, in height 8.

The shrine described by Herodotus (II: 169–70, 175), over 9 m (30 ft) in height, has not been found, but one might compare the still-standing granite *naos*-shrine, over 6 m (20 ft) tall, erected by the same king at Mendes.

Cities of the Damietta Branch

Today, one of the two remaining major branches of the Nile in the Delta, the Damietta (and its offshoots, notably the Mendesian branch serving ancient Mendes) provided the necessary preconditions for the growth of some of the most important cities of Lower Egypt, although some of these significant urban centres, such as Hermopolis Parva, have either not survived at all or do so in a very badly degraded condition.

Athribis

Strategically located in the centre of the southern apex of the Delta, **Athribis** (modern Tell Atrib, ancient Hwt-Ta-Hery-Ib), was well placed to become an important city, and is known to have existed as early as the reign of Sneferu in the 4th Dynasty. Unfortunately those same strategic advantages also apply to the modern city of Benha, which, in its rapid modern expansion, has largely consumed the remains of the ancient city – though at the beginning of the 19th century they covered an area of 1,900 by 1,500 m (6,234 by 4,921 ft). Despite its size, the mound of Tell Atrib did not attract significant archaeological activity until 1956–98 when it became the subject of a major project by the Polish Centre of Mediterranean Archaeology and University of Warsaw.

Much of the work of the Polish archaeologists concentrated on the relatively well-preserved Late Period and Ptolemaic occupation levels at 'Kom A' and Kom Sidi Yussef. It is only these late phases of occupation at Athribis that can be traced in detail, although the site has produced a significant quantity of statuary and architectural elements suggesting that Athribis had an impressive monumental core for much of its history, not least in the late 18th Dynasty when it benefited from the activities of Amenhotep son of Hapu, chief architect of Amenhotep III.

Tell Muqdam

Like Athribis, **Tell Muqdam** (ancient Ta-Remu, Classical Leontopolis) was an enormous town-mound at the beginning of the 19th century.

Unlike Athribis, it did not suffer from the expansion of a nearby modern city, but rather the extensive activities of *sebbakh*-diggers, which have resulted in its current state as a *tell* of only 0.25 square kilometres (61 acres) and a rather larger water-filled pit. Although the victim of much illegal excavation, which has generated a large number of objects said to come from this site, Tell Muqdam has not been systematically excavated in a consistent way, apart from through the work of Carol Redmount and Renée Friedman for the University of California in 1993–96. The work of this mission suggests that the city was founded no earlier than the Ramesside Period and rapidly expanded during the Third Intermediate (when it may have been the seat of the 23rd Dynasty) and Late Periods.

Mendes

Mendes is the Classical name of a city known in the dynastic period as Anpet and Per-Ba-Neb-Djedet ('House of the Ram, Lord of the Enduring Place'). Today it is an unoccupied mound, Tell Rub'a. With the adjacent mound of Tell Thmuis (see below), Mendes is *c.* 3 km (2 miles) from north to south and *c.* 900 m (2,953 ft) east to west (at its widest), making it one of the largest sites of the Nile Delta. Perhaps the sheer size of the site has historically been intimidating to archaeologists, with the first serious, systematic excavations only beginning in the 1960s with

Opposite below The extensive activities of *sebbakh*-diggers at Tell Muqdam, combined with a relatively consistent sub-soil water table in the post-Aswan Dam era, have turned much of the site into a lake.

Djedhor Honours Horus of Athribis

Like Petosiris at Hermopolis Magna, Djedhor was a high official who tried to continue traditional Egyptian religious practices – including temple-building and the burial of sacred animals – during the period of Persian occupation between the 30th and Ptolemaic Dynasties. His activities at Athribis are recorded on a group of statues in his image, which come from the site:

I caused to be built the wabet-temple of the Falcon [i.e. the god Horus] to the south of the temple of Iat-Mat, 68 cubits in length and 64 cubits wide, in perfect work and excellent in every way. A great hall is at its centre, six chapels to the east and to the west. Their doorframes are of beautiful white limestone, their doors of pine and their locks and hinges of bronze. A great portico is before the main door of this Wabet, provided with eight papyriform columns and covered by a ceiling of pine carved with the great name of His Majesty....

I caused to be built a great enclosure wall around the temple of Iat-Mat and the temple of the Wabet....

I caused to be prepared mrht-oil with which the embalming of the Falcon [i.e. a falcon sacred

The remarkable appearance of this statue of Djedhor, found at Athribis is due to its being a 'healing statue' incorporating the image of the child Horus controlling dangerous creatures – water was perhaps poured over the statue and collected in the basin underneath to be used for medicinal purposes.

to Horus] is done ... many falcons had been found in the 'Chamber of 70' which had not been embalmed and I caused them to be embalmed with this mrht-oil and to rest in the necropolis.

Queens in the Delta?

One obvious measure of the importance of Delta cities in the Third Intermediate and Late Periods is the presence of royal cemeteries indicating that the cities that housed them were to be regarded as the seats of royal dynasties. Such necropolises have been found, or are known, at Tanis (for the 21st and 22nd Dynasties), Sais (26th Dynasty) and Mendes (29th Dynasty).

However, the burials of important royal women of the same periods have been found at other cities in the Delta as well. Some of these, such as the Tell Muqdam tomb identified by some scholars as that of Queen Kamama, mother of King Osorkon III, might indicate the presence of a larger royal necropolis (in this case that of the 23rd Dynasty). Others suggest a burial in a home-city, such as the tomb of Queen Takhut, wife of Psammetichus II, in the important Late Period necropolis at Athribis.

However, the collapse of the Old Kingdom seems to have affected Mendes especially badly, indeed the end of the 6th Dynasty saw a violent episode in the history of the site, which is indicated by a major destruction layer uncovered by Donald Redford's team. The evidence includes burning in the area of the temple and the adjacent cemeteries as well as the sprawled skeletons of unburied bodies.

Remarkably, little evidence has yet been uncovered for the occupation of Mendes in

teams led by Bernard Bothmer and Donald Hansen, and more latterly Robert Wenke and Douglas Brewer, with Donald Redford carrying out an important series of excavations from 1991 onwards.

Mendes before the Late Period

Deep coring on the *tell* close to the temple has demonstrated that the mound was occupied in the Late Predynastic and Early Dynastic Periods; the evidence includes clay sealings with the names of 1st Dynasty kings and officials. The Old Kingdom seems to have been a time of great prosperity for Mendes and a substantial town grew up round the temple, the 'House of the Ram', which included substantial food production and storage facilities. The town came to occupy an area of over 100,000 sq. m (25 acres) – one of the largest settlements known from the Old Kingdom. In the early part of the 6th Dynasty, an elite cemetery of mudbrick and limestone *mastaba* tombs grew up close to the temple, which was known as Djedet – 'the enduring place', and the area grew to *c.* 150,000 sq. m (37 acres).

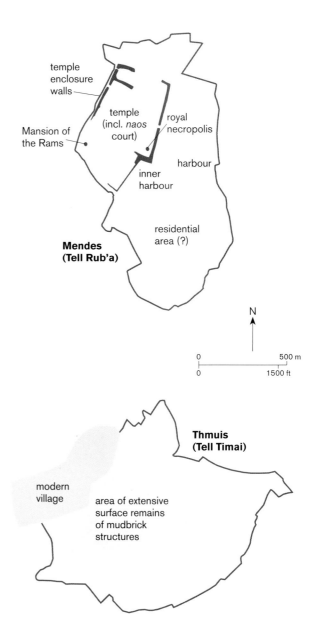

Plan showing the extent and relative locations of the neighbouring sites of Mendes (Tell Rub'a) and Thmuis (Tell Timai).

temple enclosure walls

temple (incl. *naos* court)

Mansion of the Rams

royal necropolis

harbour

inner harbour

residential area (?)

Mendes (Tell Rub'a)

N

| 0 | | 500 m |
| 0 | | 1500 ft |

Thmuis (Tell Timai)

modern village

area of extensive surface remains of mudbrick structures

the Middle Kingdom, apart from some repairs to the temple during the 12th Dynasty. In the New Kingdom, Mendes flourished once more, although not on the scale enjoyed in the Old Kingdom. The clearest evidence of this is the patronage of the Temple of the Ram by New Kingdom rulers, especially Thutmose III and the early Ramesside kings; under Ramesses II the temple was expanded to its greatest extent, 165 m (541 ft) in length.

Mendes in the Late Period

Like many Delta cities, Mendes achieved its greatest period of political prominence and monumental display during the Late Period. In a manner similar to the way in which Sais was the royal capital and focus of building work for kings of the 26th Dynasty, so Mendes served as the royal base for the kings of the 29th Dynasty.

Part of the reason for Mendes' long-lasting prosperity was the continued proximity of the Mendesian branch of the Nile. Late Period Mendes possessed a large river harbour where it met the river on its eastern side, and a secondary northwestern harbour on the Butic Canal, which ran off the Mendesian branch just to the north of the city.

As befitted a Late Period upgrading of the main temple, the central and rear parts behind the Ramesside pylons were heavily remodelled, although little now remains of this work, apart from the foundation trenches. However, to the south of the temple, King Amasis of the 26th Dynasty, in addition to his work at Sais, constructed an open court, 34 by 28 m (112 by 92 ft), which contained four huge *naos*-shrines, each cut from a single piece of granite. These were designed to house images of four deities – Re, Shu, Geb and Osiris. Unfortunately, only one remains standing today.

Other major constructions of the Late Period that would transform the sacred core of Mendes included a 'Mansion of the Rams' – a mausoleum for the burial of the succession of rams that were considered the living embodiment of the god himself. This structure consisted of a columned hall leading to a series of small, individual, mudbrick tombs, each containing a sarcophagus

The most obvious monumental remnant on the huge Tell Rub'a mound is the colossal monolithic *naos*-shrine constructed by King Amasis.

made of granite or diorite. The presence of scattered sarcophagi and their lids is further evidence.

One of the defining features of these post-New Kingdom royal cities of the Nile Delta is their royal tombs. For his royal sepulchre, King Nepherites I of the 29th Dynasty chose an area to the east of the temple where he dug a pit 11 by 19 m (36 by 62 ft) in area to form a burial chamber, on top of which the rectangular superstructure was built. Only fragments of that superstructure have survived, and today the most obvious feature of this rather desolate royal tomb is a large limestone plinth with Nepherites' black granite sarcophagus set into the top of it.

Thmuis

In the period after the late New Kingdom, Mendes expanded in a somewhat unexpected

---

Ptolemy II Visits Mendes

Around 280 BC, Ptolemy II visited Mendes. He reviewed progress on the building projects that he had ordered at the site and took part in cultic ceremonies for the Ram. This was all recorded on an enormous stela he erected in the Temple of the Ram:

Year … first month of Winter. His Majesty came to visit Banebdjed to ask for life from the Lord of Life…. His Majesty visited the living ram as the first visit he made to any of the sacred animals since he ascended the throne of his father….

His Majesty took the prow of the sacred barque of the god and guided it downstream on the Great Lake and upstream on the canal of Akhenu, as had been done before him by all the kings of Upper and Lower Egypt. He carried out for him [the god] all the rites of visitation such as he found in writing….

His Majesty inspected the Mansion of the Rams and he found that the work was in progress on the House of the Ram, as His Majesty had ordered to repair the damage the rebellious foreigners had caused. His Majesty ordered it to be completed as a work of eternity. His Majesty inspected the Residence of the Noble Ram to which he had made restoration.

---

way. To the south of the mound of Tell Rub'a, and across the river from it, new land was reclaimed from the inundation, creating what was in effect a twin settlement. This later became known as **Tell Thmuis** (from the Egyptian Ta-Mawt). It developed as an adjacent independent town rather than simply as an extension to the long-established city (Mendes) on Tell Rub'a.

The End of Mendes

Although Mendes had survived the first Persian occupation of the 27th Dynasty, the arrival of the Second Persian Period of the 31st Dynasty was a different story. The significant destruction of the site at this time included the demolition of most of the tomb of Nepherites I – the smashed fragments were thrown over the enclosure wall that had been built by Nectanebo I, which was itself mostly levelled.

Although this was a major disaster, and effectively marked the end of Mendes' period as one of the great Delta cities, the Ptolemaic Period saw some revival in Mendes' fortunes – not least because of its central position in the Nile Delta and the continued importance of its riverside location. Indeed, under Ptolemy II some reconstruction work took place at Mendes, presumably to emphasize the extent to which the Ptolemaic kings – in marked contrast to their Persian predecessors – respected native Egyptian religious traditions and structures (see box, left). The shrinkage in the flow of the Mendesian branch after *c.* 200 BC seems to have initiated a gradual abandonment of the site, or at any rate lessened its status as a major urban centre.

Sammanud

The ancient city of Tjeb-Netjer, Classical Sebennytos, lies within a substantial town-mound that is completely covered by the modern city of **Sammanud**. The Egyptian historian Manetho, himself a native of Sammanud, closely identified the city with the 30th Dynasty and it is more than possible that the royal necropolis of those kings was located there. It is difficult to get a good sense of the extent of the ancient city, although it may well have been a monumental centre to rival other major Delta cities of the

Opposite above Most of the ancient city of Sebennytos has been swallowed up by its modern incarnation, the city of Sammanud. Some remains of ancient buildings are still visible, like these granite blocks strewn around a courtyard within the city.

Opposite below The huge and jumbled collection of decorated and undecorated hard-stone blocks at Behbeit el-Hagar represents the remains of a now-destroyed major temple complex.

Late Period, such as Sais and Mendes. Evidence – including a number of large granite blocks still to be seen at Sammanud – suggests major temple-building under the 30th Dynasty, centred on the temple of the local god Onuris-Shu, perhaps completely remodelling earlier Saite work.

Seven kilometres (4½ miles) to the northeast of Sammanud is the village of Behbeit el-Hagar, notable for a massive collection of huge hardstone blocks, the collapsed remains of a temple to Isis, largely from the 30th Dynasty and the early Ptolemaic Period. The first part of its modern toponym may be a corruption of the ancient Per-Hebyt 'House of the Festival'. Although a town called Hebyt is attested as early as the New Kingdom, it is unlikely that Behbeit el-Hagar was ever a major settlement in its own right and can best be regarded as a monumental offshoot of Sammanud, where kings of the 30th Dynasty (and the Ptolemaic Period) had the space to develop a massive new temple to Isis as a counterpart to its southern equivalent on Philae Island near Aswan.

A similar distance to the south of Sammanud is the village of Abusir el-Bana (Egyptian Djedu, Classical **Busiris**), the site of the ancient northern cult centre of Osiris. The site has not been the subject of systematic excavation.

Tell el-Balamun

Traditionally regarded in some ancient texts
as the northernmost town in Egypt (with
Elephantine the southernmost), this ancient site
was known as Sma-Behdet, although its current
name seems to be a corruption of a term used
from the New Kingdom, Pa-Iw-n-Imen, 'The
Island of Amun'. The site consists of a series of
mounds, up to 18 m (59 ft) tall, within an area
of 1,000 by 800 m (3,281 by 2,625 ft), which has
had little attention from *sebbakh*-diggers, perhaps
because of the salinity of the soil in this part of
the northern Delta.

Briefly explored by Howard Carter in 1913,
Tell el-Balamun has been the subject of
systematic excavations by Jeffrey Spencer for
the British Museum since 1991. This work has
not produced any remains earlier than the New
Kingdom, most notably a Ramesside temple
enclosure. Later major temple-building took
place in the Third Intermediate and Late Periods,
especially by kings who are well represented in
other parts of the Delta such as Shoshenq III,
Psammetichus I and Nectanebo I.

Recent excavations at Tell el-Balamun by the British
Museum team have provided a greater understanding
of the history of this important site in the northern Delta.

Cities of the Pelusiac Branch

The sites described in this section are principally
those built on or near the ancient Pelusiac
Branch of the Nile, which opened onto the
Mediterranean near the city of Pelusium,
and its minor offshoots, including modern
waterways, which followed its course or run
parallel to it (e.g. the Ismailiya Canal and the
Bahr Muweis waterway). Also included here are
the fortress-towns of the Wadi Tumilat. All of
these settlements can be divided into one of
two major types: towns and cities that were
founded as 'normal' population centres and
those that had their origins as fortified military
camps. This division is especially important in

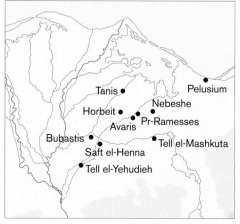

the Eastern Delta since, despite occasional and sometimes very serious problems with incursions from Nubia and Libya in the south and west respectively, it was here that Egypt traditionally experienced immigration and, particularly from the Third Intermediate Period onwards, invasion.

'The Waters of Ra'

Apart from the important city of Bubastis (see below), relatively little is known about settlement in the Eastern Nile Delta before the New Kingdom. It is likely that, as in other parts of the Delta, major settlements were located on or near major branches of the Nile, and as the course of these branches fluctuated over millennia, so did the fortunes of the towns and cities originally built alongside them. The current Pelusiac branch of the Nile roughly corresponds to the most important ancient Nile channel of the Eastern Delta: 'the Waters of Ra'. Part of the importance of settlements built on this channel was control of transport routes into northern Sinai and the Levant. Even as late as the New Kingdom, the Mediterranean coast was much further south

than it is today, making both Pr-Ramesses and its predecessor Avaris important maritime as well as riverine ports.

Tell el-Yehudieh

There are several sites in Egypt that bear the name **Tell el-Yehudieh**, or a variant of it, and it suggests a connection with a Jewish presence in Egypt – Édouard Naville named the monograph that describes his work at the site in 1886–87 'The Mound of the Jew and the City of Onias'. The second part of the title refers to the building at Tell el-Yehudieh of a Jewish temple – one of the very few outside Jerusalem – by Onias, son of a similarly named high priest, after his flight from Jerusalem around 160 BC. Built by permission of Ptolemy VI, the temple at Tell el-Yehudieh was (along with Elephantine) one of the centres in Egypt associated with resident Jewish communities during the Ptolemaic Period.

However, Tell el-Yehudieh had an even longer association with immigrants from the Levant, since its earliest attested phase of occupation

The remains of Tell el-Yehudieh give little indication of the importance of this long-lived site in the southeastern Delta.

(investigated by Petrie in his excavations of 1905–6) comprised a large, fortified settlement with ramparts typical of Syro-Palestinian towns of the Middle Bronze Age. Graves excavated at the site have produced objects associated with the Hyksos, most notably black ceramic juglets with incised and white-filled decoration called 'Tell el-Yehudieh Ware', which are one of the most distinctive cultural artifacts of the Second Intermediate Period.

Despite its strategic location, Tell el-Yehudieh seems to have been largely ignored by New Kingdom rulers until the Ramesside Period. Archaeologically, this phase of the site's history is best represented by the scant remains of a temple of Ramesses III, and the finds of polychrome faience tiles, which came from a palace belonging to the same king.

In the Classical Period the site was (like Tell Muqdam) known as Leontopolis, and in the 20th Dynasty, 'House of Ra, north of Heliopolis'.

Saft el-Henna and Suwa

Saft el-Henna (ancient Per-Soped, Classical Phacusa) is best known for an enormous black granite *naos*-shrine dedicated to the god Soped-Nektanebo I, which was discovered by Édouard Naville in 1885 on a ruin-field of considerable extent (which also included a large collection of basalt blocks, probably from the Late Period temple). Since then, as at Horbeit, a modern village has expanded over the ancient site, leaving only a few small *tell*-mounds within the village and the fields around it. Although fragments of colossal Ramesside royal statuary can still be seen on these mounds, it is uncertain whether the town was of any real size before the 30th Dynasty.

The main cemetery of Saft el-Henna seems to have been on the nearby *gezira* of Suwa, a large sandy mound, which, although it has not been systematically excavated, has produced chambered mudbrick tombs mainly of the Late and Graeco-Roman Periods, but some as early as the New Kingdom.

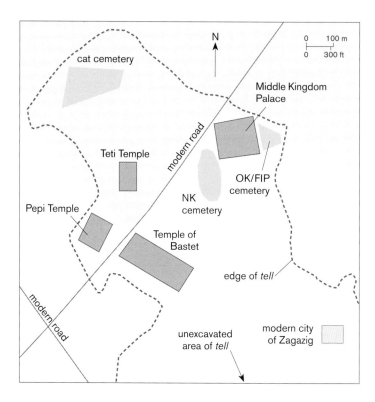

Bubastis

Unlike the *tell*s of Mendes and Tanis, the huge ruin-field of Bubastis is not conveniently isolated from major modern settlement, but is immediately adjacent to – and increasingly absorbed within – the city of Zagazig. This is a reflection of the long-term suitability of this particular spot for urban settlement owing to the stability of the Pelusiac branch of the Nile in this part of the Delta, and the site's strategic importance on the route from Memphis to Sinai, and beyond into the Levant. Today the site is referred to as Tell Basta, a name that, like the Classical Bubastis, is derived from its pharaonic name, Per-Bastet, 'House of [the lion/cat-goddess] Bastet'. It is a site remarkable not only for its size (today it occupies an area of *c.* 70 hectares, 172 acres) but also for the range in both date and type of its visible monuments, displaying a continuous history of occupation and importance from the Old Kingdom until the Third Intermediate Period. It is a site that has been sporadically excavated, perhaps most notably by Édouard Naville from 1887 to 1889.

Above Plan of Bubastis. Although much of the northern part of the site has been lost due to the expansion of the modern city of Zagazig, the site still retains the most impressive set of archaeological remains in the Delta covering the period from the Old Kingdom to the Late Period.

Bubastis before the New Kingdom

Although we know little of its early history, Bubastis was clearly an important regional centre. Royal interest in the city during the Old Kingdom is attested by the presence of two *ka*-chapels built by kings Pepi I and Teti. Although these structures are relatively modest in scale and in materials used (some limestone elements within a mainly mudbrick structure) they are remarkable as rare examples of surviving Old Kingdom monuments outside the Memphite area, and were maintained in use long after their construction. Other evidence of the status of Bubastis in the late Old Kingdom and First Intermediate Period is provided by a substantial cemetery including mudbrick *mastaba* tombs with elaborate stone elements.

Bubastis flourished in the Middle Kingdom. Although the temple from this period seems to have been swept away by later, more extensive building work, a colossal granite head of Amenemhat III found by Naville in his excavation of the temple area suggests important royal patronage of Bubastis. The most significant Middle Kingdom structure at Bubastis is a large palace complex, which covers an area of *c.* 120 by 90 m (394 by 295 ft), providing both a residential and administrative centre for the mayors of Bubastis and, perhaps, a residence for the king when he visited the city. Limestone reliefs found in association with this palace refer to a jubilee festival of Amenemhat III. The destruction of the palace by fire and its abandonment at the end of the Middle Kingdom might be related to the emergence of the Hyksos, and especially the expansion of Avaris as *the* urban centre in the Eastern Delta during the Second Intermediate Period (see below).

The extensive use of granite architectural elements in the Temple of Bastet is a clear indication of the importance of this cult and this city in the New Kingdom and Late Period.

View (above) looking southwest over the northern part of Tell Basta. In the foreground are the mudbrick walls of Old Kingdom tombs and beyond them the remains of the Middle Kingdom palace (plan, right).

New Kingdom Bubastis

There is little to suggest major expansion of Bubastis during the 18th Dynasty, though Amenhotep III built a small festival-chapel here. The extent to which Bubastis was patronized by Ramesside kings is not agreed by scholars, since many of the plentiful Ramesside monuments at Bubastis could have been reused from other sites, as is known to have been the case at Tanis (see box p. 209). The most impressive of these Ramesside monuments, which were used to embellish the monumental landscape of Bubastis, was an extraordinary colossal granite statue of Ramesses II's daughter Meritamun. This statue was not re-inscribed (as some were) with the names of individuals of the Third Intermediate Period, making it likely that Bubastis was the originally intended location for this statue, which, presumably, stood alongside one or more now-lost colossal statues of the king himself. The cemeteries at Bubastis during the Ramesside

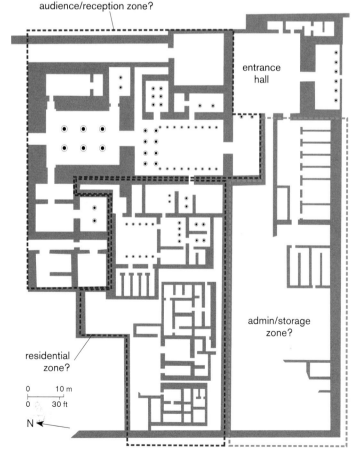

Period contained a number of large and elaborate tombs, which attest to an important local elite, including the Hori family, two of whose members served as Viceroys of Kush (Upper Nubia) during the 20th Dynasty.

Bubastis in the Third Intermediate and Late Periods

Like Sais and Tanis, Bubastis was a Delta city that achieved its greatest level of national importance during the Third Intermediate Period. The settlement at and around the city of Libyan prisoners from the wars of the Ramesside Period created local dynasties of Libyan families who came to serve as a military elite in the Egyptian army at the end of the New Kingdom, and later became the dominant force, regionally and then nationally, when the New Kingdom collapsed. Manetho describes the 22nd Dynasty as 'Kings of Bubastis' and building works of these kings are still referred to by reference to their home city, such as the 'Bubastite Portal' at far away Karnak.

Unsurprisingly the temple enclosure, which dominated the centre of the city, was extended during the Third Intermediate Period thanks to the patronage of kings who wished to enhance their home town. It came to cover an area of 200 by 60 m (656 by 197 ft), with the eastern side of the enclosure containing buildings erected by Osorkon I and his grandson Osorkon II. The most impressive of these was constructed to celebrate the *sed*-festival of Osorkon II. Although most of this work was carried out using limestone, it still required substantial numbers of huge blocks of hard stones, especially red granite, which still litter the site. Behind the Osorkons' temple was an open courtyard, and the western side of the enclosure was the site of activity in the 30th Dynasty by Nectanebo II, especially the erection of a series of large monolithic *naos*-shrines, perhaps in a similar way to the arrangement in the Late Period temple at Mendes. The Late Period – specifically the 26th Dynasty – also saw the development of a necropolis for the burial of cats sacred to Bastet.

In 2008 – over 100 years after Naville's work in the Third Intermediate Period temple at Bubastis – a team lead by Eva Lange began a fieldwork project to investigate the development of this part of the site.

The description Herodotus provides of the city during the Late Period (see box overleaf) is not entirely different from the visible remains today, especially the fact that the city was made up of areas with different heights, so that the temple enclosure was lower than the surrounding districts – this is how the ruins appear today, with some surviving vestiges of the *tell* being substantially higher than the main temple. As Naville put it,

lofty mounds, which are nothing but layers of decayed brick-houses which were always rebuilt on the same spot so that after centuries the ground was considerably raised. It is clear that one must have looked down on the stone buildings which had remained at the same level.

Horbeit and Abu Yassin

Horbeit and **Abu Yassin** are two neighbouring villages, which, respectively, occupy the ancient city and nome-capital of Shednu (Classical Pharbaethos) and the cemetery of its sacred bulls. In this bipartite arrangement they are somewhat similar to Saft el-Henna with its cemetery at neighbouring Suwa, or Kom Firin whose necropolis is at nearby Silvagou in the Western Delta. Fragments of the ancient city can be seen between the modern houses, including massive granite roofing blocks from a temple of Nectanebo II at Horbeit and five impressive granite sarcophagi from the bull-cemetery at Abu Yassin.

Avaris and Pr-Ramesses

Anyone strolling across the fields near the Eastern Delta village of Qantir will find little indication that they are walking over the remains of not one but two of the great cities of the pre-Classical world: the Second Intermediate Period Hyksos capital of **Avaris** (Hwt-Waret) and the Ramesside capital of **Pr-Ramesses** (more fully Pr-Ramesses-Mery-Imen-Aa-Nehtu – 'The House of Ramesses, Beloved of Amun, Great of Victories').

Avaris

The city of Avaris has become well known through the excavations of Austrian archaeologist Manfred Bietak at the site of Tell ed-Daba. It was founded early in the 12th Dynasty by Amenemhat I, but it developed considerably in the late 12th Dynasty as a response to Egyptian interest in Sinai and the Levant, and immigration by 'Asiatic' groups from the east. Avaris served as a point of departure for Egyptian expeditions to the east, and was partly occupied by Asiatic 'Expedition Leaders'. As an important trading centre, the city flourished, its population swelled

Herodotus Describes the Temple of Bubastis

... where there is a temple of Bubastis, which is well worth describing. Other temples may be larger, or have cost more to build, but none is a greater pleasure to look at. The site of the building is almost an island, for two canals have been led from the Nile and sweep round it, one on each side, as far as the entrance, where they stop short without meeting. Each canal is 100 feet wide and shaded with trees. The gateway is 60 feet high and is decorated with remarkable carved figures some 9 feet in height. The temple stands in the centre of the city, but the temple was allowed to remain in its original position, the result being that one can look down and get a fine view of it from all round. It is surrounded by a low wall with carved figures and within the enclosure stands a grove of very tall trees about the actual shrine which is large and contains the statue of the goddess. The whole enclosure is about a furlong square. The entrance to it is approached by a stone-paved road about 400 feet wide and about 2,000 feet long, running eastward through the market-place and joining the temple of Bubastis to the temple of Hermes. The road is lined on both sides with immense trees, so tall that they seem to touch the sky.

Herodotus II, 137–38

– especially with Canaanite immigrants – and it developed its own palace complex. When the Middle Kingdom collapsed, these Canaanites, the 'Hyksos', were in a strong enough position to establish political control of the Eastern Delta and then, indeed, of a substantial proportion of the Nile Valley.

In the ensuing Second Intermediate Period, Avaris became one of the largest and richest towns in the Near East – archaeological evidence in the form of millions of sherds of imported pottery excavated at the site indicates its importance as a major trading centre. Its main god was the Levantine storm god Baal-Zephon, who was identified with the Egyptian god Seth; the connection between this deity and this part of the Eastern Delta was to become a long one. Late in the Hyksos Period, a massive citadel was built, probably in response to the danger posed by the Theban 17th Dynasty, whose primary aim was the destruction of Hyksos power (and, perhaps, presence) in Egypt.

The conquest of Avaris by Ahmose, founder of the 18th Dynasty, did not make it disappear. Initially, however, the town was abandoned, apart from the temple of Seth, which continued to operate until the Amarna Period. In the Thutmosid Period (most likely during the reigns of Hatshepsut and Thutmose III) the old Hyksos citadel and adjacent cemeteries were covered by a massive palace complex, 5¼ hectares (13 acres) in area, built on a series of tall platforms. The presence of Minoan-style frescoes in two of the new palaces suggests a connection with the Minoan court, leading some scholars to believe that this was, in part, a residence-palace built for a royal marriage between an Egyptian king and a Minoan princess.

However, there is also clear evidence that Avaris was also an important military base at this time and up to the reign of Amenhotep II (who agreed a peace treaty with the Near Eastern state of Mitanni). However, the changing situation in the Near East (especially the emergence of the Hittites as a major rival) may have acted as a stimulus to reactivate this important eastern base. Horemheb constructed a huge fortress at Avaris, but it was under his successors, the Ramessides, that this part of the Nile Delta was to become especially important.

The Foundation of Pr-Ramesses

The existence of Pr-Ramesses – the Delta residence of Ramesside kings – was known from descriptions in ancient texts well before its physical discovery:

> His Majesty has built for himself a Residence whose name is 'Great of Victories'.
> It lies between Syria and Egypt and is full of food and provisions.
> It follows the model of Upper Egyptian Thebes and its duration is like that of Memphis.

This encomium raises a number of interesting points about Pr-Ramesses. Although it was, in essence, the personal creation of Ramesses II, it was not a barren site, like Amarna, but already had a previous national and international importance as Avaris, and also a personal connection to Ramesses, since the Eastern Delta was the home region of his family, and his father Seti I had already built a summer palace there. The strategic location of Pr-Ramesses, 'between Egypt and Syria', on the edge of the Eastern Delta, is stressed, at a time when Egyptian foreign affairs were dominated by Near Eastern issues

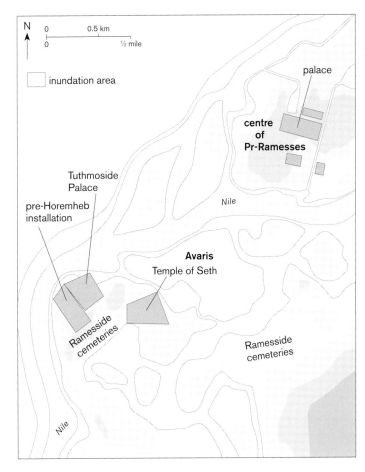

Plan of Pr-Ramesses and Avaris, based on a range of archaeological sources including both excavation and satellite imagery.

(especially competition with the Hittites over Egypt's Levantine empire) and a well-resourced ('*full of food and provisions*') military centre conveniently close to the action was desirable. But in two major respects the encomium above is incorrect – the city's layout was definitely not based on that of Thebes, nor was it to have anything like the longevity of Memphis.

The Search for Pr-Ramesses

More immediately important to the archaeologists who began to ponder the location of Pr-Ramesses in the late 19th century was its obvious size and importance, as well as its potential identification with 'Raamses' the Biblical city of Hebrew bondage. It was natural to assume that such a city would have left substantial remains. One of the first Eastern Delta candidates was Pelusium (see pp. 210–11), although this turned out to be a major city whose archaeologically attested importance only developed well after the New Kingdom. More promising was the great mound of Tanis (San el-Hagar – see pp. 206–9), especially after the excavations there of French Egyptologist Pierre Montet in the 1930s produced monumental remains – statues, obelisks and stone blocks – many inscribed with the name of Ramesses II; these indeed proved to be monuments from Pr-Ramesses.

However, the appearance of glazed tiles from a New Kingdom palace at Qantir, and subsequent excavations there by Egyptian archaeologists Mahmoud Hamza and Labib Habachi, and more recently by German archaeologist Edgar Pusch, provided ultimately conclusive evidence that *this* was the location of Pr-Ramesses. The monumental remains of the Ramesside Period at Tanis had been transported there to embellish the new regional centre only once Pr-Ramesses had been abandoned – one of the most extreme examples (along with Alexandria) of expensive stone monuments being relocated wholesale to new locations.

The Landscape of Pr-Ramesses

The identification of the Qantir locality with Pr-Ramesses was only gradually accepted, not least because its modern landscape, with its flat, level fields, gives little indication of how the Ramesside city appeared to its inhabitants. In 1250 BC, the local landscape consisted of a series of *gezira*s, sandy mounds that became islands during the inundation. Pr-Ramesses was therefore a series of districts, located on these *gezira*s, which would become physically separated

Many of the inscribed and decorated stone blocks from the temples built by Ramesses II as the monumental core of Pr-Ramesses are now visible at Tanis, like this scene of Ramesses II offering to the god Atum.

from each other during the flood. Although invisible today, these *gezira*s, and the individual Nile channels that flowed around them, have been detected and mapped by the German and Austrian archaeologists investigating Avaris and Pr-Ramesses.

The main city centre of Pr-Ramesses is under the modern village of Qantir. In the Ramesside Period this was the southern tip of a large *gezira* (G1) that was a permanent island in the river stream. The old town of Avaris was about a kilometre (⅔ mile) to the southwest of the main city centre of Pr-Ramesses, on two adjacent *gezira*s (G5 and G6) to the east of the main Nile channel; these became separate islands during the inundation.

The eastern part of the centre of Pr-Ramesses was made up of a residential area containing houses and gardens of different sizes. This area remains to be explored in detail, but it is tempting to assume it has the same 'mixed residential district' character of Amarna.

The western part of the centre was very much a royal city. The main building here included a large temple for Amun-Ra-Harakhty-Atum (a composite deity with solar associations) and

Left The only significant surface trace of the great city of Pr-Ramesses is these feet from a colossal seated statue of Ramesses II.

an even larger palace immediately to the south of the temple. South of the palace was a barracks area for elite chariot troops and a royal horse stud. Two narrow channels from the river led to two harbour basins, which served the central city.

As at other known royal cities – especially Thebes – the most important topographic features within Pr-Ramesses were its temples. Papyrus Anastasi II tells us that: 'Its west is the House of Amun, its South the House of Seth, Astarte its East, Wadjet its North.' However, how this configuration actually worked on the ground is not clear, since only the temple of Seth (near the old centre of Avaris) is known archaeologically. Indeed the main temple at Pr-Ramesses was massive and may or may not have included the monumental columned hall built to celebrate Ramesses' 30-year *heb-sed* festival, elements of which (columns and obelisks) were later transported to Tanis.

It also included several examples of a monumental feature particularly favoured by Ramesses II – colossal statues of himself, or rather colossal statues representing divine aspects of himself, which were to be worshipped by the populace:

'Ramesses Beloved-of-Amun' is in it as god, 'Montu-in-the-Two-Lands' is [its] Herald, 'Ra-of-the-Rulers' is [its] Vizier, 'Joy-of-Egypt, Beloved-of-Atum' is [its] Mayor.

The End of Pr-Ramesses

Pr-Ramesses was the major urban centre in the Eastern Delta, and one of the most important in Egypt, for less than two centuries. This may seem a long time when contrasted with Amarna's span, but is relatively short when compared with the millennia of constant building work at Memphis and Thebes. The problem at Pr-Ramesses – unlike at Thebes, but not unknown at Memphis – was its location on a Nile branch that was subject to substantial lateral movement. But, whereas the solution at Memphis was for the city to 'follow' the eastward-moving river over the centuries, at Pr-Ramesses the city was simply abandoned when its harbours became unusable. Instead the importance (along with the population and much of the monumental building fabric) of Pr-Ramesses moved downstream to the city of Tanis, which, by the end of the 20th Dynasty, had completely superseded it.

The importance of the archaeological remains being excavated at Qantir (Pr-Ramesses) and Tell ed-Daba (Avaris) is doubly astonishing given the flat, featureless fields under which they are buried.

205

Tanis

Tanis is the Classical name for a site that is today called San el-Hagar ('San of the Stone'); both names derive from the dynastic toponym Djanet. The *gezira* of San el-Hagar is the largest in Egypt, covering an area of 177 hectares (437 acres) and rising to a height of 32 m (105 ft) above the surrounding cultivation. Today the site has a rather barren appearance because problems of localized soil salinity have made this part of the Eastern Delta incapable of a level of agricultural production that would support a significant population, and therefore San el-Hagar does not suffer from problems of large-scale modern occupation in the same way as, for example, Alexandria or Bubastis. The size of the mound attracted the attentions of antiquities-diggers in the first half of the 19th century, and later of archaeologists. Auguste Mariette carried out the first major excavations at Tanis in 1860–64, followed by Petrie in 1883–84. Since 1929 the site has been excavated by various French teams,

most notably by Pierre Montet and, since 1985, by Philippe Brissaud. Archaeological attention has been concentrated on the temple enclosure and its contents. The excavation of the non-monumental parts of the city of Tanis – the areas where most of its residents lived and worked – is a major task for future archaeologists.

Tanis is unknown before the 19th Dynasty and only came to prominence in the late Ramesside Period when it became a replacement for Pr-Ramesses, which, as we have seen, had become ineffective as a major commercial and administrative hub owing to movements of the Nile, which left it harbourless. The capital of the 14th Lower Egyptian Nome, Tanis came to particular prominence in the Third Intermediate Period as the seat of the rulers of the 21st and 22nd Dynasties. Unlike similar cities of the Delta

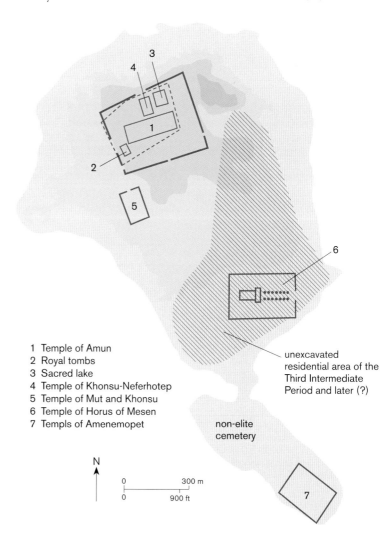

Plan of Tanis, showing the extent of the tell, the location of the major temple enclosure (including the royal tombs) and possible extent of the main area of settlement.

1 Temple of Amun
2 Royal tombs
3 Sacred lake
4 Temple of Khonsu-Neferhotep
5 Temple of Mut and Khonsu
6 Temple of Horus of Mesen
7 Templs of Amenemopet

unexcavated residential area of the Third Intermediate Period and later (?)

non-elite cemetery

N

0   300 m
0   900 ft

Wenamun Travels through Tanis

The *Tale of Wenamun* is a travel narrative that describes the adventures (and misadventures) of Wenamun, an official of the temple of Karnak at Thebes, who sets out to obtain timber from Byblos in Lebanon during the dying years of the New Kingdom. Although most scholars believe the story to be fictional, it is set in a convincing geographical and historical background, including the emergence of Smendes as effective ruler of northern Egypt. Wenamun's journey from Thebes naturally took him through the Eastern Delta and its emerging maritime and political centre, Tanis:

On the day of my arrival at Tanis, the place where Smendes and Tantamun are, I gave them the despatches of Amun-Re, king of the gods....

I stayed until the fourth month of Summer in Tanis. Then Smendes and Tantamun sent me off with the ship's captain Mengebet and I went down upon the great sea....

– particularly Sais and Bubastis – Tanis did not attract the attention of Herodotus, although it continued to be patronized by kings of the Late and Ptolemaic Periods before being finally abandoned in the Roman Period.

'Thebes of the North'

As a royal capital (albeit one of a rather restricted territory) that emerged after the collapse of the New Kingdom, Tanis needed to be shaped into an appropriate monumental setting. The overt aim of the kings of the 21st and 22nd Dynasties, for whom the old religious capital of Thebes was outside their control, was to present their Delta capital as a 'Thebes of the North'. This meant developing a monumental landscape at Tanis that paralleled the key aspects of the 'real' Thebes.

The first stage was to recreate the religious heart of Thebes, which consisted of a temple of Amun and associated temples for the other members of the Theban divine family, Mut and Khonsu. This need was satisfied by the building of Tanis' Northern Precinct, defined

by a rectangular mudbrick enclosure wall 430 by 370 m (1,411 by 1,214 ft) in area and 15 m (49 ft) thick. An inner enclosure wall was built by Psusennes I in the 21st Dynasty with a later monumental gateway added by Shoshenq III during the 22nd Dynasty. The main temple within this precinct was the temple of Amun whose ground plan was an impressively large 220 by 72 m (722 by 236 ft) in area. As with most of the temple buildings at Tanis, a large proportion of the original limestone masonry of the Amun temple was later destroyed and/or burnt for lime, but the site is today marked by an impressive collection of mostly granite blocks and monoliths whose origins were undoubtedly temple buildings at Pr-Ramesses, or even earlier Middle Kingdom monuments that had been requisitioned first for Pr-Ramesses and then later moved to Tanis. The scale of this relocation of monuments is staggering: for instance no fewer than 26 obelisks have been recovered from the Amun temple, all but one being inscribed for Ramesses II. A second major temple in the

Aerial view of Tanis, looking westwards across the temple enclosure in the northern part of the site. The main temple of Amun is represented by the cluster of much-destroyed monuments in the centre of this photograph.

The amount of colossal statuary and other large-scale monuments, such as obelisks, from the Ramesside Period found at Tanis give as much a sense of the once-impressive appearance of Pr-Ramesses (from where most of them came) as of that of Tanis itself.

Northern Precinct, at a right-angled axis from the Amun temple, was dedicated to Khonsu.

The Southern Precinct is less well understood than the Northern Precinct. It contained one temple, which is conventionally referred to as the 'Temple of Anath' because of statue groups found there which show Ramesses II with (among others) the goddess Anath. However, the Third Intermediate and Late Period material from this site indicates that this was a temple for Mut and her son, Khonsu-the-Child, thus once again stressing parallels with the deities worshipped at Thebes.

Royal Tombs at Tanis

Archaeologically, Tanis is best known for its royal tombs. The practice of burying kings within temple enclosures in the Delta during the Third Intermediate and Late Periods, as noted at Sais and Mendes, began at Tanis. Because of its location, Tanis did not allow easy access to desert valleys that would provide a royal cemetery to parallel the Valley of the Kings at Thebes. Instead, royal tombs belonging to the kings at Tanis were constructed within the Northern Precinct, as a way of providing a burial that was beneficially close to the temple of Amun, hopefully secure from unwanted disturbance, and crucially above ground water (and the inundation) on a high part of the town-mound of Tanis. These modest structures mainly consisted of little more than single-room tombs constructed below ground level from reused blocks of granite and limestone, and had burial equipment that included second-hand Ramesside objects.

The cluster of six tombs was discovered by Pierre Montet in 1939 underneath the mudbrick remains of houses of the Late and Ptolemaic Periods, which had been built over the forgotten royal burials. Although the contents of these tombs fall far short of the expectations of rich royal burials as raised by the tomb of Tutankhamun, they were far more successful than those in the Valley of the Kings at preserving their contents intact until the 20th century.

The identity of some of the royal owners of these tombs is disputed, owing in part to the change of ownership and usurpation of these tombs during the Third Intermediate Period, but the burials seem to include some of the key figures of the 21st and 22nd Dynasties. Four of the tombs may have been constructed for Psusennes I, Amenemope, Osorkon III and Shoshenq III, while Shoshenq II and Takelot II were also buried there. Other claimed (or assumed) original occupants and later interlopers include Smendes, Siamun and Psusennes II of the 21st Dynasty, and Osorkon II, Takelot I, Shoshenqs IV and V, and Pimay of the 22nd Dynasty.

Reuse of Monuments in the Delta

Tanis is the best example of a practice common in the Nile Delta, that of moving and reusing existing stone structures. This practice was not unique to the Delta, but the lack of available resources for stone quarrying there, when compared to the proximity of quarries of building stone for cities in the Valley, gave a particular impetus to reuse materials in northern Egypt.

The availability of hard stones such as granite was even more problematic. At the best of times, transporting large granite monoliths such as obelisks from the quarries at Aswan was a major undertaking, even if river travel meant that incremental distances were not as seriously onerous as they would be for overland travel. The 'best of times' included the Ramesside Period, when an efficient centralized bureaucracy operated in a politically stable country, providing the best opportunities for the founding of Pr-Ramesses. The Delta rulers of the Third Intermediate Period were faced with a less advantageous scenario: the economic resources they could draw on were significantly less than those of their New Kingdom predecessors, while access to key quarry sites in the Nile Valley – such as Aswan – was dependent on the goodwill of those southern rulers under whose political control these now came. In this situation, the reuse of what was available to hand became more a necessity than a cheap short-cut.

It is also the case that, of the four major cities with a large monumental component that needed to be created very quickly from essentially nothing, three were in the Delta. These were Alexandria, which drew on standing monuments from the Western Delta (especially Sais); Tanis, which used monuments from Pr-Ramesses; and Pr-Ramesses itself, which appears to have supplemented 'new-build' monuments with a set of Middle Kingdom structures of probably disparate origins.

The nature and style of many monuments – bearing traditional images of an Egyptian king worshipping a traditional set of Egyptian gods, whether on statues, stelae, obelisks, columns or temple walls – meant that it was easy for them to be given a re-purposing that was no more extensive than a change of royal name to make them workable in their new context. Where necessary, additional tweaks in the form of the minor manipulation of divine names or images (such as Amun instead of Seth on the Osorkon column at Tanis) would make the monuments even more appropriate to their new context. It may be that the little-disguised antiquity of these monuments (many statues had the names of their new royal owners added alongside that of their original dedicatee, rather than replacing them) was actually embraced as a mechanism for stressing continuity with one's royal 'ancestors'.

The fourth city to be designed as a monumental arena from scratch was Amarna. Given the specifically 'new' nature of that city's monumental display and iconography – in terms both of the forms of monuments and the methods of portraying god and king within an urban setting – the reuse of existing monuments would not have been appropriate.

The re-use of stone from earlier royal monuments is well illustrated by this wall, part of the gateway to the entrance to the Amun temple at Tanis, which contains blocks taken from buildings belonging to kings of the 19th to 22nd Dynasties.

Nebeshe

In the 19th century, the *tell* of **Nebeshe** (ancient Imet or Per-Wadyt, Classical Bouto) was around 1,400 by 1,000 m (4,593 by 3,281 ft) in area. Owing to the extensive exploitation of the *tell* for *sebbakh*, and the expansion of the nearby modern town of el-Husseiniya, this enormous town-mound has almost completely disappeared. In 1886 Petrie was able to observe that the western part of the site was dominated by a mudbrick temple enclosure 180 by 160 m (591 by 525 ft), containing two temples, which can be attributed, on the basis of foundation-deposits in the smaller of the two temples, to Amasis of the 26th Dynasty. The central and eastern parts of the mound have largely produced – during occasional excavations at the site – houses and cemeteries of the Late and Graeco-Roman Periods.

The earlier history of Nebeshe is problematic: traces of occupation as early as Nagada III have been found at the site, as has evidence of the Old Kingdom and First Intermediate Period. It is likely that it benefited from royal patronage in the Ramesside Period (as indicated by a granite statue of the site's patron-goddess Wadjet dedicated by Ramesses II) although the reuse of Ramesside monuments, some of which were themselves re-inscribed Middle Kingdom royal statuary brought to Nebeshe from other Eastern Delta sites during the Late Period, cannot be discounted.

Pelusium

On the mouth of the Pelusiac branch of the Nile, and giving that waterway its name, **Pelusium** controlled entry into the Nile Delta by water-borne traffic, giving the city a crucial strategic military and mercantile role.

The site, known as Tell Farama, is a substantial town-mound over 6 kilometres (3¾ miles) from east to west (including the suburban dependencies of Tell Makhzan and Kanais), despite pressure on the site from encroaching farmland. The name Pelusium survives in the name of the nearest modern settlement: the village of Balousa.

Pelusium was first excavated by Jean Clédat in 1910. The site and its environs were the subject of concentrated international archaeological attention in the 1990s when the building of the el-Salaam Canal – whose route runs immediately to the south of Tell Farama – threatened the survival of a number of sites in this area.

The date of its foundation is problematic, and depends on when this part of the Eastern Delta coastline was formed. Herodotus refers to the Persian army of Cambyses defeating Psammetichus III near Pelusium in 525 BC, but there is no archaeological evidence to suggest it existed as a major settlement as early as this and it was therefore not one of the 'Ways of Horus' fortresses (see p. 215). By the Graeco-Roman Period, Pelusium was essentially an island formed by the Pelusiac branch forking

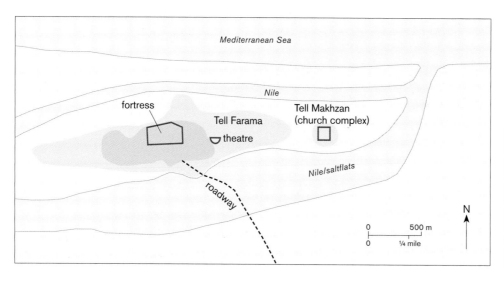

Plan of Pelusium (Tell Farama). The dynamic nature of the Mediterranean coastline, which interacted with the mouth of the Pelusiac branch of the Nile, made the landscape around the site one of constant change.

and then meeting again just before it entered the Mediterranean. At this time, it flourished as an important city of the Mediterranean world and enjoyed an appropriately Hellenistic/Roman civil infrastructure including baths, theatres and (possibly) a hippodrome. However, defence was always a concern and the most impressive remnant of the ancient city to be seen today is the 8-hectare (20-acre) Late Roman fortress, probably dating to the 6th century AD, whose red-brick walls are over 2 m (6½ ft) thick and have 36 towers and three heavily defended gates.

The role of Pelusium as the eastern gateway to Egypt from the Late Period onwards is reflected in the impressive heavily defended red-brick walls of the Roman fortress at the site.

Fortress-Towns of the Eastern Delta and Wadi Tumilat

Egypt's Eastern Delta frontier, including the Wadi Tumilat, was vulnerable to attack from unfriendly powers in the Near East. It is not surprising that a set of fortified settlements was developed during different periods of Egyptian history to guard against incursion or invasion.

Tukh el-Qaramus

One of the largest (over 30 hectares, or 74 acres) in area, **Tukh el-Qaramus** is certainly one of the least-explored town-mounds in the Nile Delta. Ancient names for the site probably included Bekhnu and Dekyt, both of which are mentioned

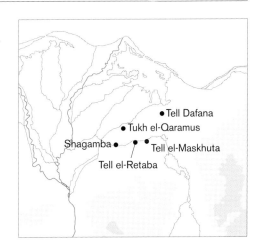

on a stela of Shoshenq III found there. Evidence for occupation before the Third Intermediate Period is limited, but this is probably a result of its archaeological under-exploration since it is unlikely that such a substantial *gezira* in the Eastern Delta would not have had a long history of settlement.

Tukh el-Qaramus was principally excavated in a period of just over a decade by Édouard Naville and Francis Ll. Griffith (1887), Georges Foucart (1892) and Campbell Edgar (1906), but the site was surveyed by Steven Snape in 1984. Although the site has largely been denuded of its stone buildings, the mudbrick platform on which its temple stood still remains, as do sections of the massive mudbrick walls that provided the outer fortifications for this fortress-town, and the internal zoning within the town. It is likely that Tukh el-Qaramus served as one of Egypt's eastern military bases during the Third Intermediate and Late Periods (the term *bḫn*, bekhen, refers to a fortification), but was abandoned at some point during the Graeco-Roman Period.

Shagamba

Shagamba (also known as Tell Miniet el-Habib) is a site that was probably similar in character to Tukh el-Qaramus, if somewhat smaller. It is located in the Eastern Delta on the route from the Wadi Tumilat to Memphis. It was visited by Petrie's team in 1906 at which time the walls of a fortress, identified as being of the Late Period, were relatively well preserved. By the 1980s most of these mudbrick walls had been removed, leaving just one fragment, a dark grey mound of degraded mudbrick over 10 m (33 ft) in height, protected by a modern cemetery sitting on top of it.

Tell Dafana

The *tell* of **Tell Dafana** (ancient Tjebnet, Classical Daphnae) is a substantial mound, 1,200 by 700 m (3,937 by 2,297 ft) in area. Largely on the basis of comments by Herodotus, Petrie (who worked at Tell Dafana in 1885–86) suggested

The major *tell* of Tukh el-Qaramus is typical of large settlement sites in the Nile Delta in having a surface largely formed by weather-worn hills of large mudbrick structures.

that it was primarily a fortress-town founded by Psammetichus I for Greek mercenaries to defend Egypt's eastern borders at a time of pressure from the Assyrians. More recent work at the site by Jeffrey Spencer and François Leclère for the British Museum has indicated that the site had a primarily Egyptian character, including a large temple enclosure, suggesting that its occupation by non-Egyptians was relatively transitory. However, occupation of Tell Dafana after the 26th Dynasty is not well attested, making it likely that the site was primarily a military outpost whose use was perhaps eclipsed by the development of Pelusium.

Tell el-Maskhuta

The site of **Tell el-Maskhuta** is probably the location of the Biblical Pithom, a name deriving from one of the site's names – Per-Tem-Tjeku, 'The House of Atum in Tjeku'. Herodotus refers to the site as 'Patoumos'. The site was first explored by Édouard Naville in 1883, who identified the massive enclosure (210 by 210 m, 689 by 689 ft) on a town-mound of 1,100 by 600 m (3,609 by 1,969 ft). Between 1977 and 1985, Tell el-Maskhuta was excavated by John Holladay for the University of Toronto, which resulted in the location of the site's earliest occupation phase, a small and short-lived Hyksos settlement and cemetery.

Excavations at the site have produced a series of monuments dating to the late New Kingdom and Third Intermediate Period, although it has been argued that these were imported during the Late Period from abandoned or diminished sites of the Eastern Delta. During the 26th Dynasty, a much more substantial phase of activity was initiated by Necho II's construction of a canal along the Wadi Tumilat, thus linking the Pelusiac Branch to the Red Sea; at this point Tell el-Maskhuta became an important trading and military centre.

The site became especially fortress-like with the construction of an enclosure wall, which was 8–9 m (26–29½ ft) thick. The strategic importance of Tell el-Maskhuta against invasion from the east – a major concern in the Late Period – is attested by destruction layers associated with the Babylonian and Persian

Despite the importance of Tell el-Maskhuta as a strategically placed fortress-town, its surface remains today are relatively limited, apart from visible sections of its external walls.

incursions of 601, 568 and 525 BC. Major revivals in levels of occupation and mercantile activity at Tell el-Maskhuta were associated with renewals of the canal under Ptolemy II (when it was known as Heroonpolis) and Trajan (when it was called Ero).

Tell el-Retaba

Briefly explored by Flinders Petrie in 1905, **Tell el-Retaba** has since 2007 been excavated by a Polish–Slovak archaeological mission led by Sławomir Rzepka and Jozef Hudec. Their work to date indicates that the site appears to have been founded in the 18th Dynasty, if not earlier, and expanded during the reigns of Ramesses II and III. In this New Kingdom phase of occupation, Tell el-Retaba was surrounded by an enclosure

wall to form a quadrilateral fortress over 400 by 200 m (1,312 by 656 ft) in area, with a massive gateway on its western side. A significant military character to the material excavated within the walls of Tell el-Retaba suggests that it functioned much as Tell el-Maskhuta did in the Late Period, i.e. it was a major fortified town guarding access into the Nile Delta through the Wadi Tumilat.

The extensive development of the infrastructure of modern Egypt in the 20th and 21st centuries constitutes another threat to the survival of archaeological sites, and increases the necessity of urgent rescue excavation, as can be seen clearly here in the road running through Tell el-Retaba.

Northern Sinai

The exploitation of mineral resources in southwest Sinai meant that a series of temporary campsites were set up attached to mining and quarrying sites, but none can be regarded as significant permanent settlements, with the possible exception of the impressive Middle Kingdom temple complex at **Serabit el-Khadim** and the small Old Kingdom fortlet at **Ras Budran**. The situation in northern Sinai was rather different, especially along the well-established 'Ways of Horus' route between the northeastern Nile Delta and the southern Levant.

Although the existence of a chain of forts and fort-towns along this route has long been known, not least through the illustration of these fortified settlements and their adjacent water sources on the northern wall of the hypostyle hall at Karnak, which shows Seti I travelling between them, their archaeological reality has only become obvious from the 1980s onwards with the work of Eliezer Oren at **Bir el-Abd** and **Haruba**, James Hoffmeier at **Tell el-Borg** and Mohammed abd el-Maqsoud at **Tell Heboua**.

The last-named site is the most substantial and refers to a cluster of fortified settlements around a lagoon at the easternmost extent of the Nile Delta, occupied from the Second Intermediate to the Ramesside Periods. Excavations here have revealed that this was the location of ancient

Tjaru, which seems to have functioned as a major mustering point for Egyptian military campaigns into the Levant.

The main purpose of the 'Ways of Horus' centres further east was to provision Egyptian armies (and possibly also merchant caravans) travelling across this difficult environment. Although badly destroyed, Tell el-Borg was a fort whose defences included a deep brick-lined moat. Haruba consists of a series of small sites clustered around a central fort and administrative centre, including a workshop for the production of pottery. Bir el-Abd likewise had a small central fort, but also an artificial water reservoir and a series of grain silos, which are estimated to have held c. 44,600 litres (9,810 gallons) of grain.

The movement of the Mediterranean coastline has resulted in the important New Kingdom 'Ways of Horus' fortress-town of Tell Heboua being left in the middle of a flat, salty plain.

The Oases

There are five major oases in the Western Desert that have witnessed substantial settlement activity: Siwa, Bahariya, Farafra, Dakhla and Kharga. These can best be regarded as independent areas, fertile islands in a desert 'sea' whose level of settlement, and interest to the ancient Egyptians, was based on a number of factors, of which size and distance from the Nile Valley were perhaps the most crucial.

With the exception of Balat in the Dakhla Oasis, none of the oases has preserved substantial settlement remains from the dynastic period. Siwa was the most distant oasis and probably unknown to the Egyptians before the Late Period, although it seems to have developed rapidly from that period onwards and became a famous oracular centre whose visitors included Alexander the Great. Farafra was of relatively marginal interest and, although known in texts from the Old Kingdom, archaeologically nothing is now preserved before the Graeco-Roman Period.

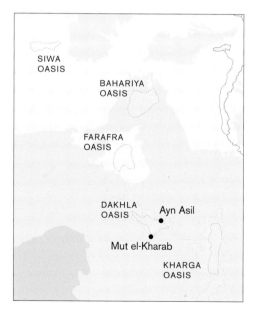

Top The contrast between the lush landscape of the Kharga Oasis and the surrounding desert is evident here in a view of Kharga's most substantial ancient remains, the Persian Period temple.

To the dynastic Egyptians the most important oases were Bahariya (known as the Northern Oasis –Wehat Mehtet), and Kharga and Dakhla (known jointly as the Southern Oasis – Wehat Resyt). Before the Late Period, Bahariya is known principally for the New Kingdom tomb of a local administrator, Amenhotep-Huy; no contemporary settlement has been discovered to date. It is Dakhla that has produced the most substantial pre-Classical settlement evidence, including **Mut el-Kharab**, which was probably the most important town in the oasis (and perhaps its capital from the New Kingdom onwards) and which has been occupied sporadically from the Old Kingdom to the present day. The extent of the modern town of Mut has hampered a wider understanding of the full extent of this important centre, which has been excavated since 2001 by the Dakhla Oasis Project and Monash University. Their work has revealed an important and long-used temple of the god Seth within a large enclosure wall (240 m (787 ft) north to south by 180 m (591 ft) east to west), probably built during the Late Period.

The Town at Balat

The modern village of Balat in the eastern Dakhla Oasis gives its name to an ancient town composed of two distinct, linked areas: a necropolis now known as Qila el-Dabba and a nearby settlement site now known as Ayn Asil.

The town was founded in the late Old Kingdom, probably to act as a regional administrative centre and a colonial town for the Egyptians who governed the Dakhla Oasis. The largest tombs in the cemetery – huge *mastaba*s with mudbrick walls up to 6 m (20 ft) in height, and with burial chambers at the bottom of enormous pits up to 10 m (33 ft) deep – belong to four governors of the Oasis in the period from the late Old Kingdom and First Intermediate Period. The largest of these belonged to Khentika who was 'Boat Captain and Ruler of the Oasis'.

Excavations at Ayn Asil, which have been carried out by the French Institute in Cairo since 1997, allow the reconstruction of the history of building work at the town, which in total covered an area of 800 m (2,625 ft) north to south and

The processes by which the town of Ayn Asil quickly disappeared after its abandonment is well demonstrated by the wind-blown sand that has already accumulated around the buildings excavated (and partially restored) by the French team.

The Governor's Palace complex at Ayn Asil provides a rare example of what must have been typical urban architecture of all periods of Egyptian history, with limited use of wood or stone for necessary parts of buildings, like these column-bases (above). The survival of significant and complex remains in mudbrick (left) is only due to the unusual location of the town which has been preserved through desertification.

500 m (1640 ft) east to west. The earliest phase of the site, during the reign of Pepi I, is represented by a square fortified enclosure with mudbrick walls 175 m (574 ft) long and with rounded towers at the corners. By the reign of Pepi II the town had expanded to the south, protected by a thick enclosure wall, including a governor's palace-complex which was 225 m (738 ft) north to south and 95 m (312 ft) east to west.

This complex contained a range of buildings that fulfilled a number of functions. They included private domestic apartments, administrative areas, storage areas and a series of *ka*-chapels, which served the cult of the governors. Ayn Asil's capacity for industrial self-sufficiency is best represented by a large pottery workshop, which seems to have satisfied local ceramic requirements, partly by reproducing fashionable contemporary vessels from the Nile Valley.

A clear destruction level, including a major fire, marks the abandonment of the palace at some point in the First Intermediate Period, although the western part of the town continued to be occupied until its final abandonment in the early Middle Kingdom.

Not far from Ayn Asil is its cemetery at Qila el-Dabba, including some impressively large tombs built for governors of the oasis during the Late Old Kingdom.

The Mediterranean Coast

In addition to the oases, the other area of the Western Desert that offered opportunities for urban settlement was the Mediterranean coast. Historically, Egypt was uninterested in this neighbouring territory and, unlike northern Sinai (see below), no attempt was made to place an Egyptian presence along the fertile coastal strip. This situation changed in the early Ramesside Period when population movements towards Egypt by the Libyan groups from further west made permanent military settlement a priority.

Zawiyet Umm el-Rakham

Traces of forts built by Ramesses II are known from **Gharbaniyat** and **el-Alamein**, but the best known fortress-town in the group is **Zawiyet Umm el-Rakham**, 280 km (174 miles) west of the Nile Delta, which has been excavated by Steven Snape for the University of Liverpool since 1994. It is clear that this fortress-town, known anciently as 'The Town (*dmi*) of Usermaatre-Setepenre', was intended for long-term and extensive occupation because of its size and the range of buildings within.

It was defended by a massive mudbrick wall, 140 m (459 ft) along each side, with a single central towered gate. A fragmentary inscription on this gate refers to *menenu*-fortresses – a type of heavily defended *dmi*/town, which is an accurate description of Zawiyet Umm el-Rakham. Inside these walls the Egyptian occupants erected a limestone temple, a series of storerooms and a 'governor's residence', which included a private chapel. Inscribed objects from

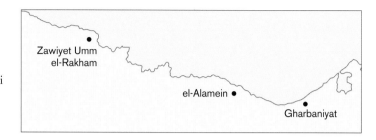

the temple and other private chapels next to it tell us that the fortress was garrisoned probably by over 500 soldiers at any one time and that their commander was a man called Neb-Re. The extent to which these soldiers brought their families with them to this most distant posting in the Egyptian empire is unknown, as is the extent to which they might have fraternized with the local population. The life of the town was relatively short, being abandoned either before or shortly after the death of its founder, Ramesses II.

Right Plan of Zawiyet Umm el-Rakham, showing the major areas excavated to date.

Opposite above Zawiyet Umm el-Rakham was deliberately placed on the narrow strip of land between the foot of the Libyan plateau (foreground) and the Mediterranean Sea (background).

Opposite below Water was the most important resource to be secured by Egypt's frontier forts. This small well at Zawiyet Umm el-Rakham was conveniently sunk where it could be used in the baking and brewing district.

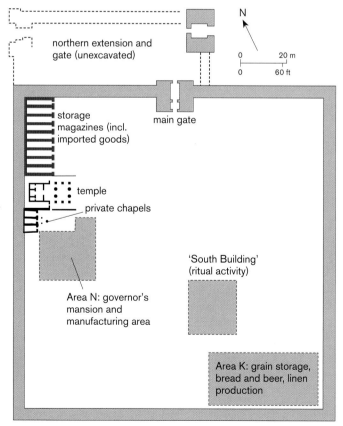

Self-Sufficiency at Zawiyet Umm el-Rakham

This fortress-town may have been partly supplied by transport barges from the Delta, perhaps especially in the early phases of its building and occupation, and exotic foreign products such as olive oil, wine and (probably) opium arrived by sea courtesy of maritime traders travelling between Crete and Egypt. However, the long-term survival of the town and its population relied much more on self-sufficiency, especially in terms of food production.

Water – the most critical requirement – was supplied by a series of wells (two have so far been excavated) and, possibly, by the water-harvesting of rainfall in cisterns. Evidence for various types of production comes from 'Area K', which took up a substantial portion of the southeast corner of the town. Here a series of granaries, mortars, saddle-querns, quern-rubbers/grinders and ovens (along with one of the wells) provided all that was needed to turn grain into flour, bread and

beer, the main dietary staples (see box overleaf). The grain itself would probably have been grown in fields on the fertile coastal strip outside the walls of the town, and watered by winter rainfall. In addition, 'Area K' has also produced both

Grain, Granaries and Population

Various attempts have been made to calculate how much of their basic staple – grain – ancient Egyptians actually ate, and to what extent population size of any given settlement correlates with estimates of the capacity of its granaries. In the case of Zawiyet Umm el-Rakham the two granaries in Area K that have so far been completely excavated have an average diameter of 3 m (10 ft), and there are indications that their original height was at least 2 m (6½ ft). These dimensions indicate an internal volume of approximately 14 cubic m (494 cubic ft) each, and therefore a total estimated storage capacity of the four known granaries of approximately 56 cubic m (1,978 cubic ft), i.e. 56,000 litres (12,318 gallons).

Calculations as to how many men these granaries could supply with grain are, like the volume of the storage capacities of the granaries themselves, a matter of evidence-based estimation. Dutch Egyptologist Jack Janssen has suggested that monthly grain rations to Deir el-Medina workmen of 4 *khar* of emmer and 1.5 *khar* of barley equate to approximately 300 and 150 litres (66 and 33 gallons) respectively, although these figures should probably be regarded as an allocation for a family, with an individual's average consumption probably closer to one litre (⅕ gallon) per day. This figure correlates reasonably well with ration distributions at the Nubian fortress of Uronarti in the Middle Kingdom, where ration dockets indicate a 10-day distribution of 60 units produced from ⅔ *hekat* of barley and 70 units from 1 *hekat* of emmer; with a *hekat* measuring

4.78 litres (1 gallon) – this approximates to 7.5 litres (1½ gallons) of grain in 10 days and somewhere between 1,458 or 2,136 per day.

However, the Uronarti distributions, although measured in terms of their grain content, were supplied as baked loaves, presumably because they were supplied from a centrally controlled military baking facility, the opportunities for individual members of the Uronarti garrison to carry out their own food-processing opportunities being presumably very limited. Nevertheless, as a rough rule-of-thumb, a garrison of 500 men requiring 7.5 litres of grain each for 10 days is a total of 3,750 litres. The known total grain store of 56,000 litres at Zawiyet Umm el-Rakham would therefore last for about 150 days.

The partially excavated granaries at Zawiyet Umm el-Rakham. The granary on the left has been adapted at some point to create a room containing a pair of ovens.

spindle whorls and 'spinning-bowls', which are associated with the spinning of linen, also sourced locally through the cultivation of flax.

In addition to consumption by the population of the town, the products of 'Area K' – including beer and linen, as well as pottery and metal objects produced in other parts of the town – could have been traded with local Libyan pastoralists in return for additional food, perhaps explaining the goat bones and ostrich eggshells that have been found in large numbers at the site.

Left A series of storage vessels excavated at Zawiyet Umm el-Rakham demonstrate the long distances travelled by visitors to the site: rear left, a Canaanite amphora; front right an Egyptian jar; rear right and front left, a pair of coarse-ware stirrup-jars, possibly from mainland Greece or Crete.

Nubia

The area of modern Sudan south of the First Cataract at Elephantine was known to the Egyptians as Nubia, subdivided like Egypt in two, as Lower Nubia (Wawat), the area between the First and Second Cataracts of the Nile, and Upper Nubia (Kush), upstream of the Second Cataract. In addition to the indigenous towns and cities of the region, the most important example being Kerma, Nubia also received Egyptian settlement in the form of forts and towns built during Egypt's imperial domination of the region during the Middle and New Kingdoms.

Fortified towns

Some of these Middle Kingdom forts were overwhelmingly military in character, especially those in naturally defended locations such as the rocky outcrops overlooking the Nile at **Semna** and **Kumma**, or islands such as **Uronarti**. Others, built in the floodplain to the north of the second cataract, were designed for a larger population,

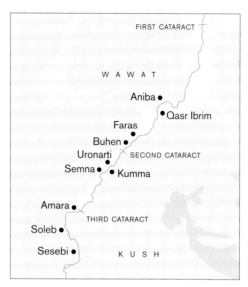

the largest and most important of which was **Buhen**, which was mainly excavated by the British archaeologist Harry Smith as part of the Nubian Rescue Campaign, which aimed to record

The intimidating multi-layered defences of Buhen were essential when the fortress-town faced a potentially substantial threat from Egypt's Nubian enemies during the Middle Kingdom.

and excavate as many archaeological sites as possible in this part of Lower Nubia in the 1960s and 1970s before the building of the Aswan High Dam and the subsequent creation of Lake Nasser.

The defences of the central 'citadel' at Buhen, which was 150 by 138 m (492 by 453 ft), are some of the most extensive and complex of any piece of military architecture anywhere in Egypt's empire, with a series of walls and ditches obviously designed against a serious potential military threat. Within these walls, the layout of the administrative centre was based on Middle Kingdom ideas of orthogonal design for centrally planned settlements (as at, for instance, Kahun and Wah-Sut at Abydos), with clearly designated blocks for a temple, a barracks or storage building, and a military command centre built in the northwest corner of the citadel. Outside this fortified core, outer defences contained an area of 420 by 150 m (1,378 by 492 ft), which was not investigated before being flooded by Lake Nasser.

New Kingdom Cities in Nubia

During the New Kingdom, the main seats of imperial power in Nubia were **Aniba** and **Faras** (capitals of Wawat, Lower Nubia), **Amara** and **Soleb** (capitals of Kush, Upper Nubia). Heavy defensive fortifications were no longer a priority, since any serious Nubian opposition to Egyptian control of the region had effectively been crushed early in the 18th Dynasty. Instead, the emphasis was on the creation of suitable Egyptian 'colonial' towns to serve a primarily imported Egyptian population. The basic model seems to have been the 'temple-town', although it should be noted that the largest and best known of the Nubian temples – those built by Ramesses II at Abu Simbel, Gerf Hussein and Wadi es-Sebua – have not produced adjoining settlement remains of any size. The same is true of the important temple built by Amenhotep III for his wife Tiye at Sedeinga.

A good example of a New Kingdom temple-town in Nubia is **Amara West**, excavated by Herbert Fairman and Peter Shinnie from 1938 to 1950, and since 2008 by Neal Spencer. The core town, which was founded by Seti I and continued in use until the reign of Ramesses IX, consisted of a sandstone temple around which

a number of tightly packed mudbrick buildings were clustered. The density of this settlement may reflect the possibility that, in the Ramesside Period, this was an island in the Nile. To the west of the town itself was a suburb consisting of large villas. **Sesebi** is 80 km (50 miles) south of Amara West and was also excavated by Fairman and Aylward Blackman in 1936–38, and since 2008 by Kate Spence for the University of Cambridge. The town was laid out on a regular, grid-iron plan within an enclosure wall, 270 m north to south and 200 m east to west (886 by 656 ft), and divided into a series of areas that can be recognized as residential housing, administrative buildings and a series of temples. Sesebi seems to have been founded by Akhenaten and continued in use until the Ramesside Period.

Although the settlement and administrative buildings of the Egyptian colonial town at **Faras** (ancient Ibshek) have not been identified, the distribution over a wide area of the tombs and temples associated with the New Kingdom town suggests that the Sesebi model – that of a compact, walled settlement – does not apply everywhere and that some Egyptian colonists felt secure enough to develop a more dispersed form of urban occupation, which they would have known well from, for instance, Thebes.

One of the most striking archaeological sites of Lower Nubia is **Qasr Ibrim,** not least because, located well above the Nile itself, it is the only site in the area to have survived the creation of Lake Nasser. The early history of Qasr Ibrim is unclear, especially the question of whether or not it was occupied during the New Kingdom. However, it seems to have become an important regional centre from the end of the New Kingdom with a long constructional history from the 25th Dynasty until the Middle Ages.

The town of Sesebi (opposite, with plan below) is a good example of the extent to which Egyptian towns in Nubia during the later part of the 18th Dynasty and Ramesside Period were built with an emphasis on well-planned settlements and monumental architecture, like in Egypt itself, reflecting Nubia's status as a pacified part of Egypt's empire rather than a dangerous frontier.

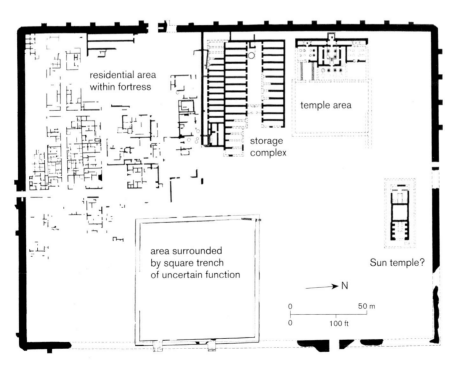

residential area
within fortress

storage
complex

temple area

area surrounded
by square trench
of uncertain function

Sun temple?

→ N

0   50 m
0   100 ft

Epilogue – Lost Cities

In our exploration of the cities and towns of ancient Egypt we have seen the different sources of evidence that can be used to interpret the places where the ancient Egyptians lived together as small or large communities. Some of that evidence comes from the visible physical remains of houses, streets and administrative buildings, but actually surprisingly little of it. In fact it is astonishing how even the largest and most impressive of ancient Egyptian cities can disappear. Of the four greatest cities of the New Kingdom – perhaps the high point of Egyptian civilization – we have seen that the obviously impressive temples and tombs at Thebes are only the monumental core of the ancient city, that Amarna was reduced to a bleak desert plain, that Memphis is only visible in tiny scattered fragments and that Pr-Ramesses had completely vanished under the fields of the Eastern Nile Delta. But we have also seen that those very cities, especially Amarna, Memphis and Pr-Ramesses, have been, and continue to be, slowly and patiently brought to light by the work of archaeologists who are using a range of sophisticated methods of site location and site investigation to recover all that can be discovered about these great urban centres.

Those same techniques are also being used to explore a great variety of settlement sites throughout Egypt and its border regions. The stories of Amarna, Memphis and Pr-Ramesses tell us how remarkably easy it is to lose an ancient city and how difficult it can be to find it again. For smaller ancient settlements the problem is often greater. Our ancient sources (such as town-lists or the presence of nearby cemeteries) might provide evidence of the existence of particular towns, but there is no guarantee that we can locate them with any accuracy, let alone explore their remains. At the same time the effort that has been put in recent years into archaeological survey and prospection in traditionally unexplored areas, especially in the Nile Delta, has revealed a wealth of interesting data, which is revolutionizing our understanding of the settlement of ancient Egypt.

The future of settlement archaeology in Egypt is both exciting and challenging, and there is still much work to be done before our understanding of the cities and towns of ancient Egypt can truly be said to be complete.

The rediscovery of the city of Avaris in the Eastern Delta is an important example of the way in which a range of different archaeological techniques can be used to explore superficially unpromising sites. Here two of these techniques – geophysical prospection and aerial photography – have been combined to provide a composite view of what is visible both above (colour) and below (black and white) the ground near the modern village of Ezbet el-Ezzawin.

Glossary

Not intended as a comprehensive list, the following guide covers the main terms and phrases that may be unfamiliar to readers. Terms that are themselves defined in the glossary appear in **bold** in other entries.

Cataract   In the context of the Nile, the term cataract refers to areas of shallow water or rapids caused by bands of hard stone crossing the river. This stone is much more resistant to weathering by the flow of the river than the surrounding sandstone, creating natural obstacles to river travel, especially when the Nile is low in its inundation cycle. The First Cataract of the Nile at Elephantine/Aswan, formed of granite, is a natural frontier that became the effective political boundary between Egypt and Nubia for most of pharaonic history. The Second Cataract of the Nile, which was heavily defended by Egypt during the Middle Kingdom, formed the boundary between Lower Nubia ('Wawat') and Upper Nubia ('Kush').

Confréries   Small group of workmen at Deir el-Medina. The term was used by Bruyère to describe the 'social clubs' for which he found evidence at the site as he was excavating.

Disembedded capital   'Disembedded capitals are urban sites founded *de novo* and designed to supplant existing patterns of authority and administration' (Joffe 1998, 549). Ancient Egypt produced a number of such non-organic urban developments, which were driven by the individual requirements of particular rulers, or groups of rulers: Itj-Tawy in the Middle Kingdom, Amarna in the New Kingdom and Alexandria at the beginning of the Graeco-Roman Period are all especially good examples. *See also* '**royal cities**'.

Encomium   A poem or prose text written in praise of a person or thing. In the New Kingdom a genre of texts generally referred to as 'In Praise of the City' gives the view of educated scribes as to the benefits of individual cities, such as Pr-Ramesses or Thebes, or city life in general (see p. 30).

Gezira   The Arabic word for 'island', the term *gezira* is also used to refer to the naturally deposited sand-islands whose most distinctive feature was that they stood above the floodwaters of the Nile, even during the **inundation**. These features, sometimes referred to as 'turtlebacks', were especially important in the Nile Delta, and could be of very considerable size, as at Tanis.

Inundation   The annual flooding of the Nile covered the fields of the Valley and Delta with silt-rich water, which contributed greatly to the fertility of Egypt's agricultural land. This widespread flooding also had a profound influence on the location and nature of settlements (and, especially, cemeteries) in ancient Egypt.

Iteru   The main measure of long distance in ancient Egypt an *iteru*, or 'river-length', was probably 20,000 cubits in length, or (since a cubit was approx. 525 mm), 10.5 km (6½ miles).

Ka   The ancient Egyptians conceived the self as being made up by several visible and invisible parts. The *ka*, roughly translated as soul, had to be nourished after death by relatives or other individuals leaving food at the tomb.

Kom   Like *tell*, the Arabic *kom* refers to a mound formed by the debris of earlier settlements. The appearance of *kom* in a modern toponym is often an indication of significant ancient settlement, as at Kom Ombo in southern Egypt or Kom Firin in the Nile Delta.

Loggia   An architectural term referring to a room or gallery on the outside of a building, where the outer wall is replaced by a series of columns in order to open it to the exterior. Such features seem to have been common in large villas such as those at Amarna where a loggia would provide a comfortable summer room that was both shaded from the sun yet open to cool breezes.

Lower Egypt   Northern Egypt, primarily comprising the Nile Delta, but also including the 1st Lower Egyptian nome, which contained Memphis and the Memphite cemeteries on the west bank of the Nile as far south as Meidum.

Mastaba   Monumental mudbrick tombs built to house elite burials from the Early Dynastic Period onwards. The massive rectangular edifices with sloping sides and a flat roof were constructed above ground over the interior underground burial chamber.They are especially known from the court cemeteries around Old Kingdom royal burials, where they are often cased with fine limestone.

Mulqaf   A 'wind-catcher' – a feature on the roofs of houses designed as a 'scoop' that funnelled cool breezes into the house itself. *Mulqaf*s are illustrated in depictions of houses on some tomb scenes and on model '**soul houses**'.

Nilometer   The Egyptians carefully monitored the rise and fall of the Nile during the **inundation** using large-scale measuring devices especially found within major temples. Linear scales cut into the walls of large stone pools or staircases running down into the river were two popular forms. The most important Nilometer – because it was the first part of Egypt where the rise in the Nile would be visible – was at Elephantine.

Nomarch   Theoretically the chief official of a **nome**. In reality, the pattern of local government and its relationship to the crown varied considerably during the dynastic period, although the general areas of responsibility – tax collection for the crown, oversight of economic activity within the nome – remained fairly constant.

Nome A Greek word used to refer to the basic geographical administrative unit in ancient Egypt, which the Egyptians themselves called a *sp3t* (sepat). The division of Upper Egypt into 22 nomes was established by the Old Kingdom, but the 20 nomes of Lower Egypt were subject to change up to and including the Graeco-Roman Period, partly because nome boundaries in the Delta were based on the dynamic branches of the Nile. The nome capitals constituted the largest group of important towns/cities of ancient Egypt.

Onomasticon (pl. *onomastica*) Ancient Egyptian texts that aimed to provide categorized lists of places and things. Two especially important *onomastica*, which list towns and cities of ancient Egypt, are the Middle Kingdom *Ramesseum Onomasticon* and the New Kingdom *Onomasticon of Amenemope*, both of which provide important information on contemporary placenames.

Ostracon (pl. ostraca) From the Greek term for a potsherd, used as casual writing material. In Egypt the term more usually refers to flakes of limestone whose smooth surface and white appearance made them suitable for short texts or illustrations written in ink, most notably from the Theban area in the New Kingdom.

Polis In Hellenistic Egypt the term refers specifically to a self-governing urban centre with its own extensive (Greek style) institutions. It would be supported by a network of smaller settlements within its agricultural hinterland (known as the *chora*). The most important of the small number of cities in Egypt that fitted, or came to fit, this description was Alexandria.

Pyramid town Sometimes used as a variant of '**Workmen's Village**', that is to say a settlement built to house workers involved in the construction of a royal project, in this case a pyramid. However, the term is also used to refer to a settlement that housed the priests, administrators and workers who were required for the ongoing functioning of the royal pyramid, especially the cultic activity in its mortuary temple. Such pyramid towns could become important centres of population and regional administration in their own right. The best example of such a settlement is the pyramid town of Kahun, part of the pyramid complex of King Senwosret II.

'Royal city' Used by Egyptologists to refer to urban projects in ancient Egypt that were the result of royal initiative and were also designed around buildings of particular importance to the king, such as major temples and palace complexes. The best known and most complete of such 'royal cities' is Amarna.

Sebbakh Being made largely of Nile silt (and usually mixed with straw), the mud brick used in the construction of Egyptian buildings was a ready-made fertilizer referred to by the Arabic term *sebbakh*. In the 19th century in particular, ancient *tells*, especially in the Delta, were tempting targets for peasant farmers who removed vast quantities of this material to spread on their fields, resulting in much destruction to ancient sites. Individuals who removed *sebbakh* are referred to as *sebbakh*-diggers.

Sed-festival The jubilee celebrations held every thirty years of a king's reign.

'Soul house' In the Middle Kingdom in particular, models of houses, workshops and other structures were an important component of the burial equipment, and were used to provide the soul or *ka* of the deceased with magical substitutes for the things the models represented. The largest and most impressive of these, such as that belonging to the Theban official Meketre

(see p. 73), were rendered in great detail and provide important evidence for the form and decoration of buildings of the period. Much simpler variants were the clay offering-trays that were partly modelled to look like houses.

Talatat Although most Egyptian monumental architecture was built from impressively large individual blocks of stone, the scale of building works undertaken by Akhenaten at Karnak and, especially, at Amarna made rapid construction a priority. One way of achieving this was the use of smaller, regular-sized building blocks of local stone that could be quarried, transported and used in building projects much more easily. These standard blocks, measuring *c.* 1 by 0.5 by 0.5 cubits (*c.* 54 by 27 by 27 cm, or *c.* 21¼ by 10⅔ by 10⅔ in.) are referred to as *talatat* from the Arabic word for 'three', possibly because each is approximately three hand-spans long.

Tell A mound formed by successive occupation layers at one settlement over a period of many years. Many settlements in modern Egypt have the qualifier 'Tell' in their name, and although not all have a distinctive ancient mound to match their toponym (although some, such as Tell Edfu, do), the term is itself an indicator that an ancient site was probably to be found in that locality.

Temenos In the context of ancient Egypt, this term is used to refer to the sacred precincts around a temple. A very significant aspect of town and city planning, in most cases this area was defined by the *temenos*- or enclosure-wall, which could be a massive construction and could form a well-fortified town-within-a-town at times of danger to the community, for example at Medinet Habu on the West Bank at Thebes at the end of the New Kingdom.

Upper Egypt Southern Egypt, primarily comprising the Nile Valley between the First Cataract of the Nile near Elephantine to as far north as Meidum on the west bank of the Nile and a little further north on the east. Although not part of the nome system until the Graeco-Roman Period, the Faiyum can be regarded as an adjunct to Upper Egypt.

Urbanization Broadly speaking, the process of urbanization sees the increase in number and size of urban centres, accompanied by a decrease in the proportion of the population living outside cities. In ancient Egypt the vast majority of the population was always rural (i.e. non-urban), but the emergence of cities in the Late Predynastic and Early Dynastic Periods was vital to Egypt's development as a politically centralized state with a sophisticated and shared elite culture.

'Villageization' The adaptation of centrally planned and sometimes monumental structures for small-scale domestic use by individual communities. The growth of the town of Djeme within the *temenos* walls of the mortuary temple of Ramesses III at Medinet Habu is a good example of this.

Vizier Term used to describe the chief official below the king. The two viziers of Upper and Lower Egypt had a wide range of administrative responsibilities for the regions they oversaw.

Wadi A dry river bed, often used as a road to travel through the desert. Two of the most famous were the Wadi Tumilat linking the Eastern Delta to Sinai and the Wadi Hammamat, a major trade route that connected the Qena bend of the Nile with the Red Sea.

'Ways of Horus' This ancient Egyptian term refers to the route from the Eastern Nile Delta across northern Sinai towards Southern Palestine. It is most famously represented by Seti I at Karnak as a series of forts and fortified settlements, which have been identified with sites close to the northeastern Delta (including Tell Heboua and Tell Borg) and along the North Sinai coast (including Haruba and Bir el-Abd).

Window of Appearances One of the public aspects of some Egyptian royal palaces, whose main functions were

primarily residential and administrative, was to provide a physical location where the king could appear to the population at large on specific ceremonial occasions, such as the presentation of rewards to worthy officials. As illustrated in New Kingdom private tombs, most notably those at Amarna, these 'Windows of Appearances' took the form of elaborately decorated raised balconies where the king, suitably elevated, could appear to best effect.

Workmen's village A purpose-built settlement to house state-controlled workers involved in royal building projects. These settlements might be short-lived for short-term projects, but the best known – the workmen's village at Deir el-Medina – was in use for as long as royal tomb builders were needed for the Valley of the Kings, a period of nearly 500 years.

Zir A large ceramic vessel, usually used for the short-term storage of drinking water.

Further Reading

Abbreviations used:
JARCE = Journal of the American Research Center in Egypt
JEA = Journal of Egyptian Archaeology
MDAI = Mitteilungen des Deutschen Archäologischen Insituts, Abteilung Kairo

General Reading

Arnold, D., *The Encyclopedia of Ancient Egyptian Architecture* (London and Princeton, 2003).
Aufrère, S., and J-C. Golvin, *L'Égypte Restituée* (3 vols; Paris, 1991–97).
Badawy, A., *Egyptian Architecture I–III* (Giza & Berkeley, 1954–68).
Baines, J., and J. Malek, *Cultural Atlas of Ancient Egypt* (Oxford and New York, 2000).

Bietak, M., (ed.), *Haus und Palast im Alten Ägypten. Internationales Symposium 8. bis 11. April 1992 in Kairo* (Vienna, 1996).
Bietak, M., E. Czerny and I. Forstner-Müller (eds), *Cities and Urbanism in Ancient Egypt: Papers from a Workshop in November 2006 at the Austrian Academy of Sciences* (Vienna, 2010).
Fairman, H. W., 'Town Planning in Pharaonic Egypt.' *Town Planning Review* 20 (1949), 32–51.
Hassan, F., 'Town and Village in Ancient Egypt: Ecology, Society and Urbanization'. in T. Shaw, P. Sinclair, B. Andah and A. Okpoko, *The Archaeology of Africa: Food Metals and Towns* (London and New York, 1993), 551–69.

Kees, H., *Ancient Egypt: A Cultural Topography* (London and Chicago, 1961).
Kemp, B. J., *Ancient Egypt: Anatomy of a Civilisation* (2nd edn; London and New York, 2006).
Lacovara, P., *The New Kingdom Royal City* (London and New York, 1997).
O'Connor, D., 'Urbanism in Bronze Age Egypt and Northeast Africa' in T. Shaw, P. Sinclair, B. Andah and A. Okpoko, *The Archaeology of Africa: Food Metals and Towns* (London and New York, 1993), 570–86.
Soulié, D., *Villes et citadins au temps des pharaons* (Paris, 2002).
Trigger, B., A. B. Lloyd, D. B. O'Connor and B. J. Kemp, *Ancient Egypt: A Social*

History (Cambridge and New York, 1983).

Tomlinson, R. A., *From Mycenae to Constantinople: The Evolution of the Ancient City* (London and New York, 1992).

Uphill, E., *Egyptian Towns and Cities* (Princes Risborough, 1988).

Texts in Translation

Lichtheim, M., *Ancient Egyptian Literature I: The Old and Middle Kingdoms* (Berkeley, 1975; London 1976).

Lichtheim, M., *Ancient Egyptian Literature II: The New Kingdom* (Berkeley and London, 1976).

Lichtheim, M., *Ancient Egyptian Literature III: The Late Period* (Berkeley and London, 1980).

McDowell, A. G., *Laundry Lists and Love Songs: Village Life in Ancient Egypt* (Oxford and New York, 1999).

Wente, E., *Letters from Ancient Egypt* (Atlanta, 1990).

Part I – The Rise of the City
Origins of Urbanism

Adams, B., *Ancient Hierakonpolis* (Warminster, 1974).

Adams, B., *Ancient Nekhen: Garstang in the City of Hierakonpolis* (New Malden, 1987).

Hoffman, M. A., *Egypt before the Pharaohs* (New York and London, 1979).

Hoffman, M. A., 'A Rectangular Amratian House from Hierakonpolis and Its Significance for Predynastic Research.' *Journal of Near Eastern Studies* 39 (1980), 119–37.

Hoffman, M. A., 'A Model of Early Development for the Hierakonpolis Region from Predynastic though Old Kingdom Times.' *JARCE* 23 (1986), 175–87.

Kemp, B. J., 'The Early Development of Towns in Egypt.' *Antiquity* 51 (1977) 185–200.

Wengrow, D., *The Archaeology of Early Egypt: Social Transformations in North-East Africa, 10,000 to 2650 BC* (Cambridge and New York, 2006).

Wilkinson, T., *Early Dynastic Egypt* (London and New York, 1999).

Location of Cities

Bietak, M., 'Urban Archaeology and the "Town Problem" in Ancient Egypt' in K. Weeks (ed.), *Egyptology and the Social Sciences* (Cairo, 1979), 97–144.

Graham, A., 'Islands in the Nile: A Geoarchaeological Approach to Settlement Location in the Egyptian Nile Valley and the Case of Karnak' in M. Bietak, E. Czerny and I. Forstner-Müller (eds), *Cities and Urbanism in Ancient Egypt: Papers from a Workshop in November 2006 at the Austrian Academy of Sciences* (Vienna, 2010), 125–43.

Hauser, P. M., and L. F. Schnore (eds), *The Study of Urbanization* (New York and London, 1965).

Joffe, A. H., 'Disembedded Capitals in Western Asian Perspective.' *Comparative Studies in Society and History* 40 (1998), 549–80.

Kemp, B. J., 'The City of el-Amarna as a Source for the Study of Urban Society in Ancient Egypt.' *World Archaeology* 9 (1977), 123–39.

Lichtheim, M., 'The Praise of Cities in the Literature of the Egyptian New Kingdom' in S. M. Burstein and L. A. Okin (eds), *Panhellenica: Essays in Ancient History and Historiography in Honor of Truesdall S. Brown* (Lawrence, 1980), 15–23.

O'Connor, D. B., 'Political Systems and Archaeological Data in Egypt: 2600–1780 BC.' *World Archaeology* 6 (1974), 15–38.

Shaw, I., 'Egyptian Patterns of Urbanism: A Comparison of Three New Kingdom Settlement Sites' in C. J. Eyre (ed.), *Proceedings of the 7th International Congress of Egyptologists* (Leuven, 1998), 1049–60.

Smith, H. S., 'Society and Settlement in ancient Egypt' in P. J. Ucko, R. Tringham and G. W. Dimbleby (eds), *Man, Settlement and Urbanism* (London and Cambridge, MA, 1972), 705–19.

Tisdale, H., 'The Process of Urbanization.' *Social Forces* 20/3 (1942), 311–16.

Trigger, B., 'Determinants of Urban Growth in Pre-industrial Societies' in P. J. Ucko, R. Tringham and G. W. Dimbleby (eds), *Man, Settlement and Urbanism* (London and Cambridge, MA, 1972), 575–99.

Wilson, J. A., 'Egypt through the New Kingdom: Civilization without Cities' in C. H. Kraeling and R. M. McAdams (eds), *City Invincible: Urbanism and Cultural Development in the ancient Near East* (Chicago, 1960), 124–36.

Building the City

Arnold, D., *Building in Egypt: Pharaonic Stone Masonry* (New York and Oxford, 1991).

Arnold, D., *The Encyclopaedia of Ancient Egyptian Architecture* (London and Princeton, 2003).

Fathy, H., *Gourna, a Tale of Two Villages* (Cairo, Chicago and London, 1969).

Fathy, H., *Architecture for the Poor* (Chicago and London, 1973).

Kemp, B. J., 'Soil (including mud-brick architecture' in P. T. Nicholson and I. Shaw, *Ancient Egyptian Materials and Technology* (Cambridge and New York, 2000), 78–103.

Kitchen, K. A., 'Building the Ramesseum.' *Cahiers de Recherches de l'Institut de Papyrologie et Egyptologie de l'Université de Lille* 13 (1990), 85–93.

Klemm, R., and D. D. Klemm, *Stones and Quarries in Ancient Egypt* (London, 2008).

Simpson, W. K., *Papyrus Reisner I: The Records of a Building Project in the Reign of Sesostris I* (Boston, 1963).

Spencer, A. J., *Brick Architecture in Ancient Egypt* (Warminster, 1979).

Egyptian Words for Towns and Cities

Brugsch, H., *Dictionnaire Géographique de l'ancienne Égypte* (Leipzig, 1879).

Erman, A., and H. Grapow, *Wörterbuch der ägyptischen Sprache* I–V (Leipzig, 1926–31).

Gauthier, H., *Dictionnaire des noms géographiques contenus dans les Texts Hieroglyphiques* (7 vols; Cairo 1925–31).

Gardiner, A. H., *Ancient Egyptian Onomastica* I–II (Oxford, 1947).

Goelet, O., '"Town" and "Country" in Ancient Egypt' in M. Hudson and A. B. Levine (eds), *Urbanization and Land Ownership in the Ancient Near East* 2 (Cambridge, Mass., 1999), 65–114.

Montet, P. ,*Géographique de l'Égypte Ancienne* (2 vols; Paris, 1957–61).

Redford, D. B., 'The Ancient Egyptian "City": Figment or Reality?' in W. E. Aufrecht, N. A. Mirau and S. W. Gauley (eds), *Aspects of Urbanism in Antiquity: From Mesopotamia to Crete* (Sheffield, 1997), 210–20.

Zibelius, K., *Ägyptische Siedlungen nach Texten des Alten Reiches* (Wiesbaden, 1978).

Estimating Population

Butzer, K. W., *Early Hydraulic Civilization in Egypt: A Study in Cultural Ecology* (Chicago and London, 1976).

Kemp, B. J., 'Temple and Town in Ancient Egypt' in P. J. Ucko, R. Tringham and G. W. Dimbleby (eds), *Man, Settlement and Urbanism* (London and Cambridge, MA, 1972), 657–80.

Kemp, B. J., 'Middle Kingdom Granary Buildings.' *MDAI* 113 (1986), 120–36.

Miller, R. L., 'Counting Calories in Egyptian Ration Texts.' *Journal of the Economic and Social History of the Orient* 34/4 (1991), 257–69.

Peet, T. E., *The Great Tomb-robberies of the Twentieth Egyptian Dynasty* (Oxford, 1930; Mansfield, CT, 2005).

Valbelle, D., 'Eléments sur la démographie et le paysage urbains d'après les papyrus documentaires d'époque pharaonique.' *Cahiers de Recherches de l'Institut de Papyrologie et Egyptologie de l'Université de Lille* 7 (1985), 75–87.

Part II – Cities for Kings and Gods

Palaces

Gundlach, R., and J. Taylor (eds), *Egyptian Royal Residences: Structure and Function* (Wiesbaden, 2009).

Kemp, B. J., 'The Window of Appearance at el-Amarna and the Structure of the City.' *JEA* 62 (1976), 81–99.

Kemp, B. J., 'The Harim-Palace at Medinet el-Ghurab.' *Zeitschrift für Ägyptische Sprache und Altertumskunde* 105 (1978), 122–33.

Lacovara, P., 'Gurob and the New Kingdom "Harim" Palace' in J. Phillips (ed.), *Ancient Egypt, the Aegean and the Near East: Studies in Honour of Martha Rhoads Bell* (San Antonio, 1997), 297–306.

O'Connor, D., 'Mirror of the Cosmos: The Palace of Merenptah' in R. E. Freed and E. Bleiberg (eds), *Fragments of a Shattered Visage: Proceedings of the International Symposium on Ramesses the Great* (Memphis, 1973), 167–98.

O'Connor, D., 'City and Palace in New Kingdom Egypt.' *Cahiers de Recherches de l'Institut de Papyrologie et Egyptologie de l'Université de Lille* 11 (1989), 73–87.

O'Connor, D.,'The King's Palace at Malkata and the Purpose of the Royal Harem' in Z. Hawass and J. Houser Wegner, *Millions of Jubilees: Studies in Honor of David P. Silverman* (Cairo, 2010), 55–82.

Reiser, E., *Der königliche Harim im alten Ägypten und seine Verwaltung* (Vienna, 1972).

Shaw, I., 'Seeking the Ramesside Royal Harem: New Fieldwork at Medinet el-Gurob' in M. Collier and S. Snape (eds), *Ramesside Studies in Honour of K. A. Kitchen* (Bolton, 2011), 453–63.

Stadelmann, R., 'Temple Palace and Residential Palace' in M. Bietak (ed.), *Haus und Palast im Alten Ägypten. Internationales Symposium 8. bis 11. April 1992 in Kairo* (Vienna, 1996), 225–30.

Fortified Cities

Dunham, D., *Second Cataract Forts II: Uronarti, Shalfak, Mirgissa* (Boston, 1967).

Dunham, D. and J. M. A. Janssen, *Second Cataract Forts I: Semna-Kumma* (Boston, 1960).

Emery, W. B., H. S. Smith and A. Millard, *The Fortress of Buhen: The Archaeological Report* (London, 1979).

Kemp, B. J., *et al.*, 'Egypt's Invisible Walls.' *Cambridge Archaeological Journal* 14: 2 (2004), 271–76.

Morris, E. F., *The Architecture of Imperialism: Military Bases and the Evolution of Foreign Policy in Egypt's New Kingdom* (Leiden, 2005).

Vogel, C., *The Fortifications of Ancient Egypt: 3000–1780 BC* (Oxford and Long Island City, 2010).

Temple and City

Lacau, P., and H. Chevrier, *Une chapelle de Sésostris Ier à Karnak* (2 vols; Cairo, 1956–69).

Routledge, C., 'Temple as the Center in Ancient Egyptian Urbanism' in W. E. Aufrecht, N. A. Mirau and S. W. Gauley (eds), *Aspects of Urbanism in Antiquity: From Mesopotamia to Crete* (Sheffield, 1997), 221–35.

Part III – Cities for People

City Government

Helck, W., *Die altägyptischen Gaue* (Wiesbaden, 1974).

The Middle Kingdom

David, A. R., *The Pyramid Builders of Ancient Egypt: A Modern Investigation of Pharaoh's Workforce* (London and Boston, 1986).

O'Connor, D., 'The Elite Houses of Kahun' in J. Phillips (ed.), *Ancient Egypt, the Aegean and the Near East: Studies in Honour of Martha Rhoads Bell* (San Antonio, 1997), 389–400.

Petrie, W. M. F., *Kahun, Gurob and Hawara* (London, 1890).

Petrie, W. M. F., *Illahun, Kahun and Gurob 1889–90* (London, 1891).

Wegner, J., 'Excavations at the Town of Enduring-are-the-places-of-Khakaure-maa-kheru-in-Abydos: A Preliminary report on the 1994 and 1997 Seasons.' *JARCE* 35 (1998), 1–44.

Wegner, J., 'The Town of Wah-Sut at South Abydos: 1999 Excavations.' *MDAI* 57 (2001), 281–308.

Winlock, H., *Models of Daily Life in Ancient Egypt* (Cambridge, MA, 1955).

The New Kingdom

Bierbrier, M., *Tomb-builders of the Pharaohs* (London and New York, 1982).

Bomann, A. H., *The Private Chapel in Ancient Egypt* (London and New York, 1991).

Borchardt, L., and H. Ricke, *Die Wohnhäuser in Tell El-Amarna* (Berlin, 1980).

Bruyère, B., *Rapports sur les fouilles de Deir el-Médineh* (Cairo, 1924–53).

Černý, J., *A Community of Workmen of the Ramesside Period* (Paris, 2001).

Davies, N. de G., 'The Town House in Ancient Egypt.' *Metropolitan Museum Studies* 1/2 (1929), 233–55.

Kemp, B. J., 'Amarna Workmen's Village in Retrospect.' *JEA* 73 (1987), 21–50.

Lesko, L. H., (ed.), *Pharaoh's Workers: The Villagers of Deir el-Medina* (Ithaca and London, 1994).

Ricke, H., *Der Grundriss des Amarna-Wohnhauses* (Leipzig, 1932).

Roik, E., *Das altägyptische Wohnhaus* (Frankfurt, 1988).

Samuel, D., 'Bread Making and Social Interactions at the Amarna Workmen's Village, Egypt.' *World Archaeology* 31 (1999), 121–44.

Spence, K., 'The Three-dimensional Form of the Amarna House.' *JEA* 90 (2004), 123–52.

Spence, K., 'Settlement Structure and Social Interaction at el-Amarna' in M. Bietak, E. Czerny and I. Forstner-Müller (eds), *Cities and Urbanism in Ancient Egypt: Papers from a Workshop in November 2006 at the Austrian Academy of Sciences* (Vienna, 2010), 289–98.

Traunecker, C., 'Les Maisons du domaine d'Aton à Karnak.' *CRIPEL* 10 (1988), 73–93.

Valbelle, D., *Les ouvriers de la tombe: Deir el-Médineh à l'époque ramesside* (Cairo, 1985).

Feeding and Supplying the City

van den Boorn, G. P. F., *The Duties of the Vizier* (London and New York, 1988).

Bowman, A. K., and E. Rogan (eds), *Agriculture in Egypt. From Pharaonic to Modern Times* (Oxford, 1999).

Eyre, C. J., 'The Market Women of Pharaonic Egypt' in N. Grimal and B. Menu, *Le Commerce en Égypte ancienne* (Cairo, 1998), 173–91.

Gardiner, A. H., and R. O. Faulkner, *The Wilbour Papyrus* I–IV (Brooklyn and London, 1941–52).

Hodkinson, A. K., 'Mass-Production in New Kingdom Egypt' in J. Corbelli, D. Boatright and C. Malleson (eds), *Current Research in Egyptology IX* (Oxford, 2011), 81–98.

Ikram, S., *Choice Cuts: Meat Production in Ancient Egypt* (Leuven, 1995).

Janssen, J. J., *Commodity Prices from the Ramessid Period* (Leiden, 1975).

Janssen, J. J., *Grain Transport in the Ramesside Period: Papyrus Baldwin (BM EA 10061) and Papyrus Amiens* (London, 2004).

Kemp, B. J., 'Large Middle Kingdom Granary Buildings (and the Archaeology of Administration).' *Zeitschrift für Ägyptische Sprache und Altertumskunde* 113 (1986), 120–36.

Miller, R. L., 'Calorie Counting in Egyptian Ration Texts.' *Journal of the Economic and Social History of the Orient* 34 (1991), 257–69.

O'Connor, D., 'The Geography of Settlement in Ancient Egypt' in P. J. Ucko, R. Tringham and G. W. Dimbleby (eds), *Man, Settlement and Urbanism* (London and Cambridge, MA, 1972), 681–98.

Working Life

Davies, N. de G., *The Tomb of Rekh-mi-re at Thebes* (New York, 1935).

Eyre, C. J., 'Work and the Organisation of Work in the Old Kingdom'. In Powell, M. A. (ed.) *Labor in the Ancient Near East* (New Haven, 1987), 5–47.

Eyre, C. J., 'Work and the Organisation of Work in the New Kingdom' in M. A. Powell (ed.), *Labor in the Ancient Near East* (New Haven, 1987), 167–221.

Water and Sanitation

Dixon, D. M., 'The Disposal of Certain Personal, Household and Town Waste in Ancient Egypt' in P. J. Ucko, R. Tringham and G. W. Dimbleby (eds), *Man, Settlement and Urbanism* (London and Cambridge, MA, 1972), 647–50.

Franzmeier, H., 'Ḥnm.t, šd.t, ḥw.t, and bꜥr: Ancient Egyptian *Emic* Terms for Wells and Cisterns' in V. Gashe and J. Finch (eds), *Current Research in Egyptology 2008* (Bolton, 2008), 31–42.

Janssen, J. J., 'The Water Supply of a Desert Village.' *Medelhavsmuseet Bulletin* 14 (1979), 9–15.

Morris, J. P., *Wells and Water Supply in New Kingdom Egypt* (Ph.D thesis, Liverpool University, 2006).

Schools

Baines, J. and C. J. Eyre, 'Four Notes on Literacy.' *Göttinger Miszellen* 61 (1983), 65–96.

Kahl, J., 'Ein Zeugnis altägyptischer Schulausflüge.' *Göttinger Miszellen* 211 (2006), 25–29.

Crime

Eyre, C. J., 'Crime and Adultery in Ancient Egypt.' *JEA* 70 (1984), 92–105.

McDowell, A. G., *Jurisdiction in the Workmen's Community of Deir el-Medineh* (Leiden, 1990).

Tyldesley, J. A., *Judgment of the Pharaoh: Crime and Punishment in Ancient Egypt* (London, 2000).

Death

Dodson, A, and S. Ikram, *The Tomb in Ancient Egypt* (London and New York, 2008).

Grajetzki, W., *Burial Customs in Ancient Egypt: Life in Death for Rich and Poor* (London, 2003).

Snape, S., *Ancient Egyptian Tombs: The Culture of Life and Death* (Chichester, 2011).

Part IV – Towns and Cities of Graeco-Roman Egypt

Alston, R., *The City in Roman and Byzantine Egypt* (London, 2002).

Bagnall, R. S., and D. W. Frier, *The Demography of Roman Egypt* (Cambridge and New York, 1994).

Bailey, D. M., *Excavations at Ashmunein IV. Hermopolis Magna: Buildings of the Roman Period* (London, 1991).

Ball, J., *Egypt in the Classical Geographers* (Cairo, 1942).

Bingen, J., *Hellenistic Egypt: Monarchy,*

Society, Economy, Culture (Edinburgh and Berkeley, 2007).

Bowman, A., *Egypt after the Pharaohs* (Oxford and Berkeley, 1990).

Crawford, D., *Kerkeosiris: An Egyptian Village in the Ptolemaic Period* (Cambridge, 1971).

Donadoni, S., *Antinoe (1965–68)* (Rome, 1974).

Fraser, P. M., *Ptolemaic Alexandria* (Oxford, 1972).

Gazda, E. K., (ed.), *Karanis: An Egyptian Town in Roman Times* (Ann Arbor, 1983).

Goddio, F., *The Topography and Excavation of Heracleion-Thonis and East Canopus (1996-2006)* (Oxford, 2007).

Husselman, E. M., *Karanis Excavations of the University of Michigan in Egypt 1928-1935: Topography and Architecture* (Ann Arbor, 1979).

Mckenzie, J., *The Architecture of Alexandria and Egypt: 300 BC–AD 700* (London and New Haven, 2011).

Müller, W., 'Urbanism in Graeco-Roman Egypt' in M. Bietak, E. Czerny and I. Forstner-Müller (eds), *Cities and Urbanism in Ancient Egypt: Papers from a Workshop in November 2006 at the Austrian Academy of Sciences* (Vienna, 2010), 217–56.

Tacoma, L. E., *Fragile Hierarchies: The Urban Elites of Third Century Roman Egypt* (Leiden, 2006).

Part V – Gazetteer

Porter, B., and R. Moss, *Topographical Bibliography of Ancient Egyptian Hieroglyphic Texts, Reliefs and Paintings* (vols I–VII; 1934–81).

Elephantine to Thebes

von Pilgrim, C., 'Elephantine – (Festungs) Stadt am Ersten Katarakt' in M. Bietak, E. Czerny and I. Forstner-Müller (eds), *Cities and Urbanism in Ancient Egypt: Papers from a Workshop in November 2006 at the Austrian Academy of Sciences* (Vienna, 2010), 257–70.

von Pilgrim, C., *Untersuchungen in der Stadt des Mittleren Reiches und der Zweiten Zwischenzeit: Elephantine XVIII* (Mainz, 1991).

Seidlmayer, S. J., 'Town and State in the Early Old Kingdom: A View from Elephantine' in A. J. Spencer (ed.), *Aspects of Early Egypt* (London, 1996), 108–27.

Michalowski, K., *Tell Edfu* 1937 (Cairo, 1937).

Moeller, N., 'The Archaeological Evidence for Town Administration: New Evidence from Tell Edfu' in A. Dodson and S. Ikram (eds), *Beyond the Horizon: Studies in Egyptian Art, Archaeology and History in Honour of Barry Kemp* (Cairo, 2010), 263–74.

Anus, P., and R. Sa'ad, 'Habitations de prêtres dans le temple d'Amon de Karnak.' *Kêmi* 2 (1971), 217–38.

Kemp, B. J., and D. O'Connor, 'An Ancient Nile Harbor: University Museum Excavations at the "Birket Habu".' *International Journal of Nautical Archaeology and Underwater Exploration* 3 (1974), 101–36.

Nims, C. F., *Thebes of the Pharaohs: A Pattern for Every City* (New York and London, 1965).

O'Connor, D., 'The City and the World: Worldview and Built Forms in the Reign of Amenhotep III' in D. O'Connor and E. H. Cline (eds), *Amenhotep III: Perspectives on his Reign* (Ann Arbor, 1998), 125–72.

Vandorpe, K., 'City of Many a Gate, Harbor for Many a Rebel: Historical and Topographical Outline of Graeco-Roman Thebes' in S. P. Vleeming (ed), *Hundred-Gated Thebes* (Leiden, 1995), 203–39.

Ventura, R., *Living in the City of the Dead: A Selection of Topographical and Administrative Terms in the Documents of the Theban Necropolis* (Freiburg, 1986).

Coptos to Amarna

Petrie, W. M. F., *Koptos* (London, 1896).

Adams, M. D., 'The Abydos Settlement Site Project: Investigation of a Major Provincial Town in the Old Kingdom and First Intermediate Period' in C. J. Eyre (ed.), *Proceedings of the 7th International Congress of Egyptologists* (Leuven, 1998), 19–30.

O'Connor, D., *Abydos: Egypt's First Pharaohs and the Cult of Osiris* (London and New York, 2009).

el-Masry, Y. S., 'Seven Seasons of Excavation at Akhmim' in C. J. Eyre (ed.), *Proceedings of the 7th International Congress of Egyptologists* (Leuven, 1998), 759–65.

Kahl, J., *Ancient Asyut: The First Synthesis after 300 Years of Research* (Wiesbaden, 2007).

Davies, N. de G., *The Rock Tombs of Amarna* I–VI (London and Boston, 1903–8).

Frankfort, H. and J. D. S. Pendlebury, *The City of Akhenaten II: The North Suburb and the Desert Altars* (London, 1933).

Kemp, B. J., 'The Character of the South Suburb at Tell el-'Amarna.' *Mitteilungen der Deutschen Orient-Gesellschaft zu Berlin* 113 (1981), 81–97.

Kemp, B. J., *The City of Akhenaten and Nefertiti* (London and New York, 2012).

Kemp, B. J., *et al.*, *Amarna Reports I–VI* (London, 1984–95).

Kemp. B. J., and S. Garfi, *A Survey of the Ancient City of El-'Amarna* (London, 1993).

Kemp, B. J., and A. Stevens, *Busy Lives at Amarna: Excavations in the Main City (Grid 12 and the House of Ranefer, N.49.18)* (London, 2010).

Murnane, W. J., and C. C. van Siclen, *The Boundary Stelae of Akhenaten* (London and New York, 1993).

Peet, T. E., and C. L. Woolley, *The City of Akhenaten I: Excavations of 1921 and 1922 at El-'Amarneh* (London, 1923).

Pendlebury, J. D. S., *et al.*, *The City of Akhenaten III: The Central City and the Official Quarters* (London, 1951).

Spence, K., 'The Palaces of el-Amarna: An Architectural Analysis' in R. Gundlach and J. Taylor (eds), *Egyptian Royal Residences: Structure and Function* (Wiesbaden, 2009), 165–87.

Tietze, C., 'Amarna: Analyse der Wohnhäuser und soziale Struktur der Stadtbewohner.' *Zeitschrift für Ägyptische Sprache und Altertumskunde* 112 (1985), 48–84.

Hermopolis Magna to the Faiyum

Roeder, G., *Hermopolis 1929–39. Ausgrabungen der Deutschen Hermopolis-Expedition in Hermopolis, Öber-Ägypten* (Hildesheim, 1959).

Spencer, A. J., *Excavations at El-Ashmunein I: The Topography of the Site* (London, 1983).

Spencer, A. J., *Excavations at El-Ashmunein III: The Town* (London, 1993).

Lopez-Grande, M., Quesada Sanz, F. and Molinaro Polo, M. A., *Excavaciones en Ehnasya el-Medina (Hercleopolis Magna) II* (Madrid, 1995).

Naville, E., *Ahnas el-Medina (Heracleopolis Magna)* (London, 1894).

Petrie, W. M. F., *Ehnasya* (London 1904).

Brunton, G. and Engelbach, R., *Gurob* (London, 1927).

Thomas, A. P., *Gurob: A New Kingdom Town* (Warminster, 1981).

Memphis and the Memphite Region

Anthes, R., *et al.*, *Mit Rahineh 1955* (Philadelphia, 1959).

Anthes, R., *et al.*, *Mit Rahineh 1956* (Philadelphia, 1965).

Badawi, A., *Memphis als zeite Landeshauptstadt im Neuen Reich* (Cairo, 1948).

Giddy, L., *Kom Rabi'a: The New Kingdom and Post-New Kingdom Objects* (London, 1999).

Jeffreys, D. G., *The Survey of Memphis I – The Archaeological Report* (London, 1985).

Jeffreys, D. G., *The Survey of Memphis V – Kom Rabi'a: The New Kingdom Settlement (Levels II-V)* (London, 2006).

Jeffreys, D. G., and A. Tavares, 'The Historic landscape of Early Dynastic Memphis.' *MDAI* 50 (1994), 143–73.

Kitchen, K. A., 'Towards a Reconstruction of Ramesside Memphis' in R. E. Freed and E. Bleiberg (eds), *Fragments of a Shattered Visage: Proceedings of the International Symposium on Ramesses the Great* (Memphis, 1973), 87–104.

Malek, J., 'The Temples at Memphis' in S. Quirke (ed.), *The Temple in Ancient Egypt* (London, 1997), 90–101.

Martin, G. T., 'Memphis: The Status of a Residence City in the Eighteenth Dynasty' in M. Barta and J. Krejci (eds), *Abusir and Saqqara in the Year 2000* (Prague, 2000), 99–120.

Petrie, W. M. F., *Memphis I* (London, 1909).

Thompson, D. J., *Memphis under the Ptolemies* (Princeton, 1988).

Zivie, A. P., (ed), *Memphis et ses necropoles au nouvel empire* (Paris, 1988),

Arnold, F., 'Die Priesterhauser der Chentkaues in Giza.' *MDAI* 54 (1998), 1–18.

Lehner, M., and Wetterstrom, W. (eds) *Giza Reports: The Giza Mapping Project 1 – Project History, Survey, Ceramics and the Main Street and Gallery III.4 Operations* (Boston, 2007).

Lehner, M., and Tavares, A., 'Walls, Ways and Stratigraphy: Signs of Social Control in and Urban Footprint at Giza' in M. Bietak, E. Czerny and I. Forstner-Müller (eds), *Cities and Urbanism in Ancient Egypt: Papers from a Workshop in November 2006 at the Austrian Academy of Sciences* (Vienna, 2010), 171-216.

The Delta

van den Brink, E. C. M., (ed.), *The Archaeology of the Nile Delta: Problems and Priorities* (Amsterdam, 1988).

Leclère, F., *Les villes de Basse Égypte au 1er millénaire av. J.-C.* (2 vols; Cairo, 2008).

The Canopic Branch

Cagle, A., *The Spatial Structure of Kom el-Hisn: An Old Kingdom Town in the Western Nile Delta* (Oxford, 2003).

Kirby, C. J., 'Preliminary Report on the Survey of Kom el-Hisn, 1996.' *JEA* 84 (1998), 36–37.

Wenke, R., *et al.*, 'Kom el-Hisn.' *JARCE* 25 (1988), 5–34.

Coulson, W. D. E., and A. Leonard, *Cities of the Delta I: Naukratis* (Malibu, 1981).

Villing, A., and U. Schlotzauer (eds), *Naukratis: Greek Diversity in Egypt* (London, 2006).

Spencer, N. A., *Kom Firin I: The Ramesside Temple and the Site Survey* (London, 2008).

Thomas, S. C. E., 'Chariots, Cobras and Canaanites: A Ramesside Miscellany from Tell Abqa'in' in M. Collier and S. Snape (eds), *Ramesside Studies in Honour of K. A. Kitchen* (Bolton, 2011), 519–31.

The Rosetta Branch

el-Sayed, R., *Documents relatifs à Sais et ses divinités* (Cairo, 1975).

Wilson, P., *The Survey of Sais (Sa el-Hagar) 1997–2002* (London, 2006).

The Damietta Branch

Mysliwiec, K., and Z. Sztetyllo (eds), *Tell Atrib 1985–95* (Warsaw, 2000).

Redford, D. B., *City of the Ram-Man: The Story of Ancient Mendes* (Princeton, 2010).

Swan Hall, E., and B. V. Bothmer (eds), *Mendes I* (Cairo, 1980).

Spencer, A. J., *Excavations at Tell el-Balamun 1991–1994* (London, 1996).

Spencer, A. J., *Excavations at Tell el-Balamun 1995–1998* (London, 1999).

Spencer, A. J., *Excavations at Tell el-Balamun 1999–2001* (London, 2003).

Vernus, P., *Athribis* (Cairo, 1978).

The Pelusiac Branch

Quirke, S., *The Cult of Ra: Sun-worship in Ancient Egypt* (London and New York, 2001).

Saleh, A., *Excavations at Heliopolis I–II* (Cairo, 1981-83).

Naville, E., and F. Ll. Griffith, *The Mound of the Jew and the City of Onias* (London 1890).

Habachi, L., *Tell Basta* (Cairo, 1957).

Lange, E., 'Die Ka-Anlage Pepis I. in Bubastis im Kontext königlicher Ka-Anlagen des Alten Reiches.' *Zeitschrift für Ägyptische Sprache und Altertumskunde* 133 (2006), 121–40.

Naville, E., *Bubastis (1887–1889)* (London, 1891).

Petrie, W. M. F., *Hyksos and Israelite Cities* (London, 1906).

Snape, S., *Six Archaeological Sites in Sharqiyeh Province* (Liverpool, 1986).

Bietak, M., *Tell el-Dab'a II. Der Fundort im Rahmen einer archäologisch-geographischen Untersuchung über das ägyptische Ost-delta* (Vienna, 1975).

Bietak, M., and I. Forstner-Müller, 'The Topography of New Kingdom Avaris and Per-Ramesses' in M. Collier and S. Snape (eds), *Ramesside Studies in Honour of K. A. Kitchen* (Bolton, 2011), 23–50.

Habachi, L., *Tell el-Dab'a and Qantir I: The Site and its Connection with Avaris and Piramesse* (Vienna, 2001).

Pusch, E., H. Becker and J. Fassbinder, 'Wohnen und Lebe. Oder: Weitere Schritte zu einen Stadtplan der Ramsesstadt.' *Ägypten und Levante* 9 (1999), 155–70.

Uphill, E., *The Temples of Per Ramesses* (Warminster, 1984).

Montet, P., *La Nécropole Royale de Tanis I–III* (Paris, 1947–60).

Yoyotte, J., 'Le Tell de San el-Hagar. Une montagne d'origine humaine.' *Bulletin de la Société Française des Fouilles de Tanis* 6 (1992), 103–21.

Petrie, W. M. F., 'Nebeshe (Am) and Defenneh (Tahpanhes)' in W. M. F. Petrie, *Tanis II* (London, 1888).

Fortress Towns of the Eastern Delta and Wadi Tumilat

Holladay, J. S., *Cities of the Delta III: Tell el-Maskhuta* (Malibu, 1982).

Northern Sinai

Abd el-Maksoud, M., *Tell Hebuoa (1981–1991)* (Paris, 1998).

Hoffmeier, J., 'The Gate of the Ramesside Fort at Tell el-Borg, North Sinai' in M. Collier and S. Snape (eds), *Ramesside Studies in Honour of K. A. Kitchen* (Bolton, 2011), 207–17.

Oren, E., 'The "Ways of Horus" in North Sinai' in A. F. Rainey (ed.), *Egypt, Israel, Sinai: Archaeological and Historical Relationships in the Biblical Period* (Tel Aviv, 1987), 69–119.

The Oases

Giddy, L.L., *Egyptian Oases* (Warminster, 1987).

Hope, C. A., and O. E. Kaper, 'Egyptian Interest in the Oases in the New Kingdom and a New Stela for Seth from Mut el-Kharab' in M. Collier and S. Snape (eds), *Ramesside Studies in Honour of K. A. Kitchen* (Bolton, 2011), 219–36.

Marchand, S., and G. Soukiassian, *Balat 8: Un habitat de XIIIe dynastie – 2e periode intermédiaire à Ayn Asil* (Cairo, 2010).

Soukiassian, G., M. Wuttmann and L. Pantalacci, *Balat 6: Le palais des gouverneurs de l'époque de Pépy II: Les sanctuaires de ka et leurs dépendances* (Cairo, 2002).

The Mediterranean Coast

Habachi, L., 'The Military Posts of Ramesses II on the Coastal Road and the Western Part of the Delta.' *Bulletin de l'Institut Français d'Archéologie Orientale* 80 (1980), 13–30.

Snape, S., and P. Wilson, *Zawiyet Umm el-Rakham I: The Temple and Chapels* (Bolton, 2007).

Snape, S., 'Vor der Kaserne: External Supply and Self-Sufficiency at Zawiyet Umm el-Rakham'. In Müller, W., 'Urbanism in Graeco-Roman Egypt' in M. Bietak, E. Czerny and I. Forstner-Müller (eds), *Cities and Urbanism in Ancient Egypt: Papers from a Workshop in November 2006 at the Austrian Academy of Sciences* (Vienna, 2010), 271–88.

Nubia

Blackman, A. M., 'Preliminary Report on the Excavations at Sesebi, Northern Province, Anglo-Egyptian Sudan, 1936–37' *JEA* 23 (1937), 145–51.

Kemp, B. J., 'Fortified Towns in Nubia' in P. J. Ucko, R. Tringham and G. W. Dimbleby (eds), *Man, Settlement and Urbanism* (London and Cambridge, MA, 1972), 651–56.

Spence, K., *et al.*, 'Fieldwork at Sesebi 2009.' *Sudan and Nubia* (2009), 38–46.

Spencer, N., 'Cemeteries and a late Ramesside Suburb at Amara West.' *Sudan and Nubia* (2009), 47–61.

Spencer, P. A., *Amara West 1: The Architectural Report* (London, 1997).

Acknowledgments

A number of people have been both helpful and particularly patient in assisting me with this book, notably Joyce Tyldesley, Colin Ridler, Alice Reid and Sally Nicholls. I would also like to thank David Jeffreys, Angus Graham, and all my colleagues at Liverpool, past and present.

Sources of Illustrations

a = above; b = below; l = left; r = right

1 British Museum, London ; 2–3 Kenneth Garrett/National Geographic Creative; 4 © 2013 Ancient Egypt Research Associates; 8–9 © 2013 Ancient Egypt Research Associates; 10 Werner Forman Archive/British Museum London; 11 Susanna Thomas; 12, 14, 15 Rutherford Picture Library; 17 Angus Graham; 18–19 akg-images/Erich Lessing; 20 Kenneth Garrett/National Geographic Creative; 21 GlowImages/ Alamy; 24a Ashmolean Museum, University of Oxford; 24b Steven Snape; 25 Garstang Museum of Archaeology, Liverpool University; 26 German Archaeological Institute, Cairo; 27 Kenneth Garrett/National Geographic Creative; 28a, 28b Rutherford Picture Library; 29a Angus Graham; 29b Rutherford Picture Library; 30 Andy Whitehead; 31, 32a Steven Snape; 32b akg-images/Bible Land Pictures; 33, 34a, 34b Steven Snape; 35 British Museum, London; 37 Rutherford Press Ltd; 39 ©: Griffith Institute, University of Oxford; 40 British Museum, London; 41 Rutherford Picture Library; 42–43 Michael Poliza/National Geographic Creative; 44 Model and photo by Eastwood Cook; concept by Mallinson Architects and Kate Spence; 45 Courtesy Barry Kemp/The Amarna Trust; 46 Steven Snape; 47l Otto Georgi; 47r akg-images/Erich Lessing; 48 Ivy Close Images/Alamy; 49 Steven Snape; 50 British Museum, London; 51 Roger Wood/Corbis; 51b, 52 Steven Snape; 53a Egyptian Museum, Cairo; 53b, 55 Rutherford Picture Library; 56a Steven Snape; 56b Heidi Grassley © Thames & Hudson Ltd., London; 57 Kenneth Garrett/National Geographic Creative; 58–59 Gianni Dagli Orti/Corbis; 60 Michael Poliza/ National Geographic Creative; 61 Steven Snape; 63a Zev Radovan/Alamy; 63b akg-images/Erich Lessing; 64 Manchester Museum, University of Manchester; 65 Steven Snape after Petrie; 66 Oxford University Press; 67 Oxford University Press; 68, 69a, 69b Josef Wegner; 70 Steven Snape; 72l British Museum, London; 72r, 73l The Metropolitan Museum of Art, New York/ Art Resource/Scala, Florence; 73r British Museum, London; 74 F. Jack Jackson/Alamy; 75 akg-images/Horizons; 76, 77a, 77b Steven Snape; 79 Rutherford Picture Library; 81 akg-images/ Erich Lessing; 82 akg-images/De Agostini Picture Library; 83 Heidi Grassley © Thames & Hudson Ltd., London; 84 Fitzwilliam Museum, University of Cambridge/Bridgeman Art Library; 86, 87, 88 Courtesy Barry Kemp/The Amarna Trust; 89 Werner Forman Archive; 90a Steven Snape after Barry Kemp; 90b, 91, 92 Courtesy Barry Kemp/The Amarna Trust; 93 Pics that fly/Alamy; 94 Gian Berto Vanni/Corbis; 95 Steven Snape; 96 British Museum, London; 97, 98, 99 Steven Snape; 100 James L. Stanfield/National Geographic Creative; 101a Musée du Louvre, Paris; 101b Steven Snape; 102 Steven Snape after Davies; 103a British Museum, London; 103b Staatliche Museen zu Berlin; 104 Steven Snape after Davies; 105a Rutherford Picture Library; 105b Abdel Ghaffar Shedid; 106 Rutherford Picture Library; 107 Steven Snape; 108 Rutherford Picture Library; 109 Heritage Images/Corbis; 110 Steven Snape; 111 Egyptian Museum, Cairo; 112 Art Archive/Alamy; 113a Robert Harding Picture Library/ Alamy; 113b Joyce Tyldesley; 114 British Museum, London;

115 akg-images/Erich Lessing; 116a Everett Collection Historical/ Alamy; 116b akg-images/Erich Lessing; 117a Daniel Mayer; 117b Steven Snape; 118a Julian Heath; 118b Heidi Grassley © Thames & Hudson Ltd., London; 119a Danita Delimont/Alamy; 119b Images of Africa Photobank/Alamy; 120 British Museum, London; 121 Kenneth Garrett/National Geographic Creative; 122–123 Kenneth Garrett/National Geographic Creative; 124 Steven Snape; 125 © J-CL. Golvin, Errance Editions; 126 Steven Snape; 127 Stéphane Compoint; 128 © Franck Goddio/Hilti Foundation; 129 Florence Maruéjol; 130a, 130b, 131 Steven Snape; 132a The Art Archive/Jane Taylor; 132b Steven Snape; 134 Kelsey Museum of Archaeology, University of Michigan; 135 Steven Snape; 136a Rutherford Picture Library; 136b from Description de l'Egypte, 1809–1829; 137 Rutherford Picture Library; 138a Steven Snape; 138b from Description de l'Egypte, 1809–1829; 139 Steven Snape; 140–141 © J-CL. Golvin, Errance Editions; 142 Steven Snape; 143 GeoEye satellite image; 144a Steven Snape; 144b Rutherford Picture Library; 145a Steven Snape; 145b Rutherford Picture Library; 146a, 146b Steven Snape; 147 Images of Africa Photobank/Alamy; 148a Rutherford Picture Library; 148b Courtesy Dr Nadine Moeller, The Oriental Institute, Chicago; 149 Steven Snape; 150 © J-CL. Golvin, Errance Editions; 151a Heidi Grassley © Thames & Hudson Ltd., London; 151b Steven Snape; 153 Rutherford Picture Library; 155, 157 Courtesy Barry Kemp/The Amarna Trust; 158 Model and photo by Eastwood Cook; concept by Mallinson Architects; 159 Courtesy Barry Kemp/The Amarna Trust; 160 Photo G. Owen; 161, 162, 163 Courtesy Barry Kemp/The Amarna Trust; 164, 165a, 165b Steven Snape; 166 Einsamer Schütze; 167 Steven Snape; 168b Einsamer Schütze; 169, 170 Steven Snape; 172 Sonia Halliday Photographs; 173 David Jeffreys/Egypt Exploration Society; 174 Rutherford Picture Library; 175 Steven Snape; 177 Rutherford Picture Library; 178, 179a, 179b, 180a, 180b © 2013 Ancient Egypt Research Associates; 181 NASA; 183, 184 Steven Snape; 186 Penelope Wilson; 187a, 187b Steven Snape; 188 Photo Scala, Florence; 189 Rutherford Picture Library; 191a Egyptian Museum, Cairo; 191b Steven Snape; 192 Steven Snape after Redford; 193 Courtesy Donald Redford, The Mendes Expedition; 195a, 195b Rutherford Picture Library; 196a Jeffrey Spencer, British Museum, London; 197 Rutherford Picture Library; 198 Steven Snape; 199 Rutherford Picture Library; 200a Heidi Kontkanen; 200b Steven Snape; 201 Courtesy Eva Lange; 203, 204a Steven Snape; 204b Iri-en-achti; 205 © Qantir-Pi-Ramesse, Edgar Pusch; 206 Steven Snape; 207 Thomas Sagory/www.du-ciel.com, 2004. Mission Française des Fouilles de Tanis; 208 Universal Images Group/DeAgostini/Alamy; 209, 210 Steven Snape; 211 Blauepics Photography; 212 Steven Snape; 213 Rutherford Picture Library; 214 Polish Centre of Mediterranean Archaeology, University of Warsaw; 215 Tara Todras-Whitehill/X01969/Reuters/Corbis; 216 Hemis/Alamy; 217, 218a, 218b, 219 Rutherford Picture Library; 220, 221a, 221b, 222a, 222b Steven Snape; 223b Paul Almasy/Corbis; 225a Egypt Exploration Society; 225b Steven Snape; 226 Österreichisches Archäologisches Institut Zweigstelle, Cairo.

Index